About the Author

Elizabeth Lesser is the co-founder of the Omega Institute in Rhinebeck, New York (www.eomega.org), which offers conferences and workshops attended by 20,000 people a year, and she has been a director and teacher at that organization. Formerly a midwife, she attended Barnard College and San Francisco State University and now lives in the Hudson Valley with her husband and three sons. She is the author of *The Seeker's Guide* and *The New American Spirituality*, and can be reached at elizabethlesser@aol.com.

ALSO BY ELIZABETH LESSER

The Seeker's Guide

(Originally published as *The New American Spirituality*)

Broken Open

Broken Open

How Difficult Times Can Help Us Grow

Elizabeth Lesser

RIDER

LONDON · SYDNEY · AUCKLAND · JOHANNESBURG

First published in 2004 by Villard Books,
an imprint of Random House Inc., USA
This edition published in 2004 by Rider,
an imprint of Ebury Press, Random House,
20 Vauxhall Bridge Road, London SW1V 2SA
www.randomhouse.co.uk

Random House Australia (Pty) Limited
20 Alfred Street, Milsons Point, Sydney
New South Wales 2061, Australia

Random House New Zealand Limited
18 Poland Road, Glenfield
Auckland 10, New Zealand

Random House (Pty) Limited
Endulini, 5A Jubilee Road
Parktown 2193, South Africa

The Random House Group Limited Reg. No. 954009

Book design by Lee Fukui

Papers used by Rider are natural, recyclable products made from wood
grown in sustainable forests.

Printed and bound by Mackays of Chatham plc, Chatham, Kent

A CIP catalogue record for this book is available
from the British Library

ISBN 1844135616

For my husband, Tom

Contents

Prelude   xiii

Introduction   xix

PART I

The Call of the Soul

What Einstein Knew   7

What Dante Knew   17

The Hands That Work on Us   20

Open Secret   24

Bozos on the Bus   27

Open-Heart Surgery   30

Heart Warrior   35

Lightening Up and Falling Down   39

When They Revolutionize the Cocktail Parties   43

Sleeping Giants and Strange Angels   46

The Rapture of Being Alive   49

PART II

The Phoenix Process

Chimidunchik   59

Here Begin the Terrors, Here Begin the Miracles   64

Fierce Grace   72

Before and After   79

A Broken Heart Is an Open Heart   86

September 11th   92

Crooked Hearts   98

PART III
The Shaman Lover

Leaving My Father's House   107

Marriage Math   111

The Shaman Lover   114

Initiation   118

The Crossroads   122

Goethe's Chain Letter   126

The Joy of Being Wrong   129

PART IV
Children

Firstborn   139

Run Away, Bunny!   143

The Great Movement of the Couch   147

Gift   153

The Vroom, Vroom Gene   160

Letting Them Go   164

Iron John   171

Widening the Circle   176

Despair and Dulcimers   179

PART V
Birth and Death

Trailing Clouds of Glory   189

The Hundredth Name   193

No Birth, No Death   198

Visitation Dreams   205

Good Grief   210

Karaoke   216

Practicing Death   221

The Turtles and the Trees   227

A Meditation for Practicing Dying   232

PART VI

The River of Change

Enjoying the Passage of Time   239

The Workshop Angel   242

When Grapes Turn to Wine   245

Ch-ch-Changes   250

Comfortable with Uncertainty   256

For Hugo   258

Peaceful Abiding   264

The Truth   269

Epilogue   273

Appendix: Toolbox   277

Meditation   279

Meditation Instructions   283

Ten-Step Meditation Practice   289

Psychotherapy   291

Working with Teachers, Therapists, and Healers 295

Prayer   297

Acknowledgments   303

Permission Credits   305

Prelude

And the time came when the risk to remain tight in a bud

was more painful than the risk it took to blossom.

—Anaïs Nin

SOME YEARS AGO, I took a trip to the city of Jerusalem, where centuries are layered in stones, and streets are carved into the layers, twisting and turning in haphazard patterns that divide and connect neighborhoods, markets, mosques, temples, and churches. One morning in that broken city, I sat alone on a well-worn wall at the base of the Mount of Olives. The day was moving forward with the kind of determination that comes from people with places to go and things to do. Religious pilgrims pushed past each other into the gates of the holy city. Men and women made their way to work and market; children ran past them to school. But I had nowhere to go.

The group I was traveling with in Jerusalem had risen early for the day's planned itinerary. I'd stayed behind. I could no longer keep up the charade that I was part of their adventure: I wasn't here to visit sacred sites, or to walk the Stations of the Cross, wail at the Western Wall, or chant the Ninety-nine Names of Allah. No, I was here to further delay making a decision about my life at home. I had come to Jerusalem only because my friend, who was leading the trip, was worried enough about me to pay my fare—which worried me enough to fly halfway around the world to a city as mixed up as myself. Now I was here, but really I was still back there, at home in New York, scared and confused about my crumbling marriage.

Wandering deeper into the walled Old City, I came to an ancient alleyway lined with shops selling religious artifacts for the Western pilgrim. Normally I would veer away from these kinds of stores. Inspirational sayings stitched in needlepoint or Virgin Mary coffee mugs seemed no different to me than those velvet Elvis paintings you see at flea markets. But I needed help. I needed inspiration—even from a coffee cup, or an embroidered pillow, or from Elvis himself.

One narrow, dusky shop appealed to me, and I went in. On the floor was a patchwork of Persian rugs. On the walls hung small paintings, some of saints and prophets, others of mountains and flowers. Was this a gallery? A rug store? A gift shop? I couldn't tell. In the back of the long room, drinking tea at a low table, sat two Arab men dressed in white caftans. One was a stooped and aged gentleman, and the other—his son perhaps—was a mysterious-looking character with gleaming eyes and long, black hair like the mane of a well-groomed horse. After a while the son put down his tea and came forward to greet me. Fixing his gaze on me, as if trying to read the secrets of my heart (or the contents of my purse), he said in perfect English, "Come, you will like this picture." Taking my hand, he led me around piles of rugs to the back of the store, near where his father was sitting.

The old man stood and shuffled over to meet me. He placed his right hand on his heart and bowed his head in the traditional Islamic greeting. "Look," he said, pointing at a small painting hanging on the wall. He touched my arm with the kindness of a grandfather. "See the rose?" he asked, turning me toward the picture. There, framed in dark wood, was the ethereal image of a rosebud, with shimmering, pale petals holding one another in a tight embrace. Under the flower was an inscription that read:

> And the time came when the risk to remain tight in a bud
> was more painful than the risk it took to blossom.

Unexpected tears stung my eyes as I read the words. The two men hovered around me, more like bodyguards than salesmen. I turned away from them, hiding my face in the shadows. I was afraid that if the old man showed me one more ounce of mercy I would break down in a stranger's store, thousands of miles from home.

"What is wrong?" the long-haired man asked.

"Nothing is wrong," I said. "I'm fine."

"No, something is wrong," the man said. "You are in pain."

"What do you mean?" I asked, suspicious yet curious. Was he a con man, trying to sell me the painting, or was my heartache that palpable, my story so easily read? I felt exposed, as if the long-haired man was a spy of the soul who knew all about my marriage, my two little boys, and the crazy mess my husband and I had made of our life together.

"What do you mean?" I asked again. I looked at the men. They stared back at me. We stood in silence, and then the long-haired man repeated, "You are in pain. Do you know why?"

"No, why?" I asked, even though I certainly did know why.

"Because you are afraid."

"Afraid of what?"

"Afraid of yourself," the man said, placing his hand on his chest and patting his heart. "You are afraid to feel your real feelings. You are afraid to want what you really want. What do you want?"

"You mean the painting? You think I want the painting?" I asked, suddenly confused and desperate to get away from the smell of the rugs and the intensity of the man. "I don't want the painting," I said, making my way toward the door. The man followed me to the front of the shop. He stood directly in front of me, took my own hand, and put it over my heart.

"I don't mean the painting," he said kindly. "I mean what the painting says. I mean that your heart is like the flower. Let it break open. What you want is waiting for you in your own heart. The time has come. May Allah bless you." Then he slipped back into the darkness. I pulled open the door, stepped out into the bright and bustling day, and wound my way through the circling streets to my hotel. Once in my room, though it was noon and ninety degrees, I ran a bath.

As I rested in the tub, the words under the painting echoed through my mind. Somehow, the long-haired man had seen into me and named the source of my pain. I was like the rosebud, holding myself together, tight and tense, terrified of breaking open. But the time *had* come. Even if I was risking everything to blossom, the man was right: It was time for me to find out what I really wanted—not what my husband wanted, not what I thought my children needed, not what my parents expected, not what society said was good or bad. It was time for me to step boldly into the fullness of life, with all of its dangers and all of its promises. Remaining tight in a bud had become a kind of death. The time had come to blossom.

Introduction

HOW STRANGE THAT THE NATURE OF LIFE IS CHANGE, yet the nature of human beings is to resist change. And how ironic that the difficult times we fear might ruin us are the very ones that can break us open and help us blossom into who we were meant to be. This book is about such times. It is a collection of stories about change and transformation in my own life, and in the lives of my friends and family, and the brave people I have met in the workshops I lead. I share these personal tales because I know that the arc of one triumphant human story traces the potential of each of our lives. There is a story in this book that can inspire and strengthen you, wherever you may be on your journey.

You may be at the beginning of a transition, feeling only a vague mood of restlessness or a nagging nudge in the direction of something new. Or maybe you are in a full-blown period of change; what you thought was your life is now over, and where you are heading is unknown. Perhaps you are coming out of the woods of a difficult time, finally able to take a breath and make sense of the journey. Or maybe you have become aware once again of the obvious yet startling fact that nothing stays the same for long; that things like the body, relationships, children, work, towns, nations, and the very earth that sustains us are fluid and fleeting—dynamic systems fueled by the breath of change.

For more than twenty-five years I have led workshops based on the subject of change and transformation. I have watched people choose growth over fear as they navigated some of life's most difficult transitions. I have seen how it is possible to approach the challenges of real life with openness and optimism—even with wisdom and joy. I have engaged in this work at Omega Institute, the retreat and conference center I cofounded in 1977. Over the years Omega has grown into one of America's largest adult learning centers, attracting close to 20,000 guests each year. Many people come to Omega's campus to study the medical and healing arts. Others attend spiritual retreats and personal growth workshops. All of them come to be around like-minded people. I often compare Omega to an oasis—a gathering place where travelers rest, learn, and tell their stories.

As a voyeur of the human experience, I have been well served by my years at Omega. It is a place rich in stories, a place where people can put down the burden of pretense and share what it really means to be human. The stories in this book are about ordinary people who, by design or disaster, decided to step boldly into the fullness of their humanity. They are tales of overcoming fear and taking risks, of hard times and difficult passages, and of buds breaking open into blossoms.

When I started writing the book, I thought I might be able to dance lightly around my own story, sharing a few personal vignettes, especially the ones about blossoming—the ones that came after the hard times and difficult passages. I thought I would write primarily about other people's dark nights of the soul, or about the ancient heroes who navigated dangerous seas or pulled a sword from the stone. But the book had other ideas. As I explored the subject of change and transformation, I was most inspired by those who were brave enough to tell the whole truth about their journeys. When people left out the dark and bewildering and shameful parts, I lost interest, and even worse, I was led astray.

And so, after more than a year of research and interviews, I took the old myths and current stories I had collected, put them aside for the time being, and got on with the harder work of telling my own story. I soon discovered that the parts I least wanted to tell—the selfish parts, the parts where my actions hurt others, the parts where I stumbled and fell—were the very tales worth telling. It was only through turning around and facing my shadow that I was able to break open into a more genuine and generous life. Therefore the story that weaves its way through the pages of this book is one of both darkness and light, dejection and rejoicing. Since I tell my story in a chronologically disobedient style, a concise overview of the "full catastrophe" (as Zorba the Greek defines a life) may serve the reader before we begin.

I was born in the 1950s, a child of an American age when the darker parts of the human story were unpopular—a time when science promised a trouble-free life and television promoted a vision of suburban perfection. I grew up in one of those "perfect" suburbs on Long Island, with only a vague and childish awareness of the shadowy woods at the edge of the weed-free lawns. At school we jumped rope on the playground but also hid under our desks during nuclear bomb drills. At home the covers of my mother's magazines showed flower arrangements and Thanksgiving Day dinners. Yet every now and then I also noticed photos of a little country called Vietnam, and of black people marching in the streets of American cities. The veneer of perfection became thinner and thinner as I left childhood and entered adolescence.

When the Beatles first crossed the Atlantic Ocean, I was waiting for them. After that, as other cultural changes dominated the sixties and seventies, I joined every revolution I could—the Woodstock nation, the antiwar demonstrations, the women's movement, and the hippie exodus back to the land. I met my first husband while building a park for homeless people in an abandoned New York City lot. I was a freshman in college, and he was a medical student. We moved in together just as the spirit of the sixties (by then it was the seventies) was losing its momentum.

We left the city, became disciples of a meditation teacher, moved to California, and then, a few years later—after he had finished his internship and I had received a teaching degree—moved back East to form a spiritual commune. We got married. I studied to become a midwife and with my husband delivered babies in our area. I had my own babies. Our little family left the commune; we bought our own home; we started a school that grew into Omega Institute. Life became complicated. Issues I never thought I would face—of love and betrayal, passion and responsibility, loss and doubt—sprouted in the hidden places of my heart and led me into the dark woods of real life. It is those stories—the ones about the journey in and out of the woods—that I tell in this book.

To be human is to be lost in the woods. None of us arrives here with clear directions on how to get from point A to point B without stumbling into the forest of confusion or catastrophe or wrongdoing. Although they are dark and dangerous, it is in the woods that we discover our strengths. We all know people who say their cancer or divorce or bankruptcy was the greatest gift of a lifetime—that until the body, or the heart, or the bank was broken, they didn't know who they were, what they felt, or what they wanted. Before their descent into the darkness, they took more than they gave, or they were numb, or full of fear or blame or self-pity. In their most broken moments they were brought to their knees; they were humbled; they were opened. And later, as they pulled the pieces back together, they discovered a clearer sense of purpose and a new passion for life. But we also know people who did not turn their misfortune into insight, or their grief into joy. Instead, they became more bitter, more reactive, more cynical. They shut down. They went back to sleep. The Persian poet Rumi says,

> *The breeze at dawn has secrets to tell you.*
> *Don't go back to sleep.*
> *You must ask for what you really want.*
> *Don't go back to sleep.*
> *People are going back and forth across the doorsill*
> *where the two worlds touch.*
> *The door is round and open.*
> *Don't go back to sleep.*

I am fascinated by what it takes to stay awake in difficult times. I marvel at what we all do in times of transition—how we resist, and how we surrender; how we stay stuck, and how we grow. Since my first major broken-open experience—my divorce—I have been an observer and a confidante of others as they engage with the forces of their own suffering. I have made note of how fiasco and failure visit each one of us, as if they were written into the job description of being human. I have seen people crumble in times of trouble, lose their spirit, and never fully recover. I have seen others protect themselves fiercely from any kind of change, until they are living a half life, safe yet stunted.

But I have also seen another way to deal with a fearful change or a painful loss. I call this other way the Phoenix Process—named for the mythical phoenix bird who remains awake through the fires of change, rises from the ashes of death, and is reborn into his most vibrant and enlightened self. I describe the Phoenix Process in Part Two of the book. For now, we need only understand it as an alternative to going back to sleep.

I've tried both ways: I have gone back to sleep in order to resist the forces of change. And I have stayed awake and been broken open. Both ways are difficult, but one way brings with it the gift of a lifetime. If we can stay awake when our lives are changing, secrets will be revealed to us—secrets about ourselves, about the nature of life, and about the eternal source of happiness and peace that is always available, always renewable, already within us.

For years I have sat in workshop rooms with people who do not want to go back to sleep. They are curious about those breezes at dawn. They hope the wind will fill their sails with courage, and with inner peace and outer purpose. Serious things, and not so serious things, are happening to these people. Some are sick and even dying; others are merely dealing with the terminal condition we call life. Some sense that an inner change is brewing, and they have been afraid to heed the storm clouds gathering in their hearts. Some have recently lost a job, or a loved one, or a fortune. Others are aware that whatever they have at this moment could be lost in the next, and they want to live as if they really know this.

In the spacious and safe atmosphere of a workshop, I have helped people grapple with questions like these: How can I stay awake even when it hurts? What might those secrets at dawn be? Why am I so afraid to slow down and listen? What will it take for my longing for wakefulness to become stronger than my fear of change? Together, we unravel ourselves, using some time-honored tools that I share in this book's Appendix: meditation for development of a quiet mind; psychological inquiry for the unveiling of a fearless heart; and prayer for the cultivation of faith. These tools are like shovels we can use to dig for the gifts buried in the jumble of our lives. All of them have made a big difference in my life. But perhaps the most profound of the tools we have at our disposal is the simple act of telling our stories to other human travelers—in a circle around the fire, at the back fence with a neighbor, or at a kitchen table with family and friends. Since the beginning of history we human beings have gathered together, talking and crying, laughing and praising, trying to make sense of the puzzling nature of our lives. By sharing our most human traits, we begin to feel less odd, less lonely, and less pessimistic. And to our surprise, at the core of each story—each personal myth—we uncover a splendid treasure, a source of unending power and sweetness: the shining soul of each wayfarer.

I offer this book in service to those in search of the shining soul—those who are willing to enter the woods of self-examination in order to retrieve what was never really lost. I have had a lot of help on my own journey, and if I can stand by you on yours, I will feel as though I am paying back the guides and friends who have lit my path. Whether you are in the midst of a big upheaval or riding the smaller rapids of everyday life, I want you to know that you are not alone, not now, or at any stage of the journey. Joseph Campbell, the great mythologist of the twentieth century, wrote, "We have not even to risk the adventure alone, for the heroes of all time have gone before us. The labyrinth is thoroughly known. We have only to follow the thread of the hero path, and where we had thought to find an abomination, we shall find a god. And where we had thought to slay another, we shall slay ourselves. Where we had thought to travel outward, we will come to the center of our own existence. And where we had thought to be alone, we will be with all the world."

The experience of change and transformation is never complete. Something bigger and brighter always calls to shine through us. We are continually challenged to change and grow, to break down and break through. The first big change made in the name of awakening can be destructive and traumatic. In the midst of my divorce, I agonized over the risks I was taking and the blows I was receiving, and wondered if so much pain could ever lead to anything good. But now, years down the road and many changes later, I trust in the twists and turns of what Joseph Campbell calls the "hero's path." Some of us need a cataclysmic event to find our way toward "the center of our own existence." Some of us don't. Some of us add up all of the smaller changes into one big lesson, and find our way home as well.

A NOTE ABOUT STORYTELLING, POETRY, AND PARABLES

I use several kinds of storytelling in this book. I use the first-person narrative to tell my own story. But because that story casts only one shaft of light on the subject at hand, I also include stories of people who have endured greater challenges than mine and still used their difficulties for growth. I tell these stories primarily in Part Two: The Phoenix Process, where I share the courage of people facing seemingly unbearable situations: grave illness, the loss of a child, the tragedy of war. Part Three: The Shaman Lover is the story of my own Phoenix Process. The stories in Parts Four, Five, and Six are about more ongoing, daily dramas—mine and others'. They are about raising children, being in relationships, growing wiser as we age, making friends with death. All of the book's stories are connected; the big ones teach us how to live the little ones every day.

Some of the sections are not really stories in a literary sense but are more like the teaching tales of older traditions. These small parables are sprinkled throughout the book, like tiny lights strung along a path. Perched at the beginning of many of the stories and parables is a quotation or poem. I realize that an opening verse is often regarded as ornamentation, but I mean for you to actually read these bits and scraps of poetry and prose. Some provide keys to the front doors of the stories; others are vehicles that can carry you all the way through the stories and back out into your life.

I have been a collector of poems and quotations for years. Some people collect antique dolls or baseball cards. I collect the words of other people. I tack them on the wall or send them to my sons, sisters, or friends, or use them in a workshop exercise I call the Poetry Bazaar. The exercise is a sort of spiritual parlor game; it's a deep icebreaker. At the start of a workshop, I spread more than a hundred slips of paper on the floor of the classroom. On each is printed a short poem or quotation by a wise thinker—people as diverse as the poet Rumi and the American comedian George Carlin. I ask the participants in the workshop to wander around the room, shopping for a poem, looking for one that tells the secret story of their heart. I encourage them to do some comparison shopping, to pick up a couple of pieces of paper and try on different sayings and quotations for style and size. Then, when the choices have been made, we gather in a circle and each person reads his or her slip aloud. Some people talk to the group about what the saying means to them. They tell us a story and let us into their lives. Others let the poems speak for themselves, something that a good poem can do. I have come to trust the power of a few well-chosen words to reveal to the world something I cannot say, or don't want to say, or didn't even know I needed to say until I saw it spelled out in front of me in the prophetic hand of the poet.

Each of the stories in this book is really your story, told by someone else, so that you may know yourself a little better. And before the story, there is the poem, or the saying. Read each quotation as a road sign, a handful of words, a pocketful of bread crumbs that have marked a way through the woods throughout the ages. Begin with this one, again from the poet Rumi, and read it as an invitation to journey with me and those whose stories are told in this book, deeper into the soul of your own life.

> *When you do something from your soul,*
> *you feel a river moving in you,*
> *a joy. . . .*

PART I

The
Call of the Soul

MANY OF US FEEL UNCOMFORTABLE revealing to others—and even to ourselves—what lies beneath the surface of our day-to-day consciousness. We get out of bed in the morning and begin again where we left off yesterday, attacking life as if we were waging a campaign of control and survival. All the while, deep within us, flows an endless river of pure energy. It sings a low and rich song that hints of joy and liberation and peace. Up on top, as we make our way through life, we may sense the presence of the river. We may feel a subtle longing to connect with it. But we are usually moving too fast, or we are distracted, or we fear disturbing the status quo of our surface thoughts and feelings. It can be unsettling to dip below the familiar and descend into the more mysterious realms of the soul.

I use the word *soul* because I have found no other word that describes as well the river of energy that animates who we are. I have heard the river called the life force, or consciousness, or God. But I prefer *soul* because of the way it sounds, and the way it tastes as it rolls around in my mouth. That reason, however, may not be good enough for some people.

Searching for the kind of data that a scientist might respect, I have read books and listened to lectures by researchers who try to explain and quantify the soul—physicists like David Bohm and Fritjof Capra, medical doctors like Deepak Chopra and Larry Dossey, and biologists like Candace Pert and Rupert Sheldrake. All of these thinkers and authors are fascinating, and I recommend their research to anyone who would find it helpful to back up a spiritual sense of the soul with some hard science.

Rupert Sheldrake's work is my favorite, although I barely understand what he is talking about in most of his books. A biochemist and cell biologist formerly at Cambridge University, he is the author of some groundbreaking books including *A New Science of Life* and *The Sense of Being Stared At and Other Aspects of the Extended Mind*. Sheldrake describes the soul as a "morphic field," or an invisible formative field that underlies the activity of all life. At an Omega lecture I once heard him say, "If we compare the dead body of a person or animal or plant with the living state that preceded it, we note that the amount of matter in the dead body is the same as in the living body. The form of the body is also the same, and so are the chemicals in it, at least immediately after death. But something has changed. The most obvious conclusion is that something has left the body, and since there's no change in weight, that which has left is essentially immaterial. That immaterial something can be called the soul."

We may not be able to hold it in our hands, but the soul is real. We may not know what form it will take when our bodies die, but I believe the soul lives on. If you are in the habit of negating the longings of the soul, or if the idea of having a soul makes you nervous, or if you regard the whole subject with raised eyebrows, you may want to consider Rumi's advice: *When you do something from your soul, you feel a river moving in you, a joy.*

If you know what Rumi is talking about, then I say that you are in touch with your soul. And if his words bring up sadness or cynicism or anxiety, then I say that you too are in possession of a living soul—one that is sending you messages on behalf of your own life.

The stories in this part of the book are about what it takes to listen to and respond to the call of the soul. Your soul is always sending messages. If you regularly paint or sing or write poetry or listen to uplifting music; or if you meditate and pray; or if you walk in nature, or move your body in sports or dance, you know what it feels like when you and your soul are in contact. *You feel a river moving in you, a joy.* You can also feel that river flowing when you reach out and help someone in need, when you are in love, when you come through the fire of a difficult endeavor, or when you finally surrender to a painful situation—when you stop fighting the fear and heartache, and you give over the reins to something greater. When you tire of your own constriction and you open, come what may, to the flow of life, you and your soul become one, and *you feel a river moving in you, a joy.*

Yet so often we resist the pull of the river. We tune out the call of the soul. Perhaps we fear what the soul would have to say about choices we have made, habits we have formed, and decisions we are avoiding. Perhaps if we quieted down and asked the soul for direction, we would be moved to make a big change. Maybe that wild river of energy, with its longing for joy and freedom, would capsize our more prudent plans, our ambitions, our very survival. Why should we trust something as indeterminate as a soul? And so we shut down. I have shut down to my soul enough times to know what it feels like when the river is dammed. I know the feeling of deadness; I know how the river diverts itself and breaks through in other ways—as a desire to blame, as an emotion of anger, as physical illness, as restlessness, or weariness, or self-destruction. The soul always speaks, and sometimes it speaks the loudest when we block its flow, when we live only half of a life, when we stay on the surface.

If we don't listen to the voice of the soul, it sings a stranger tune. If we don't go looking for what lies beneath the surface of our lives, the soul comes looking for us.

What Einstein Knew

*No problem can be solved
from the same consciousness that created it.*
—ALBERT EINSTEIN

When Route 25 leaves the mountains of northern New Mexico, the city of Albuquerque appears suddenly like a mirage—a slice of strip-mall America shimmering on a flat shelf of ancient desert. In all my years of visiting friends in New Mexico, I had not ventured into Albuquerque. I had passed by it many times, on my way to and from the airport, but never had a reason to turn off the highway until one afternoon, when I went looking for a psychic whose card had been given to me by a friend in Santa Fe. This was during the first difficult days of being separated from my husband of fourteen years, a time when people who tried to help me would eventually give up, too frustrated to continue following me around a maze with no exit. The day before I left my friend's house, she handed me the business card of a psychic and said, "Don't ask. Just go."

The front side of the card read,

> *Name: The Mouthpiece of Spirit*
> *Location: The Road of Truth*

I found more helpful directions on the other side, where three rules were printed:

1. Pay Only in Cash.
2. Bring a Blank Tape.
3. Do Not Hold Me Responsible for Your Life.

And then the address, which led me through dusty, treeless streets, past a few warehouses and truck lots, to a trailer park on a forlorn road a couple of miles from the airport. The place looked like a bad movie set—several old trailers and dilapidated outbuildings, discarded automobiles, and a dog tied to a clothesline. At a dead end I came upon the last trailer in the park, set off under a gnarled tree strung with flashing Christmas lights. Rechecking the directions, I was alarmed to discover that this indeed was The Road of Truth, the home of The Mouthpiece of Spirit.

On the steps of the trailer things got even weirder. The psychic met me at the door. She had the most hair I had ever seen—piles of bleached blond tresses arranged in a beehive on top of her head. She was wearing a red-and-white-checked cowgirl shirt, white stretch pants, and high-heeled sandals. Her eyes were clear and blue, and her nails were painted bright red to match her dangling, heart-shaped earrings. She seemed surprised to see me, as if I hadn't called earlier in the morning to confirm the appointment, as if she wasn't a psychic at all. After I established what I was doing on the steps of her trailer, she invited me in, asking me to excuse the mess. We stepped over boxes, books, magazines, and bags of pet food and potato chips. On the couch, watching TV, was a man—perhaps the psychic's husband—and a big white poodle with plastic barrettes in its hair. Neither seemed to notice me as the psychic led us to her bedroom.

The psychic sat on a king-size bed that took up most of the space in the room. She motioned to me to sit on a folding chair in the corner. I could still get out of this, I thought, as I squeezed behind the bed to sit on the chair. But before I could say anything, the psychic announced in a no-nonsense tone, "You have something in your purse for me. Something from your husband. A letter." Her voice was dusky—a smoker's voice—but it also had a regional twang, making her sound like a Texas Mae West. In fact she reminded me of Mae West, and I wondered what the hell I was doing, in a trailer near the Albuquerque airport, asking for life direction from Mae West.

"So, do you have a letter in your purse or not?" demanded the psychic.

"No, I don't," I stammered, defensively. "I don't usually carry letters in my purse."

"I am quite sure you have something, something from your husband, in your purse." Her voice softened some, and I suddenly realized that I *did* have a letter from my husband in my purse—a letter that spelled out the sad jumble of our marriage and revealed to me all the reasons for staying in it, as well as all the reasons for leaving. I had brought the letter with me to show my friend, to see if she could interpret it in a more definitive way, but I had forgotten all about it and never showed it to her. Instead, I had spent my time in Santa Fe doing exactly what Albert Einstein warns people with problems not to do. *No problem can be solved from the same consciousness that created it,* he writes. In other words, don't try to solve a problem using the same mixed-up thinking that got you into the mess in the first place. You will just keep swimming around in tight little circles of indecision and fear.

I had been in a state of indecision about my marriage for so long that my ability to move in either direction had atrophied. I had recalculated the reasons for staying and the reasons for leaving over and over, like Einstein struggling with an equation that never quite added up. Something told me I would not find my way out of this quandary using the same old arguments, but I didn't know where to look for a new perspective. It was as if I was underwater, swimming around and around in darkness. Far above me, beyond the weight of an ocean of worries, a ray of light was pointing in a luminous, new direction, but I was too distracted to notice. I was caught in waves of conflicting questions: Would I ruin my children's lives by getting divorced? Or was it worse for them to live with unhappy parents? Was I a dreamer, looking for an elusive happiness that real life could never deliver? Or were we meant to know the rapture of being alive, even at the cost of breaking the rules? The questions ebbed and flowed, back and forth, an endless exchange with no answers, no winners, just a worn-out swimmer.

How was I to break out of my tight circle of fear into a new consciousness? How did Einstein do it? How did he quiet the admonishing, skeptical voices in his head—the ones barking bad directions—long enough to hear the steady whispers of the universe? How was he able to peer beyond himself and follow the light to the more lucid answers?

I opened my purse, and there was the letter. I leaned over the bed and gave it to the psychic. She held on to it with her eyes closed, not even opening the envelope. After a few moments she asked, "Would you like to tape the session, dear?" sounding no longer like Mae West but more like a kindly waitress at a diner. I took the blank tape out of my jacket pocket, leaned across the bed

again, and gave the psychic the tape. She popped it into a tape recorder that
had seen better days, pushed the record button, and the session began—an
hour-long mix of wacky chatter, astute philosophy, and unexplainably accurate information about me, my husband, my children, my whole mixed-up life.
She jumped around from epoch to epoch: a past life with my husband in
China; the destiny of my youngest son; the next man I would marry; and the
eventual "last days" of earth time.

Sitting in the corner, I felt as if I had left my body and The Mouthpiece of
Spirit had taken up residence. This was the only way I could explain her sudden
knowledge of my life. Otherwise, how would she have known that I had a letter from my husband in my purse? How, just from holding on to that letter,
did she know that my marriage was crumbling? She sat cross-legged on the bed,
squeezing her eyes shut, clutching the letter, mumbling to herself: "*He* wanted
to leave, but now he's changed his mind. Hmmm." She fluttered her eyelids,
then shut them tight again. "He's desperate to come back, but now *she* wants to
leave. She feels guilty; he is angry. Okay, okay," she whispered, as she opened
her eyes and studied the return address.

"Rick-shaw, Rick-shaw," she drawled, mispronouncing my husband's last
name in her Texas twang. Closing her eyes again, she said, "I see you pulling a
rickshaw. I see you serving your husband in China. He is a nobleman; you are
his servant girl. You have served him in many lifetimes. You served him then,
and you hid yourself. You serve him now, and still you hide yourself. Still you
do not claim your power. Do you understand?"

I nodded my head. Regardless of her dubious methodology of determining
past lives, I did understand how I gave away power to my husband, how I re-
sented him for steering our marriage, how I had so little trust in my own voice.

"Well, it is time to break the cycle. For you and for him. But you must be
the one to do it. You must take back your power. Do you understand?"

"It's complex," I complained. "It's not his fault that I lack confidence and
he doesn't."

She looked at me hard. "Write this down," she said, tossing me a pen and
a pad of paper with a border of little bluebirds and flowers. "Those with power
never willingly concede their control. Do you understand? Your husband will
never, ever be able to let you grow into who you are supposed to be. It is not
in your karmic contract. It's not a matter of fault. The truth is that, in order to
find yourself, you must leave him. This is your quest. And in order for your

husband to find himself, he must lose you. Y'all have lessons to learn—lessons that are more important than the marriage itself. The soul comes to earth to learn lessons, not to get married, or stay married, or to take this job or that job. You have been asking the wrong question. It's not whether or not to stay married. *The question*," she said, leaning closer to me, "*is what lesson does your soul want to learn? Do you know?*"

What lesson did my soul want to learn? I liked this question. It was new. Right then and there I felt it pointing me in a different direction. I felt it leading me up toward the light.

"Well, I'll tell you then," the psychic said when I didn't answer. "Your lesson in this lifetime is to find and trust your own precious voice. Your husband has his own lessons to learn. You cannot help each other on your quests anymore as husband and wife. Write that down. His grief at your leaving is also his fear of losing the power he has had for lifetimes. Those days are over for him, and he is in turmoil. But if you are to help him on his soul's quest, you will leave him. It is your job—your sacred contract—to free him, and to free yourself. Write that down too."

She sat patiently as I scrawled her astonishing speech on the little pad of paper. When I was done, she explained that human beings were coming into "the last days." This period of earth time could extend for a decade, or a century, or more. She didn't know; but things were speeding up and people were finally learning that only those who love themselves can love others, that only people who claim their own voice can hear the true song of another.

"It is time for you to answer the call of your soul," the psychic said emphatically. "It's calling, but you're too scared to listen. You think you know what's important, but you don't. You think it's important to keep things safe, but that's neither here nor there. What's important in this life is to learn the soul lessons.

"My dear," she said with great tenderness, "what feels like such a painful loss now will become something beautiful later on. You cannot escape your destiny. You can certainly try. People do so every day. They hold on tight, and the river just dries up.

"Now, I have more things to tell you," she said, handing back my husband's letter.

"But wait," I said. "Can I ask you another question?"

"Just one," she answered, looking at her watch.

"What about my children? I don't want to ruin their lives. Don't kids need a stable family and a safe—"

The psychic interrupted me with a wave of her hand and said, "Phooey. You're not listening. Your children are *fine*. They are telling me that if you are strong, then they are safe. If you are sure-footed, they are stable. That is all. We're moving on now." I wanted to ask her more about my husband, my kids, my fear, my grief, but she was done with that subject. "Just look at your notes," she said. "That's all you need to know. You married your husband for soul reasons then; you're leaving him for soul reasons now. You're on The Road of Truth, my dear. You've put the truck in forward, but you're looking out of the rearview mirror. It's a dangerous way to drive, you know. If you choose to stay with your husband, you will be living in dead time. Dead time. If you leave, you'll be born again. As my mother said, 'Things may get worse before they get better, but they'll only get better if you let them get worse.' " She chuckled and closed her eyes.

Quite suddenly, she sat up straight on the bed and shook her head so that her earrings made a tinkling sound. "Now I am getting a name vibration," she announced. "Yes, I am getting a name vibration, and it is T-O-M," she said, spelling out the name. "The name vibration is Tom. Do you have a Tom in your life?"

I almost fell off the chair. I certainly did have a T-O-M in my life; in fact, I had three Toms in my life. In the past year, I had gone from being a most serious and principled wife and mother to being the kind of woman who had three other men in her life, all of them named Tom! The first was a man with whom I was having a doomed love affair. The second was a novelist I had never met but whose letters and phone calls were sources of mirth and sweetness in an otherwise desperate life. And the third was a man I had recently met. Although we had talked to each other only a few times, this new Tom seemed to know me, to see me, all of me—the part of me that was a big mess, and the part that was beginning to come out from behind the shadows. He wasn't frightened by my messy self, or my liberated self. I had never before met anyone quite like him. His personality was less dense than those of most people I knew. Perhaps this was because he had been born in a little town in West Texas, where the sky is a lot less confining than in New York, or maybe it was due to the fact that he was several steps ahead of me on the divorce path. His wife had left him a few years previously, taking his wealth and his young son. He had lost everything.

Now he was emerging, like a phoenix from the ashes, with new wings and an open heart.

I didn't know what to think about this new T-O-M. I didn't know what was in store for us.

"Do you have a Tom in your life?" the psychic asked again.

"I have three." I laughed, smiling for the first time since our conversation began. "But I had never really noticed that they were all named Tom." I described my relationship with each of them to her, and she nodded her head as if she knew them quite well, waving me on with an impatient hand when she had heard enough.

"You are finished with the first T-O-M, your lover, but you will remain indebted to him, throughout all of your lifetimes," she said. "He gave you back your body, your heart, your voice. Do you understand? When you found him, you found your own precious voice. This is the contract you had with him; he has had this contract with many others. He freed the song of your soul. He comes with fire to awaken the dead. And yet he burns himself with his own heat. You cannot stay with him or you will burn yourself as well. I know you love this man, so write this down: Tom, throughout all eternity, I am grateful to you for the gift of my soul's voice."

I wrote that down, and then asked, "But, why does he—"

She waved her hand again, and said, "Don't worry about this man. He is learning his soul lessons too. He will find the peace that his soul is searching for. You have given him the key to this. You have fulfilled your contract with each other." Her eyes closed, and her earrings tinkled. "The next T-O-M is not yours," she said, shaking her finger at me. "He belongs to someone else, and that is all you need to know. Stop writing him letters." She paused and tipped her head back, as if basking in the sunlight. "But this new Tom—the one with the light above his head. Yes, this is him, the name vibration, T-O-M. You will marry this man. His light will guide you. You will help each other become your True Selves, capital *T,* capital *S.* This is the contract you signed long ago. You have been looking for each other through many lifetimes. The name vibration T-O-M has led you to him."

Now the psychic leaned over and took my hands in hers. "My dear, karma is over with your husband. You must leave your marriage in harmony, because you will continue to work with the man who once was your husband. You missed nothing by marrying young. You were true to your soul's destiny in finding your first karmic mate, and now you have more years to give to your second karmic mate, Tom. So you are on The Road of Truth. Do not waver. May all be released without any negative karma. May friendship and brotherly love prevail."

That's where the tape ends. I do not remember leaving the trailer, or driving back down the dusty road, or flying to New York. Funny the way the mind can forget so much, yet retrieve a white poodle wearing barrettes and a blue-eyed psychic whose ruby red nails matched her heart-shaped earrings.

Almost twenty years later, I came across the tape and the psychic's business card when I was going through a box of old letters and photographs. Now that I knew how the story turned out, the psychic's predictions were even more uncanny. So I sent her a note, using the street address on the card and the only name I had: "The Mouthpiece of Spirit." I told her that my first husband and I had divorced, and that we continue to work together to this day. I told her that we had parented our children together and well. And that, amazingly, I had married the T-O-M with the light above his head, and when I paid attention, I could sense his light guiding us toward our True Selves, capital *T*, capital *S*.

But my letter never reached the psychic. It was returned from the post office with a message stamped across the envelope: "Person moved. No forwarding address provided."

Who was The Mouthpiece of Spirit? If there is one thing the psychic taught me, it's that people and events are rarely who and what we think they are. They are more meaningful, more worth our attention—part of some finely choreographed, eternal dance that we would be wise to bow down before in gratitude and humility. For all we know, an eccentric woman living in a trailer on a dusty road near the Albuquerque airport may know more about the workings of the world than a professor or a poet or a president.

The philosopher Friedrich Nietzsche wrote, "If our senses were fine enough, we would perceive the slumbering cliff as a dancing chaos." He meant that literally: A rocky cliff is indeed a mass of dancing atomic particles, spinning and vibrating at tremendous speeds. This book you are holding, the chair you are sitting on, your own body—none are what they seem to be. Book, chair, body—everything is circling in a cosmic dance, appearing to us as solid form, yet if our senses were fine enough, we would stand around with our mouths hanging open at the glory and grace of it all. We would sense the presence of mystery everywhere: the angels keeping us safe as we drive home from work; the spirits hovering around our children; the thin waft of light pointing us in the direction of The Road of Truth. All we can do is try to refine our senses. We can try to quiet the noise in our minds, listen for deeper instructions, and leap without fear beyond what we think is so.

In his published journals, Einstein wrote about his life in Princeton, New Jersey, where—despite criticism from his contemporaries and years of unsuccessful research—he struggled to find a grand unifying theory of physics. "I have locked myself into quite hopeless scientific problems," he wrote, "the more so since, as an elderly man, I have estranged myself from the society here." I can just imagine Einstein, perplexed and lonely, walking in the prim neighborhoods of Princeton, engaged in impossible, circular dialogues with himself. Perhaps when he reached a low point, hopeless about ever resolving his scientific problems, he confided in a young student. Perhaps that student suggested that the old professor visit a tarot card reader who lived somewhere down the New Jersey Turnpike, beyond the closed orbit of the university. And Einstein said, "What the hell? I could use a change of scenery."

I imagine him driving out of Princeton on a blustery day, his hair blowing wildly as he speeds south, past scruffy pine forests and cultivated fields. I can see him squinting at the directions, exiting at a little town, and pulling into the driveway of a ramshackle farmhouse. No one is around. The wind whips through the trees and sings a strange and melancholy song. Einstein wonders what he's doing out in the boondocks. What will a tarot card reader know about the laws of physics? But he feels he has nothing to lose, nowhere else to turn. His mind is cluttered with the voices of other people. He hears his mother's voice warning him to stay out of trouble; his father's voice doubting his practical ability; his colleagues' voices questioning his judgment; the rest of the world, telling him to think like everyone else. He senses that, somewhere beyond the noise, he will find his soul's voice, which will lead him to unravel the mysteries of the universe. Perhaps the tarot cards will point the way.

He enters the little house and spends an hour with a strange, barefooted gypsy whose head is wrapped in a sequined scarf. She spreads the cards out on her bed, studies them carefully, and tells Einstein all about himself—about his parents, his first sweetheart, the Nazis, the theory of relativity, his failed marriage, his children, his nagging guilt about the atomic bomb. She asks him probing questions that bypass his troubled mind and soften the tightness he feels in his heart. He lets down his defenses, and once again he remembers that it is his soul that has always unlocked the most hopeless scientific problems. He feels the fresh wind of the universe stirring his creativity. He prays that he will live long enough to discover what the gypsy woman says is hovering close by.

Before he departs, the gypsy serves Einstein sweet tea and then reads the leaves left at the bottom of the cracked white cup. She looks directly into his eyes and says, "No problem can be solved from the same consciousness that created it. Do you understand? Write that down."

What Dante Knew

In the middle of the journey of our life
I found myself within a dark woods
Where the straight way was lost.
—DANTE ALIGHIERI

The story about my trip to Jerusalem, where I chanced upon the long-haired man, has a mythic flavor to it. So does the tale of the blond-haired psychic—The Mouthpiece of Spirit. Our own life stories are myths in the making, stories as profound as the most oft-told tales: the Phoenix myth, Dante's *Inferno,* Homer's *Odyssey,* the Greek myth of Persephone, the Sumerian tale of Inanna, the Arthurian grail legends. We can all find ourselves in the Old and New Testaments of the Bible, in the parables of the Buddhist and Hindu traditions, and in the shamanic stories of indigenous people, from the Americas to Africa. We can reframe past events and experience our present life as if we too are gods and goddesses, heroes and heroines, warriors and wanderers.

A woman who came to one of my workshops after a difficult few years likened her experience to the journey described by Dante in his *Inferno:* "I came into those dark woods that Dante talks about," she said. "In a brief span of time, my husband left me, my child went to college, and my father died. Every role that defined me was lost: wife, mother, daughter, and simultaneously, my fertility. I had nothing left to lose. In that dark place I uncovered qualities I had forgotten I had. I retrieved my soul. I reinvented myself. I call it my 'ashes to wings' experience. It was as if I was born a second time."

The philosopher William James wrote that there are two kinds of people in this world—the Once-Born and the Twice-Born. Once-Born people do not stray from the familiar territory of who they think they are and what they think is expected of them. If fate pushes them to the edge of Dante's famous dark woods—*where the straight way is lost*—they turn back. They don't want to learn something new from life's darker lessons. They stay with what seems safe, and what is acceptable to their family and society. They stick to what they already know but don't necessarily want. Once-Born people may go through life and never even know what lies beyond the woods—or that there are woods at all.

Perhaps a Once-Born person awakens one morning and feels the beckoning finger of fate loosening disturbing questions: "Is this all there is to life? Will I always feel the same? Do I not have some purpose to fulfill, some greater kindness to give, some inner freedom to taste?" And then he gets out of bed and dresses for work, and he doesn't attend to the soul's questions. The next morning, and all the next mornings, he lives as if the soul was a figment of a flighty imagination. This inattention makes him confused, or numb, or sad, or angry.

A Twice-Born person pays attention when the soul pokes its head through the clouds of a half-lived life. Whether through choice or calamity, the Twice-Born person goes into the woods, loses the straight way, makes mistakes, suffers loss, and confronts that which needs to change within himself in order to live a more genuine and radiant life.

But let's be careful here. Sweeping distinctions like Once-Born and Twice-Born are often misleading. They can make you feel like a failure if you perceive yourself as a stuck-in-the-mud Once-Born. Or they can inflate the ego if you fancy yourself a White Knight, swashbuckling your way through the boring landscape of everyday life. The journey into the woods of change and transformation is an inner one. The outer story line need not be a soap opera, since the real drama is being carried out in the heart of the traveler. The most ordinary-looking lives are often being lived by the most extraordinary spiritual warriors—people who have chosen the road less taken, the road of self-reflection. Twice-Born people use the difficult changes in their outer lives to make the harder changes within. While Once-Born people avoid or deny or bitterly accept the unpredictable changes of real life, Twice-Born people use adversity for awakening. Betrayal, illness, divorce, the demise of a dream, the loss of a job, the death of a loved one—all of these can function as initiations into deeper life.

The journey from Once-Born to Twice-Born brings us to a crossroads where the old ways of doing things are no longer working but a better way lies somewhere at the far edge of the woods. We are afraid to step into those woods but even more afraid to turn back. To turn back is one kind of death; to go forward is another. The first kind of death ends in ashes; the second leads toward rebirth. For some of us, the day arrives when we step willingly into the woods. A longing to wake up, to feel more alive, to feel *something* spurs us beyond our fear. Some of us resist like hell until the forces of fate deliver a crisis. Some of us get sick and tired of filling an inner emptiness with drugs or drink or food, and we turn and face our real hunger: our soul hunger.

Twice-Born people trade the safety of the known for the power of the unknown. Something calls them into the woods, where the straight path vanishes, and there is no turning back, only going through. This is not easy. It is not a made-up fairy tale. It is very real and very difficult. To face our shadow—the dragons and hags that we have spent a lifetime running away from—is perhaps the most difficult journey we will ever take. But it is there, in the shadows, that we retrieve our hidden parts, learn our lessons, and give birth to the wise and mature self. From my personal experience, and from the work I have done with men and women in my workshops, I know that the difficulty of the dark journey is matched only by its rewards. I also know that every single person in this whole wide world is offered—over and over—the chance to take the voyage from Once-Born innocence to Twice-Born wisdom.

Since that fateful day in Jerusalem, when the long-haired man dared me to break open and blossom, I have noticed that the most generous and vital people are those who have been broken open by change, or loss, or adversity. And not just broken open on the outside. Indeed, it is the internal transformation that matters most. If there is one thing that has made a difference in my life, it is the courage to turn and face what wants to change within me.

The Hands That Work on Us

In the difficult are the friendly forces,
the hands that work on us.
—RAINER MARIA RILKE

I settled down pretty young for a girl of my times. I met my first husband when I was nineteen, was married a few years later, and had a baby at twenty-three. Although I was a proud child of the sixties, and a card-carrying hippie, there is a chance that in my twenties I was one of the most morally minded members of the entire baby boomer generation. In 1975 my husband and I moved from California to the East Coast with our spiritual teacher and about a hundred other young people. From the outside looking in, we were just another bunch of middle-class kids going back to the land to form one of those ill-fated counterculture communes. But we had high hopes for our peaceable abode. We would be different; we would live in harmony and simplicity; we were in for a surprise.

After searching for land from North Carolina to Vermont, we settled in upstate New York, on the north side of a mountain, in a magnificent, broken-down Shaker village. A friend of a friend had inherited the property from his parents and could no longer afford the upkeep and taxes. Pooling our resources, we bought the place—the village and several hundred acres of woods and farmland—and set out to do everything for ourselves, from birthing babies to repairing buildings. What we couldn't fix, find, farm, or finagle, we figured we'd do without.

The Shaker village was a collection of ten enormous structures—all architectural wonders in various stages of ruin. Built in the late eighteenth century, the whole property—the buildings and basements, the courtyards and barns—was haunted by the ghosts of the Shakers, an austere people devoted to hard work, shared belongings, and out-of-body religious experiences. I found more of a kinship with the Shaker ghosts than with many of my contemporaries around the country who were busy climbing financial ladders and delaying marriage and parenthood, or worse, snorting cocaine and swapping partners.

Tucked away in a forgotten rural area, meditating and praying three times a day, studying up on Shaker crafts and herbal remedies, and raising my children with a gaggle of other commune babies, I regarded the emerging yuppie culture out in the "real world" with disdain. In fact, I perceived our experiment in communal living as a vote against modern culture and its destructive methods of so-called progress. Unlike the rest of the world, we would live lightly on the earth, in tune with a natural rhythm. My mother-in-law saw the whole commune thing in a different light: She accused us of "setting hygiene back fifty years."

My husband and I agreed that we would never make the undisciplined, greedy, and morally hollow choices of many of our other friends. We would never have a dishwasher, never live in suburbia, and never get divorced. We would not trade spiritual enlightenment for personal gratification. We wanted to build a better world. Later, I would be humbled by our naïve brand of arrogance. Later, I would stumble upon the path to a better world not in spiritual theories or in the rarefied heights of my idealism but in the softness of a broken heart, and in the fires of daily life.

Later came sooner than I ever would have imagined, but it still took a long time. Looking back on the fires that made me who I am today, I know now that the person who rose from the ashes of my most difficult times is far more interesting, joyful, brave, and honorable than the young woman who thought she knew what the world needed. The poet Rilke writes, *In the difficult are the friendly forces, the hands that work on us.* The hands of those friendly forces quietly worked on me all during the seven years I lived on the commune, as I married, became a midwife, had my children, and studied with great heart and diligence the teachings of my spiritual mentor. The hands worked on me during unhappy times with my husband, frustrating times as a young mother, and *all* the time in the bewildering conflict of communal living. The friendly forces were gathering, yet I was only vaguely aware of their rumblings, caught up as I was in creating a better culture, a better life, a better me. I believed that if I only tried hard enough, I could rise above the common sordidness and sorrow of the world.

And then the forces intervened, as they always will. My untested heart was broken. What I thought was certain—my marriage—became uncertain. What I thought was beyond reproach—my teacher—showed undeniable signs of humanness. What I wanted to believe was different from the rest of the world— the commune—wasn't. Thus began my descent. On the way down, I turned and met the friendly forces, and felt the hands of transformation begin to work on me.

Certainly, I am grateful for the uncommon intensity of communal life, for the guidance of my spiritual teacher, and for the profound friendship of those with whom I shared that period of my life. I would not trade those years for anything. But had I never stumbled down the mountain of my ideals, had my ego not been humbled by loss, and my heart not broken open by pain, I would not have discovered the secret treasure that lies waiting for each one of us at the bottom of our most difficult times.

Every shift in our life comes courtesy of the friendly forces; every catastrophe can hand us exactly what we need to awaken into who we really are. It's difficult, though, when you're in the middle of a painful transition, to mine the experience for inner growth. And when your life falls apart, it's a lot easier to blame someone else, to rail against fate, or to shut down to the hopeful messages carried on the winds of change. Sometimes, when friends try to help by saying, "There's a reason for everything," or "It's a blessing in disguise," you just want to run away, or you want to say, "Yeah, if it's such a blessing, then why does it hurt so much?"

So, please forgive me when I say that everything that happens to us in life is a blessing—whether it comes as a gift wrapped in happy times or as a heartbreak, a loss, or a tragedy. It is true: There is meaning hidden in the small changes of everyday life, and wisdom to be found in the shards of your most broken moments. At the end of a dark night of the soul is the beginning of a new life. But it's hard to accept that when you're in pain, and it's tiresome to hear about it from someone who's not.

When I am on a bad stretch of the journey, I am comforted most by the stories of other travelers who have made it past the bumps and potholes. It helps me to remember that everyone is confused when the friendly forces come knocking; that there is no one alive who has not wanted to go back to sleep instead of make a big change; and that the journey from Once-Born innocence to Twice-Born wisdom is never easy.

Open Secret

Learn the alchemy
true human beings know.
The moment you accept
what troubles you've been given,
the door will open.
—RUMI

How do we begin that journey from Once-Born innocence to Twice-Born wisdom? Where do we find the courage to make a big change? How do we use the forces of a difficult time to help us grow? There are many ways, but the first way, the gateway, is to know that we are not alone in these endeavors. One of the greatest enigmas of human behavior is the way we isolate ourselves from each other. In our misguided perception of separation, we assume that others are not sharing a similar experience of life. We imagine that we are unique in our eccentricities or failures or longings. And so we try to appear as happy and consistent as we think others are, and we feel shame when we stumble and fall. When difficulties come our way, we don't readily seek out help and compassion because we think others might not understand, or would judge us harshly or take advantage of our weakness. And so we hide out, and we miss out.

We read novels and go to movies and follow the lives of celebrities in order to imbibe a kind of full-out living we believe is out of our reach, or too risky, or just an illusion. We become voyeurs of the kinds of experiences that our own souls are longing to have. Here's the oddest thing about living life as a spectator sport: While the tales in books and movies and *People* magazine may be created with smoke and mirrors, our own lives don't have to be. We have the real opportunity to live fully, with passion and meaning and profound satisfaction. Within us—burning brighter than any movie star—is our own star, our North Star, our soul. It is our birthright to uncover the soul—to remove the layers of fear or shame or apathy or cynicism that conceal it. A good place to start, and a place we come back to over and over again, is what Rumi calls the Open Secret.

Jelalluddin Rumi wrote poems so alive and clear that even today—eight centuries later—they shimmer with freshness. Their wisdom and humor are timeless; whenever I have an aha moment with one of Rumi's poems, I feel connected to the people throughout the ages who have climbed out of their confusion on the rungs of Rumi's words.

In several of his poems and commentaries, Rumi speaks of the Open Secret. He says that each one of us is trying to hide a secret—not a big bad secret, but a more subtle and pervasive one. It's the kind of secret that people in the streets of Istanbul kept from each other in the thirteenth century, when Rumi was writing his poetry. It's what I imagine Einstein tried to hide from his neighbors in Princeton, and they from him. And it's the same kind of secret that you and I keep from each other every day. You meet an old acquaintance, and she asks, "How are you?" You say, "Fine!" She asks, "How are the kids?" You say, "Oh, they're great." "The job?" "Just fine. I've been there five years now."

Then you ask that person, "How are you?" She says, "Fine!" You ask, "Your new house?" "I love it." "The new town?" "We're all settling in."

It's a perfectly innocent exchange of ordinary banter; each one of us has a similar kind every day. But it is probably not an accurate representation of our actual lives. We don't want to say that one of the kids is failing in school, or that our work often feels meaningless, or that the move to the new town may have been a colossal mistake. It's almost as if we are embarrassed by our most human traits. We tell ourselves that we don't have time to go into the gory details with everyone we meet; we don't know each other well enough; we don't want to appear sad, or confused, or weak, or self-absorbed. Better to keep under wraps our neurotic and nutty sides (not to mention our darker urges and more shameful desires). Why wallow publicly in the underbelly of our day-to-day stuff? Why wave the dirty laundry about, when all she asked was "How are you?"

Rumi says that when we hide the secret underbelly from each other, then both people go away wondering, How come she has it all together? How come her marriage/job/town/family works so well? What's wrong with me? We feel vaguely diminished from this ordinary interaction, and from hundreds of similar interactions we have from month to month and year to year. When we don't share the secret ache in our hearts—the normal bewilderment of being human—it turns into something else. Our pain and fear and longing in the absence of company, become alienation and envy and competition.

The irony of hiding the dark side of our humanness is that our secret is not really a secret at all. How can it be when we're all safeguarding the very same story? That's why Rumi calls it an Open Secret. It's almost a joke—a laughable admission that each one of us has a shadow self, a bumbling, bad-tempered twin. Big surprise! Just like you, I can be a jerk sometimes. I do unkind, cowardly things, harbor unmerciful thoughts, and mope around when I should be doing something constructive. Just like you, I wonder if life has meaning; I worry and fret over things I can't control; and I often feel overcome with a longing for something that I cannot even name. For all of my strengths and gifts, I am also a vulnerable and insecure person, in need of connection and reassurance. This is the secret I try to keep from you, and you from me, and in doing so we do each other a grave disservice.

Rumi tells us that moment we accept what troubles we've been given, *the door will open.* Sounds easy, sounds attractive, but it is difficult, and most of us pound on the door to freedom and happiness with every manipulative ploy save the one that actually works. If you're interested in opening the door to the heavens, start with the door to your own secret self. See what happens when you offer to another a glimpse of who you really are. Start slowly. Without getting dramatic, share the simple dignity of yourself in each moment—your triumphs and your failures, your satisfaction and your sorrow. Face your embarrassment at being human, and you'll uncover a deep well of passion and compassion. It's a great power, your Open Secret. When your heart is undefended, you make it safe for whomever you meet to put down his burden of hiding, and then you both can walk through the open door.

Bozos on the Bus

We're all bozos on the bus,
so we might as well sit back
and enjoy the ride.
—WAVY GRAVY

One of my heroes is the clown-activist Wavy Gravy. He is best known for a role that he played in 1969, when he was the master of ceremonies at the Woodstock festival. Since then, he's been a social activist, a major "fun-d"-raiser for good causes, a Ben & Jerry's ice-cream flavor, an unofficial hospital chaplain, and the founder of a camp for inner-city kids. Every four years he campaigns as a candidate for president of the United States, under the pseudonym Nobody, making speeches all over the country with slogans like "Nobody for President," "Nobody's Perfect," and "Nobody Should Have That Much Power." He's a seriously funny person, and a person who is serious about helping others. "Like the best of clowns," wrote a reporter in *The Village Voice*, "Wavy Gravy makes a big fool of himself as is necessary to make a wiser man of you. He is one of the better people on earth."

Wavy (I'm on a first-name basis with him from clown workshops he's offered at Omega) is a master of one-liners, like the famous one he delivered on the Woodstock stage: "What we have in mind is breakfast in bed for 400,000"; and this one, on why he became a clown: "You don't hear a bunch of bullies get together and say, 'Hey, let's go kill a few clowns.'"

But my all-time favorite Wavy-ism is the line that opens this chapter, about bozos on the bus, one he repeats whenever he speaks to groups, whether at clown workshops or in children's hospitals. I have co-opted the phrase, and I use it to begin my workshops, because I believe that we *are* all bozos on the bus, contrary to the self-assured image we work so hard to present to each other on a daily basis. We are all half-baked experiments—mistake-prone beings, born without an instruction book into a complex world. None of us are models of perfect behavior: We have all betrayed and been betrayed; we've been known to be egotistical, unreliable, lethargic, and stingy; and each one of us has, at times, awakened in the middle of the night worrying about everything from money, kids, or terrorism to wrinkled skin and receding hairlines. In other words, we're all bozos on the bus.

This, in my opinion, is cause for celebration. If we're all bozos, then for God's sake, we can put down the burden of pretense and get on with being bozos. We can approach the problems that visit bozo-type beings without the usual embarrassment and resistance. It is so much more effective to work on our rough edges with a light and forgiving heart. Imagine how freeing it would be to take a more compassionate and comedic view of the human condition— not as a way to deny our defects but as a way to welcome them as part of the standard human operating system. Every single person on this bus called Earth hurts; it's when we have shame about our failings that hurt turns into suffering. In our shame, we feel outcast, as if there is another bus somewhere, rolling along on a smooth road. Its passengers are all thin, healthy, happy, well-dressed, and well-liked people who belong to harmonious families, hold jobs that don't bore or aggravate them, and never do mean things, or goofy things like forget where they parked their car, lose their wallet, or say something totally inappropriate. We long to be on that bus with the other normal people.

But we are on the bus that says BOZO on the front, and we worry that we may be the only passenger onboard. This is the illusion that so many of us labor under—that we're all alone in our weirdness and our uncertainty; that we may be the most lost person on the highway. Of course we don't always feel like this. Sometimes a wave of self-forgiveness washes over us, and suddenly we're connected to our fellow humans; suddenly we belong.

It is wonderful to take your place on the bus with the other bozos. It may be the first step to enlightenment to understand with all of your brain cells that the other bus—that sleek bus with the cool people who know where they are going—is also filled with bozos: bozos in drag, bozos with secrets. When we see clearly that every single human being, regardless of fame or fortune or age or brains or beauty, shares the same ordinary foibles, a strange thing happens. We begin to cheer up, to loosen up, and we become as buoyant as those people we imagined on the other bus. As we rumble along the potholed road, lost as ever, through the valleys and over the hills, we find ourselves among friends. We sit back, and enjoy the ride.

Open-Heart Surgery

At the end of a workshop I was recently leading, a class member lingered behind to speak with me. He was a handsome man with a sharp sense of humor who had done equal amounts of joking and crying during the weekend. Workshops always attract at least one member from every known personality type, and this man had been the weekend's official "stressed-out driven professional" (except that he was beginning to soften around the edges). A heart surgeon at a major teaching hospital in New York, he was reeling from his father's recent death and his impending divorce.

"I just wanted to thank you," he said, shaking my hand. "I crack open people's hearts every day for a living, but you do the real kind of open-heart surgery." He went on to tell me that before the workshop he hadn't cried for years, even when his father died, even when his wife told him she was leaving. "I am so glad to finally feel something." He sighed, touching his heart. "Even if I have to cry every day for a couple of years, it's better than having a frozen heart."

Ever the researcher, I asked him what he thought had allowed him to thaw out here, in this workshop. The doctor dug for words. "I guess it was seeing that everyone in the room was going through something. Some version of what I'm going through. And nobody really knew what to do. It made me feel less alone. And they were people I could relate to. They were people just like me."

"And what kind of a person is that?" I asked.

"Well, intelligent people. Usually you think that people who cry in front of each other are, you know, sentimental. The kind of people who weep at lame movies or weddings. But these people were very intelligent," he said, puzzled by this seeming contradiction. "They were smart, but they weren't necessarily cynical, if that's possible. They were smart 'bozos on the bus'!"

"Welcome aboard," I said.

"This better not get back to my colleagues at the hospital," the doctor joked. "For the official record, I never admitted to being a bozo. Surgeons are supposed to be the smartest people on Earth. We never make mistakes; it's never our fault. My colleagues wouldn't buy the 'Open Secret' stuff. They don't think they're bozos on the bus. They think everyone else is."

"That sounds like an exhausting way to live." I laughed.

"It is," he said, quite seriously, tears coming to his eyes. "I gotta try to do it another way. It's killing me." He wiped his face, gave me an awkward hug, turned to leave, but then turned back again and blurted out, "Hey, I have an idea! I've watched you do your work. Would you like to come to my hospital and watch me perform heart surgery?"

"Wow, that's not an invitation I get every day," I said. I remembered how life altering it had been to see my first cesarean section when I was a midwife— to see the uterus positioned so perfectly in the pelvis, and the ovaries, curling upward like two flowering vines. After seeing that operation, I had never approached my body or the birth of a baby in the same way.

"Will I get to see a heart beating?" I asked, wondering how that experience might change my perception of my own body and of life itself.

"Yes, you'll see the heart beating, and the lungs filling with air, and the blood pumping back and forth between the two."

"Yes, I definitely want to see that," I said, having little idea of what I was getting myself into, not stopping to imagine what it takes to open the chest of a human being, to cut through the breastbone, expose the heart, stop the bleeding, and perform the meticulous and miraculous work of a heart surgeon.

A month later I scrubbed into an open-heart operation at 7:00 A.M., wondering what in the world I had been thinking. In the center of the chilled operating room—which was already humming with activity—lay the patient. She was naked, still as a corpse and the color of chalk. Already under general anesthesia, she was being prepped for surgery. Nurses were sterilizing her torso and her left leg, which a member of the surgical team would open in order to remove a vein. That vein would be sewn into the open heart to replace corroded arteries. The operating room was crowded with stainless steel stools, tables, and machines. Huge overhead lamps flooded different areas with a strong, colorless light. I retreated to a dim corner, shivering in a surgical gown and mask, feeling out of place and in the way.

My friend the doctor entered the room with another surgeon. They studied the patient's chart and murmured to each other, "Obese, sixty-year-old woman, referred from Brooklyn Hospital . . ." "Poor eating habits; smoked one pack of cigarettes a day for forty years . . ." "Previous myocardial infarction." "Valvular stenosis; atherosclerosis . . ." I stopped listening and concentrated on the woman asleep on the table. As the nurses draped her, I tried to commit her face to memory so that I wouldn't forget that the operation was being performed on an actual person—someone's mother, grandmother, wife. An image of her sitting on the stoop of an apartment building in Brooklyn came to me. I saw her chatting with friends, keeping an eye on her grandchildren, waiting for her husband to come home. I said a hasty prayer for her and her family as the nurses covered her in white sheets.

Now two more nurses scrubbed in and began readying trays and trays of tools, gloves, and sutures. The second surgeon had already begun opening the woman's leg; the anesthesiologist, like an air-traffic controller, was keeping a vigilant eye on his monitors; and the nurse who would be supervising the heart-lung machine stood at alert. My surgeon friend motioned to me to stand right next to him, and as I wedged myself between the operating table and a huge vibrating and beeping machine, he made his first cut into the woman's chest and announced in a jocular tone, "All right people, let's fix this old gal."

For six hours I bent over the old gal from Brooklyn, gazing intently at her heart, just as a parent would stare at the face of a newborn. My overwhelming emotion was awe—even when the surgeon sliced into the skin, and when he sawed through the breastbone and used huge metal clamps to pull apart the rib cage. For those six hours I knew what Albert Einstein meant when he said that the most appropriate response to life is "Sacred Awe." There was the heart! It seemed so small and tender to me, blub-blubbing with a trustworthy and endearing steadiness. And there were the lungs! They looked like underwater plants gracefully pulsating as they filled and emptied, filled and emptied. I watched the lungs and heart partnering in a well-rehearsed dance, enriching the blood with oxygen and pumping it to the rest of the body.

The surgeon—who in my awestruck eyes now seemed like a mythic figure, a knight in green scrubs—patiently explained to me every step he and his team took. From cutting back the layers of muscle and fat and tissue to closing off veins to carefully examining the condition of the heart, the team worked with a kind of swift yet scrupulous precision that I had never before witnessed. And all the while, as the surgeons discussed which arteries were salvageable, or if they could repair or would have to replace a faulty valve, the magnificent heart beat to its own spongy rhythm, working in tandem with the equally extraordinary lungs, each organ trying so valiantly to sustain life.

After several hours of determining their strategy, the surgeons undertook the dangerous task of attaching the patient to the heart-lung machine, which for the rest of the operation would keep her alive. Without the flow of blood, the heart deflated from the size of a grapefruit to something so small and insignificant looking that I was afraid the nurses would lose it as they cleaned and swabbed and changed the pads and drapes surrounding the woman. But the surgeons took the little heart and packed it in ice, and using magnifying glasses and tiny scalpels, they cut away the malfunctioning arteries and replaced them with delicate sections of the vein they had taken from the patient's leg. Finally, they removed the faulty valve and stitched in a new metal one, which would remain inside the woman for the rest of her life.

All during this courageous procedure the surgeons and nurses showed signs of being both heroes and bozos on the bus. The nurses were saints at one moment, then just grouchy, overworked women, each with her own beating heart and pulsating lungs. The doctors were skilled professionals as well as a bunch of jerky guys, complaining about their wives and work, and joking disdainfully about the patient's condition—her obesity, her diet, her cigarette habit. "Yeah, she'll be pulling into McDonald's in a few days," one of them griped as he bent over her open chest and, with great sensitivity and care, sewed hundreds of tiny stitches to secure her new valve.

By 1:00 P.M. I had been standing in the same spot for six hours. The operation was not going the way the doctors had anticipated and would take several more hours to complete. My friend decided to have a colleague take over for a while, so I stepped out too. I said a dazed good-bye, somehow found my car in the hospital lot, and drove home with the image of an open heart blazoned in my mind's eye. It was a drizzly spring afternoon, and all around me I sensed the open heart of nature, the steady beat of life, the utter vulnerability—and also the dignity and significance—of it all. For days afterward I was in an altered state. Every person I saw, from my husband and friends to strangers on the street, had a heart, had lungs, was breathing and pulsating and participating in a rhythmic dance. After a while, my ecstatic vision dimmed, and the people closest to me breathed a sigh of relief. I was getting hard to take.

But I still shut my eyes sometimes and see that woman from Brooklyn lying on the operating table with her heart wide open to the world. I sense her spirit hovering between her body and the other worlds. I see my friend the surgeon doing the best he can to help a stranger live. The scene fills me with tenderness for all of us bozos on the bus. It reminds me of our dual nature: our spirit, which beats to the big sound of the universe, and our human form, which relies on the perseverance of the heart and the lungs. I have fallen in love with hearts and lungs. While I am here, contained within bones and muscles, organs and skin, I want to take care of the gift of my body. I want to feed it well, move it gracefully, and rest it deeply. I know that the life force beats on, even when the heart has stopped, but while I have a heart and lungs, I want to treat them with sacred awe. And while I dwell with others who are just like me, I want to see them for who they really are, in all of their fragility and all of their majesty.

Heart Warrior

I have read more spiritual texts and self-help books than is probably legal. So when I say that one paragraph changed my life forever, I am comparing it with hundreds of thousands of words, arranged into all sorts of poetry and philosophy and prose. I remember exactly where I was when I first read the paragraph, what I was feeling before I read it, and how those words cleared a pathway in my heart upon which I have been traveling ever since.

It was 1981. I was twenty-nine years old. My husband and I had recently left the commune and were doing something we had never done before as a family: We were taking a vacation. We were on a picture-perfect Caribbean island with our two little boys, and I was sitting on a beach towel as the boys splashed in the sparkling ocean. I was reading in the way that a mother reads, with one eye on her children and one eye on the words. The book in my lap, covered with a thin film of sand and sunscreen and the kids' apple juice, was *Shambhala: The Sacred Path of the Warrior,* by the Tibetan Buddhist Chögyam Trungpa. Trungpa was one of my first meditation teachers. I met him when I was a nineteen-year-old college student in New York City—the same year I met my boyfriend, who would become my husband and the father of my children, the same ones I was watching while reading on the beach.

But before then, before marriage and children, back when I was in college, my husband-to-be and I liked to read Chögyam Trungpa's early books aloud to each other. We would do so while taking the bus downtown in New York, on our way to a funky loft in the Village where we would sit in meditation under the puzzling and electrifying guidance of the man himself. Trungpa had recently arrived in the United States. He was forced by the Chinese to flee Tibet when he was twenty. Escaping torture and death, he led his fellow monks on a perilous winter journey over the Himalayas. After living in exile in India, then studying at Oxford, the young Chögyam Trungpa was picked by the Dalai Lama to bring the Buddhist teachings of Tibet to the West. He would become one of the most important Buddhist teachers of the twentieth century.

I knew Trungpa was a brilliant man and a powerful teacher. But there was something out of control about him, something that scared me. At that point in my young life, I was looking for an anchor. I wanted a practice that would keep me from drowning in the ocean of my emotions. I thought I was an over-sensitive and romantic girl who needed some sense knocked into her dreamy head. I thought that maybe meditation or yoga would guide me safely out of the fog, away from the storms and into the Promised Land of peace and clarity.

But Trungpa had other ideas about the spiritual quest. He was a wild guide. His directions led right into the inner ocean, and smack into the waves of longing, fear, anger, restlessness, or whatever else one found in the churning nature of the heart. He taught meditation as a way of swimming fearlessly in any ocean. He was not interested in spirituality as a form of escape. He was training people to become "sacred warriors"—not so that they could do battle with others but so that they could develop the kind of courage one needs to be kind and happy and radically alive in the midst of the world. There is no dry land, he said; there is only fearlessness, which is to be found in the heart. This is the path to freedom.

At nineteen I wasn't ready to follow that path, and I didn't stick around long enough to see where it led. I stopped studying with Chögyam Trungpa, but I continued to read every book he published. It wasn't until I was sitting on the Caribbean beach, several years into marriage and motherhood, that I figured out what Trungpa had been talking about. I was now close to thirty, and things were not going well in my life. Although I didn't know it at the time, I was drowning in an ocean of unexplored feelings. What I did know was that I often was scared and confused. If I stopped to examine my anxiety, I would sense an undertow pulling me downward, as if a monster from the depths was dragging me beneath the surface. But I was loath to look at what lay beneath. What if I found something terribly wrong there? Something wrong with me, or wrong with the way I had arranged my life? What if I found I wanted to make some big changes? What if I started crying and couldn't stop? These were the kinds of thoughts I entertained but never followed through to any kind of con-clusion. I was too busy with my little boys, too overwhelmed at work, too unsettled about my marriage. There was just too much going on to slow down and feel the pull.

Wiggling my toes in the sand, watching my boys swim in the clear blue water, I arrived at this paragraph where Chögyam Trungpa wrote:

Going beyond fear begins when we examine our fear: our anxiety, nervousness, concern, and restlessness. If we look into our fear, if we look beneath the veneer, the first thing we find is sadness, beneath the nervousness. Nervousness is cranking up, vibrating all the time. When we slow down, when we relax with our fear, we find sadness, which is calm and gentle. Sadness hits you in your heart, and your body produces a tear. Before you cry, there is a feeling in your chest and then, after that, you produce tears in your eyes. You are about to produce rain or a waterfall in your eyes and you feel sad and lonely and perhaps romantic at the same time. That is the first tip of fearlessness, and the first sign of real warriorship. You might think that, when you experience fearlessness, you will hear the opening to Beethoven's Fifth Symphony or see a great explosion in the sky, but it doesn't happen that way. Discovering fearlessness comes from working with the softness of the human heart.

I sat on the beach with those words resonating throughout my body. Reading them was like looking into a mirror and loving my face for the first time. "You feel sad and lonely and perhaps romantic at the same time," Trungpa had written. "That is the first tip of fearlessness, and the first sign of real warriorship." Was he saying that the peace and clarity I was searching for was already within me, waiting in the liquid gold of my feeling heart? That I had been repressing the very parts of myself that could liberate me? This was revolutionary, yet at the same time, completely obvious.

Everything I knew to be true about life was in that paragraph. How many times had I felt a mysterious link between my small, tender heart and the vast spirit of the universe? How many times had genuine tears of sadness made me feel strangely bold and alive? How many times had I almost awakened from dullness and self-doubt while in the chambers of beauty and love? Trungpa was telling me to trust what I already knew, to dignify the longings of the human heart, and to respect its romantic, quixotic nature. He was saying that life as a human being here on Earth could not be sanitized, rationalized, or tranquilized into a rigid vision of the way it's "supposed to be." Life would always be quirky, dynamic, changing, and messy. The way of the heart—that inner instinct that draws us creatively into the chaos of life—is, ironically, also the way out of confusion, anxiety, and suffering.

Certain moments are like swinging doors that lead from one room of a life to another. In that moment, sitting on the Caribbean beach and imbibing Trungpa's words, I took my first steps beyond the room of trying to be someone I wasn't. The door swung open into the long hallway of becoming myself. Trungpa's teachings convinced me to use my heart's compass on the journey. Perhaps that compass would lead me into the unknown. Perhaps I would have to make some big changes. I was still afraid, but now I sensed where to look for courage.

It would take years for me to integrate what I had read into my life. But at least now I understood the roots of my inability to make big and powerful decisions at home or work. I had been asking only one organ—my poor brain—to carry the full weight of my life. It was time to give some of the work over to my heart. Why had I been so afraid to peer into its depth? Perhaps it was because intellectual understanding is lionized in Western society, and emotional intelligence is berated as an untrustworthy way of experiencing reality. Perhaps it was because I had grown up in a culture and a family that valued thinking and doing over feeling and loving. But here was Chögyam Trungpa, this brilliant thinker, this advanced scholar, and this brave warrior, whispering like a spiritual Cupid in my ear: "Follow the tender girl who longs for love. She knows the way. Don't be afraid."

"For the warrior," says Trungpa, "the experience of sad and tender heart is what gives birth to fearlessness. Conventionally, being fearless means that you are not afraid or that if someone hits you, you will hit him back. However, we are not talking about that street-fighter level of fearlessness. Real fearlessness is the product of tenderness."

Lightening Up and
Falling Down

When I first started leading workshops, my self-esteem as a teacher was pretty low. It didn't take much to throw me off and leave me wondering if I had what it took, or if I really knew anything worth sharing. There was a person or two in every workshop who attacked my "Open Secret" theory for being too depressing. These same people rejected Trungpa's notion of "the warrior's heart of sadness" and did not appreciate being identified as just another bozo on the bus. It wasn't that they couldn't accept that all of us have our flaws and foibles, but why, they would wonder, should we focus on that? What about positive thinking? What about rising above your problems instead of wallowing in them? What about teaching the group how to be more playful instead of pushing them toward embracing their grief? What a gloomy way to live! I'd hear these people out and wonder if I wasn't too deep for my own good. Should I lighten up?

Looking back over twenty years of teaching personal growth workshops and leading meditation retreats, I see now that part of my own growth has been to lighten up. While some people come into this world needing to learn how to tame their inner party animal, I've had to learn how to spice up my profundity with a dash of play here and a touch of joy there. Over the years, I've become much better at splashing around like a happy kid in the shallower water.

But I have also learned something else in my years of teaching. I know now that many people are scared to death of their deeper nature. I no longer take it personally if a workshop student suddenly withdraws his attention when I talk about the warrior's heart of sadness, or if he vociferously rejects being a bozo. Now I see gold in the glazed-over eyes, and I hear "Eureka!" in the persistent complaints. Now I know that these people—more than the others, who sit nodding their heads in agreement—are longing to connect with their warrior's heart and with the hearts of their fellow humans.

I have stayed in touch with some of my workshop students—Christmas cards, wedding announcements, e-mail greetings. Some have searched me out when they needed support during a rough time. Surprisingly, the students who have leaned on me the most were the ones who initially resisted the notion that sorrow and grief are natural aspects of the human condition. It has been the anti-bozos who have ended up calling me in the middle of a crisis, exhibiting undeniable bozo behavior. Some I have not been able to help; some I have.

When I first met her, Karen was in her late twenties and just finishing graduate school. She was a resolutely cheerful person—an athlete with enviable energy and a dazzling smile. She had won several rock-climbing competitions, and now she taught swing dancing. Just being around her made me feel dowdy.

Something attracted her to my workshops, even though she was one of those students whose eyes glazed over when I talked about going *through* pain in order to find sustainable joy. "I've been bebopping past pain so far," she said in one class, "and I aim to keep on dancing." Yet Karen kept dancing back to my classes, where all I could do was witness her resistance and gently point out that her failed relationships and her complex feelings toward her family and her unhappiness at work would persist until she stopped trying so hard to bebop past pain.

One year I heard through a mutual friend that Karen was suffering from a potentially terminal thyroid disorder that was completely curable when caught in time and treated by medication. This friend was afraid that Karen's shame about being sick was going to kill her. She begged me to call her. I hadn't seen Karen in a few years, and when I spoke to her on the phone, she insisted that her positive attitude and her dancing steps could pull her through this crisis. But her situation became life threatening. One day she telephoned me in a panic. After we hung up I was afraid for her life, and I called an ambulance against her will. Later her doctor told me that she had been hours away from dying. I had never seen anyone go to such lengths to keep the supposed secret of her humanness from the world. It took nearly dying for Karen finally to surrender her goal of perfection. She still sends me Christmas cards thanking me for saving her life as well as for sticking with her until she was able to join the other bozos on the bus.

I have also had to accept that there are some people I cannot help. Last year I received the sad news that a student had taken her own life. On the surface, Amy was a real live wire—a bright and zealous force of nature who was always smiling. She came to one of the first workshops I taught. When we went around the circle and introduced ourselves, Amy announced that she was a dancer and a martial artist who was there to learn how to teach workshops herself. During the week she sat in the front row, took copious notes, and held herself tall during meditation. But she would leave the room when it was time for small group interactions. At breaks, when others would relax and chat, she would dance around the room by herself. Her favorite parts of the workshop were the silent meditations and the movement exercises. She told me in private that she had nothing of interest to share with the group, that through spiritual practice she had risen above all of her negativity and unhappiness.

As Amy got older, things became more complicated—money, career, marriage. I saw her from time to time when she came to Omega to teach martial arts to our staff. I noticed that her smile now seemed pained, as if it was an uncomfortable mask that was beginning to chafe. Although she never attended another of my workshops, she came to see me a few years ago, when she and her husband were having difficulties. It was terribly hard for her to admit to me that things weren't as rosy as once reported. None of my assurances that her problems were identical to those of 99 percent of the human population seemed to relieve her. When I asked her what she was doing for her depression, she said she wasn't depressed. She was mad at herself and ashamed that she had forgotten how to be happy. "Everyone else seems to remember," she said with a rigid smile. "I'm such a wimp."

Over time Amy became agoraphobic, embarrassed to leave her home and reveal to the world who she had become. She wrote me letters comparing herself negatively with others and apologizing for having let me down. I urged her to get psychiatric help, and for a while she seemed to respond to medication. And then I got the news that she had committed suicide. I keep my memory of Amy alive through a photograph tacked on the wall of my writing room. There she is now, dressed in her white martial arts uniform, dancing close to the edge of the abyss as the sun sets over the Grand Canyon. It's more of an apt metaphor than I had suspected.

In the past when I would meet someone like Amy or Karen, I would wonder if I hadn't gotten it wrong. Maybe one *could* defy the odds and frolic through life without a big fall. When I noticed someone teetering near the edge, I would pray for her to walk around the abyss. Now I pray for something different. I pray that each one of us stays awake as we fall. I pray that we choose to go into the abyss willingly and that our fall is cushioned by faith—faith that at the bottom we will be caught and taught and turned toward the light. I pray that we don't waste precious energy feeling ashamed of our mistakes, or embarrassed by our flaws. After years of teaching, I know only a few things for sure. One is this: We are chunks of dense matter that need to be cracked open. Our errors and failings are chinks in the heart's armor through which our true colors can shine.

When They Revolutionize
the Cocktail Parties

We are built to make mistakes,
coded for error.
—LEWIS THOMAS

I was once asked to speak at a conference exploring the intersection of science and religion. Many of the conference participants were scientists, as were most of the other speakers. I don't know exactly what the organizers had in mind when they invited me to deliver a keynote address, but I decided to talk about the root of genius in both scientific exploration and spiritual enlightenment.

I started my talk with the quotation above from Lewis Thomas, one of the great physicians and science writers of our time. Thomas used research from cell biology to show how species evolve and thrive by making, and learning from, their mistakes. His own mistakes, he wrote, were his best teachers. "Why then," I asked the scientists in the packed ballroom of a New York City hotel, "if we are biologically coded for error, do we expend so much energy trying to appear as if we never make mistakes, that we know it all?" The scientists squirmed in their uncomfortable folding chairs. I continued. I told them that the Zen master Shunryu Suzuki instructed his students to approach every meditation session—even if they had been practicing for twenty-five years—with Beginner's Mind. He said that "in the beginner's mind there are many pos-

sibilities, in the expert's mind, there are few." The people who contribute the
most important wisdom to both science and spirituality approach their disci-
plines with Beginner's Mind. They start like children start, unafraid to admit to
themselves and the world that they don't know—that they are beginners. They
are the opposite of know-it-alls. They are I-don't-know-it-alls. They are not
afraid to look dumb or make mistakes. Because of that, they go places others
won't and try things others don't. That is where the new discoveries are lurking.

"So," I asked again, "if mistakes provide the best opportunity for discovery
and evolution, why do we go around trying to look so sure of ourselves all the
time?" I invited the crowd of left-brain thinkers to put down their notebooks
and papers and join in an exercise. There was a palpable sense of panic in the
room. "Don't worry," I said, "this isn't going to hurt." And just to put them at
ease, I asked, "How many of you know five other people in the room?" A few
people tentatively looked around, then raised their hands. "How many of you
know two other people in the room?" A couple of more hands went into the
air. "How many of you came alone and don't know anyone?" This time almost
everyone in the ballroom raised a hand. "See?" I reassured them. "Since you'll
probably never see each other again, you don't have to worry about doing
something foolish. Go ahead, make a fool of yourself.

"Now, turn to someone in the room you have never met. Introduce your-
selves and tell each other why you have come to this conference." Relieved at
the benign nature of the exercise, the participants broke into pairs, and a buzz
of chatting and laughing swirled around the room. After a few minutes I interrupted and said, "Now, turn back to your partner and answer this question:
Why are you *really* here? This is a conference about spirituality. What really
drew you here? What's going on in your heart of hearts that caused you to take
the time to join this group of people, in this room, on this day? Why are you
really here? Remember, you can say whatever you want—anything you've always wanted to tell a stranger but were afraid to admit. And one more thing,"
I told the scientists. "This exercise will not jeopardize your work. You can become soft in the heart without becoming soft in the head."

Again the crowd broke into pairs. This time they leaned in a little closer,
and the talking was quieter. I gave them more time to travel a few layers beneath the surface, a few layers down into the soul realms. Then I called the
group back together. In closing, I suggested that the point where science and religion meet could be called the soul.

"What is the soul?" a man in the audience asked.

"The soul," I said, "was the one who just answered the question 'Why are you *really* here?' It is the wise and whole and brave part of the self. The soul is the ageless longing for truth that sends scientists into the lab and seekers onto the spiritual path."

And that was the end of my speech.

A couple of weeks later I received a letter from a woman who had been at the conference. She wrote:

I was truly astounded by the real talk you inspired in your presentation to the large group at the conference. When I spoke to the woman sitting next to me for a few minutes, I felt I knew her better than I know some of my friends. Would that we could bring whatever it was you did to encourage such honesty into our everyday lives. Wouldn't the world be better! Here is a poem I wrote, stimulated by that conversation.

When They Revolutionize the Cocktail Parties
By Marilyn Sandberg

"Hello, what are you afraid of?"
"Death."
"Me too."
"When you hear a Mahler symphony?"
"No, when I wake up in the night."
"Me too."
"Nice meeting you."
"Same here."

Sleeping Giants and
Strange Angels

What is the knocking at the door in the night?
It is somebody wants to do us harm.
No, no, it is the three strange angels.
Admit them, admit them.
—D. H. LAWRENCE

If you have spent a long time on the surface of your life, you will begin to hear a knock at the door in the night. You may already know what that knock sounds like. It sounds as if someone you don't want to see has come for a visit. It sounds like—as the author D. H. Lawrence says—someone who *wants to do us harm.* But Lawrence begs you to pay closer attention. Perhaps you've been turning angels away from your door. Perhaps the dangerous desires—the Sleeping Giants in the basement of your life—are really angels come to deliver you from your shrunken dreams and your anxious self-doubts.

The soul's knock in the night can take many forms. You may experience it as a deep sense of longing. Not the kind of longing that leads to the mall or the refrigerator but the kind that moves downward, to a soft ache in the heart. It's the kind of longing that leads you to ask, "Is this all there is to my life? Is this what I am supposed to be doing, feeling, giving, getting?" This kind of longing can feel threatening. And so you silence its rumblings over and over until it demands to be heard—until it morphs into something else: a crisis or an illness or an addiction or some other Strange Angel.

The knock at the door can come as a disquieting dream or as a secret plan that you pray you'll never enact: leaving a job or a marriage, finally telling your mother off, revealing a hidden truth to the world. Are these bad ideas, or are they Sleeping Giants and Strange Angels? Perhaps it is best to leave these kinds of questions unanswered. Perhaps it is best to stay away from the underworld where Giants sleep and Angels knock.

But the soul wants you to go beneath. It leads downward. It says, "Don't ignore the signs. Follow your longing down. Go beneath the surface of your troubled mind, your bad moods, your repetitive mistakes. Go beneath the surface questions to even deeper questions." The soul asks questions like these: "What is that weight that holds you back? What inside of you is saying *no!*? Are you willing to look at yourself? To take responsibility for your own life? Are you willing to let something die, in order for something new to arise? What must die? What wants to live?" The soul tells you to root around in the dark stuff for the deeper questions, and to let those questions lead you from the darkness to the light.

When you feel chronically confused, or stuck, or enraged, or afraid, you can be sure that Sleeping Giants are rumbling under the surface of your life. They want to awaken. Soon they'll be knocking at the door. You are welcome to turn them away. You can spend a lifetime turning them away and going back to sleep. Or you can open the door and admit them. The Sleeping Giants and Strange Angels may bring with them risky advice. If you listen, your life may change; you will certainly change. If you turn a deaf ear, you'll stay the same. It's up to you.

Giants have been slumbering within us throughout our life. Some people go about their business for years and years before paying attention to what lies beneath. They may be forty or fifty or sixty before the Giants begin to stir. Others hear the call early on. Why is this? I don't know. It doesn't matter. It's not a race. All that matters is that when you hear the soul's call—the Sleeping Giants, the knock in the night, the Strange Angels—you pay attention.

The poet and author Robert Bly writes: "During all the time we were busy going to college, or getting up a career, or longing for purity, a mysterious force was invading the kingdom. How often men and women in their twenties feel suddenly in danger. A secret voice says, 'You must make a change, son. If you don't, it will be too late.' . . . Observers have noticed for centuries that when the effort for change heats up the psyche, the heat itself attracts demons, or sleeping complexes, or bitter enemies of the spirit—trouble of some sort." Bly calls this trouble "the Hideous Damsel time," the time when we meet the ugly hag in the woods and confront all that wants to change within us. He says, "In our tranquilizer age it is the general opinion that the Hideous Damsel time should be avoided and treated as an illness to be cured." But, he warns, "to banish her darkness is to sterilize one's chance at the evolution she brings."

Hideous Damsels, Sleeping Giants, and Strange Angels may seem the stuff of fairy tales, but fairy tales are really stories about our own lives—stories that dip beneath the surface and venture into the deeper, darker landscapes. That's why children love them. Children are still at home in the soul realm. They are in touch with both the fearsome and the fantastic nature of life. They are growing every day—learning, changing, and evolving. Go back to the fairy tales and myths you loved as a child and reread them from the perspective of an adult. Take note of the ways in which the evil witches and nasty gnomes always appear and always lead the children back into life, all the wiser for having confronted them. Go back to the Bible and read about Daniel in the lions' den, or Jacob wrestling an angel, or other Old and New Testament heroes who brave the dark places in order to discover the light.

So many of the crises we bring upon ourselves are Angels trying to get our attention. An illness or loss or heartbreak is often a Hideous Damsel, or a Sleeping Giant, or a Strange Angel who wants to help us evolve. In times of upheaval, we have two choices: We can relate to our circumstances as messengers from the deep, or we can shut down, defend our position, and add another layer of protection to the castle wall. If we defend against the Strange Angels, we will become more and more numb to life. We will remain unchanged. If we allow the Angels entry, we will open the door to change and evolution. As in a fairy tale, the moral may be a simple one, but the story maps a dangerous, fantastic, and transformational journey.

The Rapture of Being Alive

People say that what we're all seeking is a meaning for life.
I don't think that's what we're really seeking.
I think that what we're seeking
is an experience of being alive . . .
so that we actually feel the rapture of being alive.
—JOSEPH CAMPBELL

Joseph Campbell spent more than half a century mining the wisdom repositories of religion, myth, and art. At the end of Campbell's long career, when Bill Moyers asked him about the meaning of life, Campbell surprised Moyers by saying that it isn't *meaning* people have been seeking down through the ages but something he called "the rapture of being alive." After years of not only research but also participation in organized religious traditions and indigenous rites of passage, Campbell affirmed that each human being—whether from ancient Greece, or tribal Africa, or modern America—is not really hankering for a special vocation or an Earth-saving mission or some scholarly understanding of enlightenment. Rather, what we want are vibrant, full-bodied experiences of being alive. And if a desire to serve humanity or to find God comes from a rapturous engagement with life, then our service and our search will bear fruit. But if we try to love or lead, or work or pray, from a dry well, then we will serve a bitter cup to those around us and never really live the life we were given.

When I look at the pinched faces of television evangelists or the rigid bodies of angry activists marching in mobs, I want to take them aside and rub their shoulders, wipe the furrows from their brows, feed them something delicious, and make them laugh. I want to say, "It doesn't have to be so intense, so fierce, so acrimonious. You can work to ease the ills of society, and at the same time you can love the world with all of its sorrow and beauty. You can serve your God without being so uptight about it. You can feel the simple rapture of being alive and let that rapture be your North Star. You can be led by a quiet joy."

It may seem that living for rapture is a selfish act reserved for the elite, or that it's a fancy phrase for hedonism. But it isn't. Rapture is not a selfish emotion. It is pure gratitude, flowing freely through the body, heart, and soul. Gratitude for what? For breath, for colors, for music, for friendship, humor, weather, sleep, awareness. It is a willing engagement with the whole messy miracle of life. The world suffers more from unhappy, stifled people trying to do good than it does from those who are simply content within themselves.

In the end, it is the people at home in their own human skins—people who love the wounded world and its broken family—who can move mountains when called out of themselves and into a work in the world. The founders of the great religions were such people. Their ability to heal and awaken the masses sprang first and foremost from their personal experiences of being broken open. Every great hero—past and present—took a difficult journey of self-awareness before finding his or her rapture. Buddha spent several years alone in the forest, where he grappled with suffering. His enlightenment has illuminated the path for millions of others. Jesus broke from tradition, left his family and community, and went into the desert for forty days and nights, as the Hebrew prophets did before him. In the forest, in the desert, they confronted their inner demons, and there they found themselves. What they sought to right in the world, they righted first within their own hearts, and in doing so gained humility and authenticity. They went deep into the darkness—into an acceptance and transformation of their own capacity for sin—and emerged with a rapture that was theirs forever.

How odd that if we reject what is painful, we find only more pain, but if we embrace what is within us—if we peer fearlessly into the shadows—we stumble upon the light. "Once, as we were discussing the subject of suffering," Bill Moyers said about his conversations with Campbell, "he mentioned in tandem James Joyce and Igjugarjuk. 'Who is Igjugarjuk?' I said, barely able to imitate the pronunciation. 'Oh,' replied Campbell, 'he was the shaman of a

Caribou Eskimo tribe in northern Canada, the one who told European visitors that the only true wisdom lives far from mankind, out in the great loneliness, and can be reached only through suffering."

The great loneliness—like the loneliness a caterpillar endures when she wraps herself in a silky shroud and begins the long transformation from chrysalis to butterfly. It seems that we too must go through such a time, when life as we have known it is over—when being a caterpillar feels somehow false and yet we don't know who we are supposed to become. All we know is that something bigger is calling us to change. And though we must make the journey alone, and even if suffering is our only companion, soon enough we will become a butterfly, soon enough we will taste the rapture of being alive.

I have a card stuck on my refrigerator that shows a woman standing in reverence before an open freezer door, saying, "Amazing! Perfect ice cubes again." That's the kind of simple rapture I am talking about. I realize we are not put on this earth to stand around open freezers ranting like idiots about ice cubes. But a good question to ask yourself is this: If perfect ice cubes or an evening sky or an old song on the radio has not made your heart flip-flop lately, why not? What is keeping you from feeling the rapture? I can assure you, you won't find the answer in a lighted room. What stands between you and a full-bodied life can be found only in the shadows. What wants to live in you may be waiting—as it was for me—at the end of a long loneliness.

PART II

The
Phoenix Process

THE TRANSFORMATIONAL JOURNEY is a voyage with a hundred different names: the Odyssey, the Grail quest, the great initiation, the death and rebirth process, the supreme battle, the dark night of the soul, the hero's journey. All of these names describe the process of surrendering to a time of great difficulty, allowing the pain to break us open, and then being reborn—stronger, wiser, and kinder. Every religion includes in its texts stories of descent and rebirth. From Jonah in the whale to Jesus on the cross, and from the Hindu hero Arjuna on the battlefield to the prince Siddhartha losing everything to become the Buddha, the great ones have gone before us on this journey. When Bill Moyers asked Joseph Campbell about the hero's journey, Campbell said, "A legendary hero is usually the founder of something—the founder of a new age, the founder of a new religion, the founder of a new city, the founder of a new way of life."

In response, Moyers asked, "But doesn't this leave all the rest of us ordinary mortals back onshore?"

"I don't think there is any such thing as an ordinary mortal," Campbell answered. "I always feel uncomfortable when people speak about ordinary mortals because I've never met an ordinary man, woman, or child. . . . You might say that the founder of a life—your life or mine, if we live our own lives, instead of imitating everybody else's life—comes from a quest as well."

I have my own name for the quest. I call it the Phoenix Process—in honor of the mythic bird with golden plumage whose story has been told throughout the ages. The Egyptians called the bird the Phoenix and believed that every five hundred years he renewed his quest for his true self. Knowing that a new way could be found only with the death of his worn-out habits, defenses, and beliefs, the Phoenix built a pyre of cinnamon and myrrh, sat in the flames, and burned to death. Then he rose from the ashes as a new being—a fusion of who he had been before and who he had become. A new bird, yet ever more himself; changed, and at the same time the eternal Phoenix. Of the Phoenix bird, the Roman poet Ovid said, "Most beings spring from other individuals, but there is a certain kind that reproduces itself."

You and I are the Phoenix. We too can reproduce ourselves from the shattered pieces of a difficult time. Our lives ask us to die and to be reborn every time we confront change—change within ourselves and change in our world.

When we descend all the way down to the bottom of a loss, and dwell patiently, with an open heart, in the darkness and pain, we can bring back up with us the sweetness of life and the exhilaration of inner growth. When there is nothing left to lose, we find the true self—the self that is whole, the self that is enough, the self that no longer looks to others for definition, or completion, or anything but companionship on the journey.

This is the way to live a meaningful and hopeful life—a life of real happiness and inner peace. This is the Phoenix Process.

To start a fire you need a spark—an ember, or a match, or the steady and stressful rubbing of one object over another. Once the fire is ignited, you need a different sort of heat to turn the flames of adversity into the wisdom of a Phoenix Process. We all experience change and loss throughout our lives—through big and dramatic life-quakes and in smaller, more habitual ways. It takes work to use crisis and stress as vehicles for transformation. All the stories in this part of the book are about the sparks that have started fires in other people's lives, and about the hard work they did to turn the fire into a Phoenix Process. The next part of the book is the story of my Phoenix Process. While my tale is hardly as traumatic as the following stories, the moral is the same. I am a different sort of person in the aftermath of my divorce, and while I would never recommend the breaking of hearts and of a family as a path toward transformation, I am still grateful for the lessons learned along the way.

The Phoenix Process is a journey that is different for everyone, and therefore it is a trek into uncharted territory. It is erroneous, and even unhelpful, to compare one person's journey with another's—all are different, and one is not more profound or important than another. The most momentous situation—the loss of a child, a serious illness, a national tragedy—has the power to transform one's life, but so do less traumatic events. It's all in the way we approach the changing nature of life; it's all in the courage to say yes to whatever comes our way; it's in the way we listen for the messages in the flames and dig for the treasure in the ashes.

Each one of us, regardless of our situation, is looking for the same treasure in the ashes. We are in search of our most authentic, vital, generous, and wise self. What stands between that self and us is what burns in the fire. Our illusions, our rigidity, our fear, our blame, our lack of faith, and our sense of separation: All of these—in varying strengths and combinations—are what must die in order for a more true self to arise. If we want to turn a painful event into a Phoenix Process, we must name what needs to burn within us. I have observed people in the workshops I lead grappling with a rich variety of issues as they name the specific elements of their Phoenix Process. Some people realize that what must burn in the fire is their fear—fear of their own power, fear of change, fear of loss, fear of others. Some people name an inability to feel, a crippling cynicism, a sense of shame, a stance of anger.

I have noticed that for many women a Phoenix Process starts when they admit to themselves that they are tired of doing things only to please other people. They realize that they have little respect for their own needs and their own opinions. In the flames of a crisis, they suddenly understand what must burn. When the new Phoenix arises, they have claimed their positive power. They know and trust themselves, and therefore they are more dependable and trustworthy to others. Men often go into the flames because they are numb or because their inability to feel love and compassion has backed them into a half-lived life. There is within them a treasure trove of unfelt joys and grief just waiting for the heat of the fire. They arise from the ashes with the gift of openness, empathy, and a more potent experience of being human.

Of course, your particular process depends less on gender and more on personality, upbringing, timing, and needs. Each one of our descents and rebirths will look as unique as our faces. And throughout our lives, as we change and grow, we will bring different parts of ourselves to the fire, and arise each time with new gifts.

Although I understand that each person's process is different, when I am going through a difficult transition or a painful change, I take great strength and solace from the stories of others who have survived and prospered in the flames of a Phoenix Process. Those who are broken open by the kinds of experiences that seem impossible to bear inspire me. It is in that vein that I offer these stories.

Chimidunchik

The last of the human freedoms
is to choose one's attitude
in any given set of circumstances.
—VICTOR FRANKL

M y best friend's mother and father survived the Holocaust, escaping with their lives and not much more. Ruth, my friend's mother, was the only member of her family to survive. She was nineteen when she arrived in Canada, where she met Julius, who was to become her husband and my friend's father. Julius was a tall man, with a big sense of humor and a commanding presence. He was quite a bit older than Ruth. He had lost not only his parents and siblings in the concentration camps but also his first wife and their five-year-old child, although my friend would not learn about this until her father was an old man and close to death.

Most people who fled the Nazis and came to America took their grief and memories, tied them tight in a sack, and hid them somewhere, anywhere, in order to assimilate into the upbeat era of the 1950s. Julius put his memories high up on a shelf, where no one could find them, and then went about the business of living. He made a lot of money; he surrounded himself with friends and the happy things of an American life; and he did everything he could to steer his family onward, away from the dark shadows of the past.

Ruth tried to bury her memories deep in the chambers of her heart. She was a small and beautiful woman, with delicate features and translucent skin.

She was the youngest child of a wealthy and cultured Jewish family in Poland. When the Nazis began rounding up the Jews and moving them into the Warsaw ghetto, Ruth's father devised a plan for his family's survival. He paid a man he knew—a Catholic man who had worked for him—to build a room in the basement of his house. Ruth and her parents and siblings would one by one escape from the ghetto and hide in the room, where the Catholic man and his wife would care for the family.

Ruth was the first sent to the basement refuge. Her mother sewed diamonds into the hem of her coat. She gave her forged papers, attesting to a new name and a Catholic identity. Her father told her to be brave; the rest of the family, he said, would follow. He brought her to the edge of the ghetto, where a resistance fighter secreted her away.

Ruth stayed in the basement for weeks, waiting for her family. They never came. Someone else did, though. The resistance fighter arrived one morning looking for the diamonds in Ruth's coat. He told the Catholic man and his wife that if Ruth didn't give him the diamonds, he would turn them all in to the SS guards. Frightened, the couple asked Ruth to leave. As the bombing in Warsaw began, Ruth hid in the streets; her mother and father and sisters and brothers all died in the ghetto or concentration camps.

The Nazis eventually tracked Ruth down and sent her to a work camp for Catholic orphans. She told my friend little about the years in the camp—only that she labored on a farm, and that when the war was finally over she landed in a displaced persons' camp until a distant relative sponsored her trip to Canada. There she met Julius, who married her, took her to New York, and helped her put the past behind her, "where it belonged," as she said. But her eyes told another story—a more brutal one, which she took with her to her grave just a few years ago.

There was one happy story from Ruth's past that she told her daughter— a joke from her childhood about a man and a suitcase. Over the years my friend and I had referred to the joke so many times that we no longer knew if we had it right, or if what we thought it meant was what Ruth thought it meant. A few years before Ruth died, my friend and I asked her to tell us the joke again.

"Oh, it's not a good joke," she protested. "Something about a man on a crowded train who gets mad at the passenger beside him because he won't move his bag from the seat. I don't know why you girls like this joke so much," Ruth said, waving her hand as if to shoo the story away.

"It has a deeper meaning to us," I explained.

"A deeper meaning? What kind of meaning could a joke have?"

"Tell us the joke, and we'll tell you the meaning," my friend said.

"Well, there is this man on a train," Ruth began. "It's crowded on the train, and the man asks the fellow next to him to move the bag from their seat. It's a Polish joke . . . or maybe it's Russian . . . or it could be Yiddish . . . I forget, it's too long ago. Anyway, the old word for baggage was *chimidunchik*. 'Would you please move your chimidunchik?' the man says to his seatmate. But the seatmate ignores him. More people get on the train, and it gets more crowded, until there is nowhere for anyone else to sit. The man politely asks his seatmate another time to move the bag, but he gets ignored again. Finally he just starts yelling: 'Move your chimidunchik! Move your chimidunchik!' Still no answer. Finally the man gets so angry that he grabs the chimidunchik and throws it out the window. Satisfied, he turns to his seatmate and asks him, 'Now what are you going to do?'

" 'Nothing,' the guy says finally. 'It was not my chimidunchik.' "

Ruth laughed at the joke. "See? It wasn't the other guy's luggage! That's why he wouldn't move it. The man threw someone else's suitcase out the window. It's a little joke. It's funny. Now, what could the deeper meaning be?"

I told Ruth that we had assigned a meaning to the word *chimidunchik* that expanded the scope of the joke. "You know how everyone in the world has a burden to carry? Something heavy they are carting around from the past?"

"Like what?" Ruth asked, not liking where the conversation was heading.

"Like baggage from childhood," I said. "Misfortunes we suffered as kids. Or, if your childhood was easy, you pick up baggage as you go along through life. Maybe you get a serious disease, or you lose a child, or your marriage falls apart. That becomes your particular baggage. Everyone has a burden to bear, and no one else can carry it for us. It's our very own chimidunchik."

"That is not what the joke means," Ruth responded. "You girls read too much into everything." But as much as we would like to honor Ruth's interpretation, my friend and I (and a growing number of others, including our husbands and children) have been unable to excise the word *chimidunchik* from our vocabulary. There is no other word—at least not in English—that better describes the heavy baggage packed with the potential to teach us life's most important lessons.

Some people are handed weighty baggage to lug through life. Victims of abuse, people who survive terrible accidents, parents who lose a child—these people have heavier baggage to carry than most. Understandably, many cave under the weight, or become bitter and dark. Others, like Ruth, swallow the past, put on a brave face, and unwittingly pass their grief on to the next generations, like a mournful message in a bottle. Repressed pain never goes away. It is stored in the heart, in the body, and even in the genes, like deposits of oil deep within the earth. Unexplored and unexpressed memories become combustible fuel that may be used for a daughter's or a son's, or even a grandchild's, Phoenix Process. Many people whose parents survived the Nazi concentration camps must do the inner work that their grief-stricken parents were unable to do themselves.

And then there are those remarkable souls who not only withstood the horror of the camps but also were able to carry their burden with a sense of hope for the human spirit. In doing so they showed us how we too might lift ourselves out of despair. Victor Frankl was one of those people. A brilliant Austrian psychiatrist, he survived the Nazi death camps, and wrote *Man's Search for Meaning*, one of the most transcendent books of the twentieth century. In it, he developed a revolutionary theory of psychological thought called "logotherapy," which, in a nutshell, is about searching for the meaning packed in one's baggage, something he knew quite a bit about. During the Holocaust, Frankl lost his beloved wife and his entire family to the Nazis. He lived through three years of starvation, torture, and heartbreak in four concentration camps. When the camps were liberated, he returned to Austria, married again, and opened his chimidunchik for the world to see.

In the course of his long and extraordinary life, Frankl was the head of neurology at a Vienna hospital, a professor in several American universities, including Harvard and Stanford, the recipient of twenty-nine honorary doctorates from universities around the globe, and the author of thirty-two books. He received his pilot's license at age sixty-seven, was an avid mountain climber, and taught at the University of Vienna until he was an old man. He was ninety-two when he died. In his *New York Times* obituary, the mayor of his city was quoted as saying, "Vienna, and the world, lost in Victor Frankl not only one of the most important scientists of this century but a monument to the spirit and the heart."

Why was the world so touched by Victor Frankl? Why did *Man's Search for Meaning* sell more than nine million copies? Here is the answer: Frankl said that he wrote the book "to convey to the reader by way of concrete example that life holds a potential meaning under any conditions, even the most miserable ones. And I thought that if the point were demonstrated in a situation as extreme as that in a concentration camp, my book might gain a hearing. I therefore felt responsible for writing down what I had gone through, for I thought it might be helpful to people who are prone to despair."

People who are prone to despair—that's all of us. If Victor Frankl was able to transform the despair of the death camps into a search for meaning, then we can do this too, even in our darkest moments, when we are sick or troubled or afraid. In the midst of his nightmare, Frankl discovered that "it did not really matter what we expected from life, but rather what life expected from us. We needed to stop asking about the meaning of life, and instead to think of ourselves as those who were being questioned by life—daily and hourly. What matters, therefore, is not the meaning of life in general, but rather the specific meaning of a person's life at a given moment."

At this given moment you have exactly what Frankl had in Auschwitz. You have what no Nazi SS guard was able to take from him. You have your soul— what Frankl called *the last of the human freedoms, the freedom to choose one's attitude in any given set of circumstances.* When you exercise the last of the human freedoms—when you choose to learn and to grow from the weight of the world—you are putting your soul in charge of your life. You are choosing not the attitude of your smaller and more fearful self but rather the attitude of your soul, which is hopeful, expansive, and eternal. You are living for the deeper truth hidden in the pain of circumstance—your soul's lessons packed in your chimidunchik.

Here Begin the Terrors,
Here Begin the Miracles

Here is the Book of thy Descent,
Here begins the Book of the Holy Grail,
Here begin the terrors,
Here begin the miracles.
—THE GRAIL LEGEND

In the course of a few years, my friend Judi was handed a bag filled with more trauma and suffering than most people receive in a lifetime. I once asked Judi how she was able to handle the weight of her chimidunchik with so much courage. "I don't know how," she said. "I don't know if there even is a how. There's only the trust that we are given what we are given for a good reason. And we don't need to understand the reason. We don't have to ask: 'Why me?' What keeps me going is the faith that with the pain comes something greater. I am always looking for the greater thing. And I am forever finding it."

I know Judi because our kids are the same ages. We share one of the only kinds of tribal connection left to modern people; we're linked in the old ways, through place and children. We used to see each other every morning at the school bus stop, then when our children were teenagers, at the end of summer vacation, when we would pick them up at camp. These days we pass each other in town every now and then, and catch up at our yearly New Year's party, like we did last year. It was then, for the first time after twenty years of side-by-side living, that Judi and I had one of those conversations that sweep two people out of the ordinary and into a deeper friendship. Afterward, I spent more time with Judi, listening to her remarkable story, asking questions, and taking notes. I realized that someone like a saint had been living in our midst all these years. I suggest that someone like a saint is living in your midst too. If you take the time to look beyond the surface images that we present to each other in the rush and blur of daily living, you will probably find a whole cast of remarkable characters.

Like anyone's, Judi's story is a tapestry of family threads, inborn traits, and childhood gifts and hurts. Pull on one thread, and you find they're all attached. To tell only one part of a life story may seem to leave the others out, but they are all there, hiding in the fiber of a person's character. I know only a little about Judi's early life: that her father died in a car accident eleven days before she was born; that she was a dancer and a musician from an early age; and that she met Richard—her future husband—in her teens, and together they pursued dance, theater, and music. Later, they became successful psychotherapists in our community, built a house in the woods with a barn full of animals, and had their first child. When I first met them, they seemed to have everything: a good marriage, a beautiful home, meaningful work.

And then life intervened. Other threads wove into the fabric of Judi's life. Terrible threads and miraculous threads. *Here begin the terrors, Here begin the miracles* is how one translation of the medieval Grail Legend begins. The Grail Legend is the story of the young prince Parsifal, whose longing for insight causes him to leave his sheltered life and to endure many tests until he becomes the man he was meant to be. The story has been interpreted in hundreds of ways, but most Grail scholars would agree with Joseph Campbell, who says that the core meaning of the Grail myth is "the search for the inexhaustible fountain, the source of one's life, even if that search should take us through the most terrible suffering. In fact, as the Grail teaches us, it is the suffering itself that prepares us to receive the miracles."

Here begin the terrors . . . When their second baby was born, Judi and Richard's world fell apart. Denied oxygen in the birth canal, the baby almost died during her first week of life. The diagnosis was unclear; all the doctors could say—besides confirming that little Marion had brain damage and life-threatening epilepsy—was that she was suffering from "an incurable chronic condition."

For weeks in the hospital, Judi and Richard hovered over their new baby as she struggled to hold on to life. When it became clear that Marion would live, they took her home and tried to return to the way it would have been. The way it *should* have been. Judi stayed in bed as if the baby had just been born. She tried to rest in the blissful state she remembered from her first daughter's birth. But it was not to be this time around. Everyone in the family, including their jealous and frightened four-and-a-half-year-old, could taste the terror in the air.

Richard and Judi were determined to get their life back to normal. He returned to work, and she tried to stabilize Marion's health and restore a sense of calm to the family. After a few months, they were closing in on that goal. But once again, life had other ideas.

Here begin the terrors . . . One morning Judi awoke to a numbness in her leg and an overall feeling of exhaustion. She had been tired for weeks, with good reason, and had made and broken an appointment with an ophthalmologist after she experienced tunnel vision for a few days. The receptionist agreed with Judi that it was probably only "new mother fatigue." But as the days went on, her lower back began to ache, and the numbness spread further down her leg. Perhaps she had pinched a nerve while mucking out the horse stalls with Marion in the backpack. Then the other leg began to feel numb.

In a corner of her mind, Judi kept the nagging fact that her mother had multiple sclerosis, so she was relieved when the first medical professional she spoke with optimistically assured her that she was merely exhausted. But the numbness steadily got worse. When she lay in bed with her eyes closed, her awareness stopped at her navel. Finally, she ended up at the office of her mother's neurologist. And after exams and tests, the doctor gave her the bad news: "Multiple sclerosis," he said. "You have MS."

After the diagnosis, numbness and fear crept deeper and deeper into Judi's body, until her legs were like two wooden logs connected clumsily to the rest of her. She could barely stumble up the stairs and didn't dare carry the baby. She slept as much as she could and never awoke refreshed. It seemed as though there was a hole in her body, where her life was seeping out. Family and friends helped enormously, but they had their own busy lives, and at the end of the day, Judi was left with a feeling of helplessness that was almost as difficult as the disease itself. What would happen? When would it happen? Would she be able to care for her family and continue her work? Would she become a complete cripple, bound to a wheelchair? Would she die? The doctors had no answers for her. All they could say was that MS is an unpredictable illness. Its course can be slow and subtle, or swift and crippling. An initial attack can mysteriously subside, and just as mysteriously return. Every renewed attack can leave extensive nerve damage.

Over the next few years, Judi struggled to deal with her changing symptoms. Often she had difficulty standing or walking for more than fifteen minutes; her sense of balance was unreliable, and her immune system was damaged; her energy level rose and plummeted wildly. As Judi learned how to manage her disease, and as she tried to maintain a positive, healing attitude, she watched her mother's health worsen and bring her close to death. All the while, Marion grew into a little girl. As she grew, her epilepsy escalated into frequent and severe convulsions. The doctors put her on a round of drugs to control the seizures. But with the new drugs came daily psychotic episodes. It was agonizing for the family to witness Marion's violent outbursts, to watch helplessly as her eyes rolled up into her head and her body twisted and wrenched on the floor. After an episode, she would wake up with a severe headache, exhaustion, and sometimes a poignant look of love that radiated through the tears rolling down her face.

The doctors insisted that the drugs were not causing Marion's psychosis. They told Judi and Richard it was time to accept that they had a brain damaged child. When she had a violent episode in a neurologist's waiting room, the doctor commanded them to commit Marion to an institution. But during a hospitalization, a team of psychiatrists verified what Judi and Richard had suspected: Marion did not have a mental illness. It *was* the drugs that were causing the episodes.

Fed up with the lack of responsiveness by the medical community, Judi took matters into her own hands. She took Marion off the drugs and put her on a controversial regimen called the ketogenic diet, which had been used successfully by the Johns Hopkins Hospital and Medical School. The strict diet required that every morsel of food and each drop of water Marion ingested be measured and monitored. After a few months, the frequency and intensity of the seizures diminished. Eventually Marion was cured of her epilepsy.

Here begin the terrors, Here begin the miracles . . . When Judi talks about the early years of Marion's life, about her own descent into MS, and about her mother's eventual death, she describes them as any one of us would—as times of tremendous stress and darkness, one long nightmare. No Pollyanna, Judi says that she went through periods when she raged against the world, when it seemed as if terror, like an evil guest, had moved in and taken over her home and family. But she also describes something else, something that transformed the evil guest into a miracle, and the nightmare into a Phoenix Process. Most of us will not be tested in fires as relentless as Judi's, but we can lean on her faith and understanding during our own difficulties, as I have many times. When I am scared or sick or faltering in my faith, I think of the morning I sat in Judi's house and she told me about what she calls "digging for the soul in the ashes":

Since her birth and the onset of my MS, Marion and I have been travel-ing the same path. We are mutually entwined around saying yes to life, in spite of the obstacles of our illnesses. The miracle of Marion's recovery from epilepsy was an inspiration for me, as I hope to be an inspiration for her as I continue to ride the waves of having my own "incurable chronic condition." Looking back over those early, trying years, I see two equally real stories: the sacrifice involved on all of our parts, and also the miracle of who each one of us became by not shrinking back from the challenges.

We still process stray pieces of shrapnel that work their way to the sur-face from time to time, but my own health issues now seem mild in com-parison to the worst life story that I could imagine writing. Our trials have taught us lessons that have made the rest of our lives all the more precious. The first lesson is as old as the hills: "This, too, shall pass." Everything passes and changes and turns into something you would never have imag-ined, if you will only let it. I have learned how suffering only increases when I demand of life that "this should not be happening to me."

That is the second lesson—not to dwell on whether or not something *should* be happening to me. In the process of grappling with the fact that I had a debilitating illness for the rest of my life—and that my daughter would struggle with her situation for her whole life too—I realized that my only hope was to give up the life that had been, in order to make room for the life that is. I call it my "choiceless choice." Making that choice, over and over again—to accept what is, and to release what was—has become the major focusing agent for my spiritual work. My spiritual practice deep-ened because my life and my child's life depended on it.

When I say "spiritual" I don't mean a practice that is in any way separate from the rest of my life. I mean an emotional, intellectual, and physical process that is ruthlessly real and adventurous and full of death-defying risks. I mean a process that is patient, surrendered, and openly embracing of what is before me every day when I wake up in the morning to my changing body, and when I help my daughter deal with hers. I mean learning to acknowledge the powers of the universe that are far greater than, and all inclusive of, my journey on this planet.

Denial is a common first reaction to disease and disaster. It took me so long to abandon my desperate desire to continue my life "as usual." Despite protest from family and friends, at first I refused to give in and say, "I can't do that anymore." I struggled against my own body as I tried to maintain my therapy practice and to take care of everything—my mother, the children, the animals, the house—on my own. I justified my insistence on being "normal" by claiming it as a positive attitude, even though this so-called positive attitude was battering my already beleaguered system. But gradually I began to see that my need to be indispensable and my inability to ask for help were working against the whole family.

Eventually, having MS gave me permission to ask for help. Even though it was an uncomfortable stance at first, I came to realize how powerful it is when I and, I would imagine, every human being admits to our weaknesses, admits to needing help.

In the early stages of accepting my disease, I would go into my room to rest as if I was about to face the firing squad. I didn't want to feel the level of exhaustion that kept shooting me down, day after day. I didn't want to face my despair. So I devised little rituals for myself to ease the transition from "I must keep on going" to "I must rest and heal." I put my spiritual beliefs and practices to the test.

Anger is another common reaction after denial begins to fade. Alone in my room day after day, resting and thinking and praying, I realized how angry I was about Marion's birth, my illness, my mother's death, and the whole catastrophe that had visited our family. I didn't want to take responsibility for my healing; I didn't want to learn anything from Marion's afflictions; I just wanted to go back to the way it had been before. I looked around for someone to blame, and it certainly wasn't going to be me. That left God. And then it hit me—right below that childish feeling was the old, secret guilt I carried for my father's death. I realized that I would remain trapped in pain and unhappiness as long as I took the age-old stance of guilt and blame that had dominated my worldview since childhood.

And so I went deeper and deeper into a period of self-investigation, working with a variety of healing modalities, teachers, and helpers— including my heroic husband—until my illness naturally became my teacher. As I learned to hold my disease in the light of truth and heightened awareness, I experienced a new outpouring of self-love and the love of God. I discovered that God and I were on speaking terms as long as no one was to blame. Alone in my room, I poured out my sorrows, my confusions, and my daily wrestling matches with life. After yelling or crying or quietly praying for clarity and courage, there came a sense of relief in surrendering to my fatigue and to the sleep that followed.

And so I surrendered my MS and Marion's condition and all of my losses and fear and blame and guilt to the flames of what *is*. And in the ashes of what had been, I began to dig up my soul. I discovered that the soul requires a lot more interior time than we normally give it in our jam-packed schedules. Before MS I was always overriding a whispered invitation to just "be" with a whole lot of doing. I began to notice how so much of what we do each day is really a way of avoiding the deep and quiet voice of the soul. Of course, not all of my past doing—my work and parenting and family life and dance and theater—had been a way to avoid looking within. To the contrary, and that is what has made my healing journey so fascinating and so detailed. During my strong periods, I watch very carefully to see which aspects of myself I choose to pick up again and which I will leave behind forever.

Today I value every nuance of despair and every trill of joy, as I was never able to before. I still lose my way and take day trips down the side streets of anxiety over money, personal conflicts, my children, or my health, but mostly I am content with the unfolding skein of my life threads. I have already met some of the worst fears I could conjure up and am a kinder, humbler, more patient, and I hope more loving woman as a result. I awake each morning, and whether or not I can make it to the bathroom without stumbling over icy numb legs, I say a prayer of gratitude for everything that has come my way. I cannot think of my life being any different, any more than I can imagine life without my husband or either of my daughters.

I am learning to hold health and sickness, weakness and strength, and even life and death side by side—two sides of one coin. In fact, it is the acceptance of death that has finally allowed me to choose life. I am learning that it is never either-or, but both, and more. Not life *or* death, but life *and* death, health *and* sickness, good *and* bad. Both, and something more. I am learning to love the human condition, to say a full and rousing yes to it all, to work with it, to choose it, just as it is, every day.

Recently, Judi and Richard brought Marion to our New Year's party. I hadn't seen Marion for several years, since she entered a boarding school for kids with special needs. At first I hardly recognized her. At sixteen, she could have been any lovely and lanky young woman visiting her family for the holiday. But when I gave her a hug, she looked right at me, with the same eyes that I had admired when she was little—eyes that have the boldness of a wildcat. Without sharing the usual party pleasantries, Marion took my hand and led me to the back door.

"Do you want to see the moon? It's full and there's going to be an eclipse. That's unusual," she said dramatically.

"I certainly do," I said, following her out of the crowded house.

"We have to get away from the lights," Marion explained, pulling me up the hill and into the freezing cold night. The sky was alive with wind and moonlight. Wispy clouds, illuminated by the full moon, raced past the naked branches of the trees. Marion seemed fearlessly at ease in the dark luminosity. Her wildcat eyes were as bright as the moon.

"See?" she asked, pointing at the sky. She laughed heartily at a thin shadow beginning to form at the edge of the moon. We both laughed. Back in the house, my guests were gathered around the hearth, drinking and eating. I was up on the hill, freezing my butt off and laughing at the moon. I was with a girl who had known the terror of nature in her own body, and was now at home with the night. I felt brave in her presence. We laughed some more, and then Marion took my hand again and we ran back toward the warmth of the house.

Fierce Grace

In the 1960s, a young psychology professor named Richard Alpert left his teaching position at Harvard in a blaze of infamy. The son of a wealthy Boston Railroad magnate, and a brilliant scholar and teacher, he was the first twentieth-century professor to be fired from Harvard. His radical research with Timothy Leary into the use of LSD for psychological healing and the expansion of consciousness did not endear him to that staid academic community.

Alpert went on in life to become Ram Dass, named by a guru in India who saw in him someone who could live up to the meaning of his name, "Servant of God." And he did. He has been a guide for a generation of spiritual seekers. In 1971 his groundbreaking work, *Be Here Now,* was the bestselling book in the English language, outselling even Dr. Spock's *Baby and Child Care.* More than anyone—more than the Beatles, more than the Dalai Lama—Ram Dass deserves the credit for translating the ancient spiritual wisdom and practices of the East into the vernacular of the West.

I have known Ram Dass for many years: first as his student when he returned from India in the early 1970s; then as a colleague when he led retreats at Omega Institute and sat on our board of directors; and later as a friend who helped me weather the storms of my divorce. Most recently, Ram Dass has needed help. This is a new position for him to be in—to be the one who needs help rather than the one who gives it. He is in the middle of a Phoenix Process, and he is the first to admit it. He is learning to be helpless.

Many people know only the Ram Dass they read about or see from a distance at a conference or retreat. They know him as a wise, compassionate, and utterly brilliant man. I know that man, and I also know a different man: I know the man who hated to depend on anyone, who fled the scene if relationships became too sticky, who was used to running the show. I knew two Ram Dasses. The first Ram Dass uttered just a few of his well-chosen words, and dark corners of my mind were suddenly flushed with light. That Ram Dass was instrumental in my own Phoenix Process. As I went into the flames, he was a touchstone for me; I knew he would be there if things got too hot, too painful. And as I emerged from the ashes, he helped me stay on track; he kept me honest when I wanted to blame others; over and over he turned me toward the truth—the truth of the moment, and the truth of the cosmos.

The other Ram Dass infuriated me. I fought with that Ram Dass at board meetings and threw my hands up in exasperation during retreats when he resisted my attempts at organization. He accused me of being controlling. I told him that he had issues with powerful women, that he liked to play the wild boy and assign me the role of his overbearing mother. For years we danced between appreciating each other and keeping our distance. As I once heard him say to a thousand people at a conference, "Human interactions reflect a dance between love and fear." That certainly described our relationship.

Then something happened that changed Ram Dass, and changed my relationship with him. It began one evening in 1997, when he was in bed at his home in California, thinking about how to end a book he was writing on the subject of aging. "Lying there in the dark," he writes in his book *Still Here,* "I wondered why what I'd written seemed so incomplete, not quite rounded, grounded, or whole. I tried to imagine what life would be like if I were very old—not an active person of sixty-five, traveling the world incessantly as a teacher and speaker, caught up in my public role—but as someone of ninety, say, with failing sight and failing limbs. . . . I was trying to feel my way into oldness." In the middle of his fantasy, the phone rang. He got up to answer it, but his leg gave way under him and he fell to the floor. He grasped for the phone, clumsily picked it up, and found he couldn't speak. His friend on the other end of the line sensed something was terribly wrong. He asked Ram Dass if he needed help, but there was no answer. "Tap on the phone once for yes if you need help," his friend said, "or tap twice for no." Ram Dass tapped "no" over and over again. His friend called for help.

By the time help arrived, Ram Dass was still on the floor. "There I was," he writes, "flat on my back, still caught in my 'dream' of the very old man, who had now fallen down because his leg wouldn't work. . . . My next recollection is of a group of firemen, straight out of central casting, staring into the old man's face while I observed the whole thing as if from a doorway to the side." Through the next few hours, as he was rushed to the hospital, attended to by doctors and nurses, and treated for a massive cerebral hemorrhage, he stood to the side, witnessing his stroke with perplexed fascination.

It was later, when he began to feel the pain of his condition, that Ram Dass understood the gravity of the situation. Only 10 percent of people who suffer his type of stroke survive. Being who he was—someone practiced in the art of prayer and mindfulness, someone who had lectured for years on accepting suffering as "grist for the mill"—he did not take his survival for granted. There was a reason he was still alive, and he set about to discover what it was.

"Three hospitals and hundreds of hours of rehabilitation later," Ram Dass writes,

> I gradually eased into my new post-stroke life as someone in a wheelchair, partially paralyzed, requiring round-the-clock care, and a degree of personal attention that made me uncomfortable. All my life I had been a "helper"; I had even collaborated on a book called *How Can I Help?* I now found myself forced to accept the help of others. . . . Illness had shattered my self image and opened the door to a new chapter in my life. . . . The stroke was like a samurai sword, cutting apart the two halves of my life. It was a demarcation between two stages. In a way, it's been like having two incarnations in one: This is me, that was "him."

I had not seen, or even talked to the old "him" for several years. My last communication with Ram Dass had been in a letter sent after a board meeting. I wrote to complain about something he had said in the meeting, something that had hurt my feelings. He never wrote back. The next time he came to teach at Omega, I was out of town. Then he left Omega's board of directors and I had even less reason to see him. And then he had the stroke.

During his recovery, friends kept me updated on his setbacks and his progress. At first he was hooked up to oxygen; he couldn't talk, he couldn't eat. His right side was completely paralyzed. The doctors did not know if he would ever walk or speak again. Friends rallied to his side. But I didn't because I was occupied with something else. The week before Ram Dass's stroke, my father— who at eighty-five was in better shape than I will ever be—went skiing, as he often did, came home, ate dinner, went to sleep next to my mother, and never woke up. Out of the clear blue sky, my father died. He was one of the 90 percent that did not survive a massive stroke.

For months there was little room in my heart for anything but the enormous grief I felt from the sudden loss of my father. I couldn't bear even to think about Ram Dass confined to a wheelchair, learning to talk again, dealing with physical pain and his own sense of loss. But the time came when I sorely wanted to see my old friend. And I hoped he would forgive my absence.

A year after his stroke, I went to California to meet the "new" Ram Dass. Crossing over the Golden Gate Bridge, I was brought back in time to when I first met Ram Dass, when I was living in San Francisco. I mulled over the experiences that made me who I am today and realized that Ram Dass had been a part of almost all of them. In many ways he reminded me of my father—the guy out in front on the hiking trail, clearing the brush and setting the pace, never looking back, assuming that the other wayfarers could make it on their own, *should* make it on their own. When I was four years old, my father took me to the top of a ski trail, pointed my skis downhill, and said, "Follow me!" And when I was nineteen, and I read *Be Here Now,* there I was again, at the top of the mountain with my guide dancing away from me, beckoning me to follow, never turning around.

Now my father was dead, Ram Dass was in a wheelchair, and I was dancing on my own. I walked up the path to his cottage in Marin County, the bright California sunshine shimmering through the oak trees, and saw Ram Dass sitting on the porch. He was slumped over in the wheelchair, his trembling right arm tied to the chair's railing, his white hair in Einsteinian disarray. He looked up at me and waved with his good hand. "Elizabeth!" he called with delight. I caught my breath, and tears came to my eyes. My heart broke open. I felt as if I had come home after a long exile.

"I'm home, dear!" I joked.

"Yes, you're home," Ram Dass said sincerely. "Welcome home."

What ensued will go down in the record of my heart as one of those rare times in life when you finally rest—when you put down the burden of striving and a sense of well-being spreads like honey into every corner of your consciousness. There was nowhere else to go, nothing to do, no one to be—just now, just this precious day, these shared breaths with a friend. I learned something that afternoon that will serve me for the rest of my life. All along in my relationship with Ram Dass, I had been aware of two sides of the man—the brilliant teacher Ram Dass and the frustrating friend Ram Dass. But now I was with a third Ram Dass, one who seemed to be both simpler and grander than the other two combined. This was not yet another side of the man—this was his soul, his core, his true self. The other Ram Dasses stepped aside in deference, as if they were merely surface-level apparitions; as if the "good" Ram Dass was a temporary ghost, formed of genetic gifts and karmic awards, and the "bad" Ram Dass was made of learned defenses, coping mechanisms, and old wounds. This new Ram Dass, this soul version, contained the other two and transformed them into a whole and luminous being. Of course, the Ram Dass I was now greeting had been there all the time. It was not just something in him that had changed to allow the soul to shine through. Something had shifted in me too, so that my soul was greeting his, and we both had come home.

Ram Dass and I would have many more opportunities in the years to come to chafe up against each other's personalities, but sitting there on the porch, in the warm and dappled sunlight, we communed, soul to soul. Not just for a moment, but for a couple of hours, as we sat holding each other's hands like two school friends.

It was difficult for Ram Dass to form full, flowing sentences; the words came out slowly, each one separated from the one before—like solitary, naked thoughts, standing all alone on the stage, shivering in the spotlight; naked thoughts without the costumes of language. Most of the time Ram Dass struggled for the words to clothe the thoughts, yet every now and then a fully formed sentence would emerge in the finery for which he was famous. Early on in the visit, as Ram Dass searched for the words, I began to fill in the blanks for him. After one such awkward exchange, he turned to me, and out popped one of his one-liners: "I speak more slowly now. Now people finish my sentences and answer their own questions."

I asked him questions about the stroke and its aftermath. He answered a few. When he could not find the words, I finished his sentences for him, and in doing so, answered most of the questions myself. It was funny, fishing for words for a master orator. I felt like an impostor, stealing his thoughts and turning them into speech. And he asked me some questions—about my life, my kids, and my husband. He complimented me on a book I had just published. He would not have done that in the past. He wanted to hear all about the circumstances behind a Christmas photo I had sent him of my family and me on a trip in Ireland.

"You look like drunk monkeys." He laughed. "So happy."

I said, "Ram Dass, I think the stroke has made you more human. More a real human being, and more an eternal soul—both at the same time."

His eyes filled with tears. He squeezed my hand. "Grace," he said. "Stroke is heavy grace. Fierce grace."

We sat in silence for a while, digesting the words.

"Before . . . before stroke," Ram Dass continued in his halting speech, "before—happy grace . . . love grace . . . good things kept happening to me. Then, stroke . . . lose things . . . also grace . . . fierce grace."

"I understand," I said. "What did you lose? What did fierce grace take away?"

"Ego," Ram Dass said, making the motion of a blade slashing his throat. "Ego, gone. Nothing more to lose. Ego breaks open—then you see who you *really* are."

Perhaps I was finishing his thoughts now, and not just his words, but I looked into Ram Dass's eyes and I understood what he was trying to tell me. He was saying, "This is the real me. Please always know that behind all of my human behaviors—behind the best of me and the worst of me, behind the ego struggling to survive—is my soul, longing to mingle with yours." And he was telling me that behind everyone's learned behaviors and odd eccentricities lurks a soul, ready to make contact if only coaxed out through a crack in the ego. Would that it take something less than fierce grace to break us open.

Later on, I read in Ram Dass's book a less jumbled description of fierce grace:

For me to see the stroke as grace required a perceptual shift. It was a shift from taking the point of view of the Ego to taking the point of view of the Soul. I used to be afraid of things like strokes, but I've discovered that the fear of the stroke was worse than the stroke itself. . . . I've now been given a fully rounded understanding of grace. What was changed through the stroke was my attachment to the Ego. The stroke was unbearable to the Ego, and so it pushed me into the Soul level, because when you "bear the unbearable", something within you dies. My identity flipped over and I said, "So that's who I am—I'm a soul!" I ended up where looking at the world from the Soul level is my ordinary, everyday state. And that's grace. That's almost the defi-nition of grace. And so that's why, although from the Ego's perspective the stroke is not much fun, from the Soul's perspective it's been a great learning opportunity. When you're secure in the soul, what's to fear? Since the stroke I can say to you with an assurance I couldn't have felt before, that faith and love are stronger than any changes, stronger than aging, and, I am very sure, stronger than death.

"The ego. The ego," Ram Dass said. "It's like this wheelchair. It's a . . . it's a beautiful wheelchair. Use it. Enjoy it! Just don't think it is you. . . . Don't take yourself so, so . . . personally."

We laughed at that. And then we sat silently together in the slanting light until it was time for me to leave.

"So now what?" I asked Ram Dass, thinking about our friendship, about his life. "What's next?"

"Enough is enough," Ram Dass said. "That's what next. This is enough." He squeezed my hand again. Tears rolled down his cheeks—tears that said more than he could ever have said before the stroke. Tears that spoke of forgiveness and love and wonder. There was nothing more to say. I got up. I kissed his cheek, hugged him, and patted the wheelchair. "Good wheelchair," I said.

As I walked down the path, Ram Dass called to me. I turned around. "Good-bye, Elizabeth," he called, waving like a fool. "Come home soon!"

Before and After

In our sleep, pain, which cannot forget,
falls drop by drop upon the heart,
until, in our own despair, against our will
comes wisdom through the awful grace of God.
—AESCHYLUS

At the end of a talk I gave on the subject of death and grief, a man and his wife stayed behind to speak to me. Several hundred people had been in the audience, but my attention had been drawn all during the talk to these two. They were listening intently, as if their lives depended on it.

Before we said anything, the man handed me a laminated card. On the front was a drawing of a young man being held by an angelic figure against a sky blue backdrop. On the other side was a copy of their son's obituary. "He was twenty-one," the man said, as I read the card. I caught my breath. One of my own sons had turned twenty-one just a few days previously. Suddenly, after spending all afternoon talking, I could find no words. I put my hands on the shoulders of the man and his wife, and we just stood there looking at each other, nodding our heads as if we were speaking in some secret, silent language.

I stayed in touch with Glen and Connie. When Glen heard that I was writing a book of stories that focused on being broken open by change, he asked if he could send me his own. Many people have done this, and I have been touched by every story, and have woven strands of many of them into this book. But Glen's story needs to be shared more fully. It is the story of a man who rose from the ashes of one of the most difficult Phoenix Processes a person can be asked to make. Glen divides the process he and his family went through into two sections, "Before" and "After." These are his words:

Before . . .

Eric and his identical twin brother, Ryan, were born on New Year's Eve. My wife, Connie, and I were so busy and so happy. And when Katie, our beautiful little girl and final child, was born five years later, our lives were complete. And life was very good. A well-paying job for me allowed Connie to stay home with the kids and manage the endless activities of a big family: sports and scouts and school and backyard play. We lived life fully and happily.

As the years went on our kids excelled. They were Eagle Scouts, state champions in sports, high honorees in academics, accomplished musicians. So many blessings, so easily taken for granted. Then Eric and Ryan went off to college, one to study mechanical engineering, the other electrical engineering. Summers were spent hard at work earning college tuition for the coming year, but we always found time to enjoy each other and the Maine summers at the lake and coast.

Eric earned an opportunity, through good grades and hard work, to apply for a semester abroad and was accepted at the University of Melbourne in Australia. He flew off on his adventure one beautiful summer morning. We communicated often over the next five months and shared in the adventure he was having. He was recruited to play rugby for his college team. He formed a jazz combo and played the drums and the sax. Rock climbing in Brisbane; sheepherding in Adelaide; dirt biking in the outback. Eric loved people and made wonderful friends from around the world. And he kept a journal which—later, during the "after" part of the story—was such a bittersweet blessing for our family. The school semester ended in November, and Eric took three weeks to travel in New Zealand. He traveled as students do, with a backpack, sleeping in youth hostels and reveling in the joys of being young and in some of the most beautiful nature on God's earth. His letters were frequent and filled with awe at the majesty of New Zealand's Southern Alps and ice blue glaciers.

Right before he was to return home, Eric and two school friends did the longest bungee jump in the world. We found a videotape of his jump in his belongings two weeks later. He was tanned and muscular and smiling broadly as he faced the camera with arms around the shoulders of his friends. He was filled with the joy of living. The next day he got on his rented motorcycle to make his way back to Christchurch to catch a flight back to the States, back home to us.

The police officer that attended the scene of the crash said, "He was traveling near Mount Cook, on a dry, straight stretch of road, with an incredible view of the snowcapped mountains. As near as we can determine, he must have had his eyes on the distant view when he drifted into the ditch." He was unconscious when a man who saw the crash ran to his aid. And he died in that beautiful place.

After . . .

The agony of the days that followed shocked me to the core. I had never dared to dream of such darkness. I clung to my friends and family as we plummeted into the depths of despair. The awful pain of having to tell my wife and children of Eric's death will live in my heart for the rest of my days.

The days began and ended with sounds of sorrow. The time between troubled bouts of sleep was filled with previously unimagined tasks of sadness—arranging for Eric's body to be returned from the other side of the world; buying a casket and burial plot; preparing his clothes and planning a service; receiving telephone calls and visitors and flowers and food and books and cards. We walked as if in a terrible dream, praying to be awakened from the reality of it all. In those weeks and months, our minds reeled and recoiled from the horror.

And we awoke, each of us, in our own time.

In hindsight, my life "before" was about quantity and velocity. Bigger jobs, larger houses, more things . . . quicker, sooner, now. I justified my lifestyle as a way to be the best provider I could be for my family. It came at a price, and yet I paid it. As my family grew, I abandoned my former career path in environmental biology and took a better-paying position with a paper manufacturing company. In that decade especially, the paper industry had much work to do to clean up their operations, and I told myself, with some truth, that I was not "selling out" but rather working for change from the inside.

But then came the opportunity to climb the competitive career ladder. Two years in technical, five years in production, two years in sales and a master's degree from MIT. By the age of thirty-eight, I was so successful that I was positioned to take the next step to the top. Even though I had grown to hate my job, I worked long and frantic hours, accepting thankless tasks (as well as big bucks). My thought process was a constant countdown: "Just ten more years, and if the stock market cooperates, then I will have my life back." I had discussed my dissatisfaction with my family, and they all told me they supported me in changing course. But I didn't. I was controlling the universe, keeping my family safe and prosperous, and if sacrificing my values and happiness was the price I had to pay, then so be it. By the fateful summer of Eric's death, I was being courted to accept the president and CEO position at a newly acquired manufacturing facility in Chicago.

My delusions of control were destroyed on the day Eric died. My family fell apart. None of us knew we had been living life on the surface of a bubble until it popped. Katie, who had been a talented and happy sophomore in high school, found it impossible to go back to life-as-usual. Ryan did not return to college. Connie, who had always been active in school, church, and community, stayed close to home. My greatest agony was in having no ability to "fix" the despair of my family.

My colleagues at work desperately wanted me to put the past behind me and "get back in the saddle." For most of them it had to do with their extreme discomfort in having to confront my pain. Others were more concerned about my productivity and the profitability of the company. I became furious as the attempt was made to shoehorn me back into the mold. I was outraged that the world had not changed for others as it had for us. I was stunned at the people who placed profit and the status quo of the system above my family's loss.

I began to devour books searching for words of wisdom to face each day. I discovered there are entire sections of bookstores and the public library dedicated to loss. As we reached out, we began to understand that we were not alone in our pain. Many others had walked this terrible path before us. A wise and sober understanding came over me. Before Eric's death I had suffered relatively little of life's losses. I had thought I was in control of my life; now I knew I most certainly was not. I looked around at others now—those who were living the way we had before—and I knew that they too, in their own time, in their own way, would have to learn what we were learning.

We tried to learn it from the books. They helped. But we learned that the lessons of grief, like music or medicine or art or parenting or marriage, must be lived to be fully understood. And so began our journey through the "awful grace of God."

At one point in history, mankind believed that the world was a flat table, and that those foolhardy enough to venture too near the edge would fall off into a terrible world of fierce sea monsters and destruction upon the rocks. They were right. Eric's death pitched us headlong off our daily plane of existence into the darkness to be wrecked upon the rocks. For weeks and months, we roiled and thrashed in pain, submerged in agony, not sensing the light or knowing in what direction to turn. We fought to hang on to each other. Lifelines tossed to us from above were not recognized or were purposefully ignored. Each of us prayed at times to simply drown and be done with it. Were it not for friends and family—who flung themselves into our brokenness, to hold our heads above the water—we may well have drowned in our sorrow.

This place of hopelessness and fear is real, not a cute little allegory. Some people never leave that place and are broken on the rocks. Some people stop fighting and slip into the depths. We came to understand that, although we do not have control, we do have choice. God or Spirit or Creator or Insert Name Here wants us to go down into the dark waters, but also wants us to come up to the light. God will not force us to do so. We are free. We are made so, and it is our great gift. We can choose darkness, fear, addiction, and despair. We can choose light, hope, meaning, and joy.

By the grace of God, I chose life. I chose to find a way back up. It helped me to visualize myself climbing out of the dark sea, and back up onto the table of daily life. I actually began drawing pictures of tables as I attempted to communicate my deepest emotions to my wife, son, and daughter. I named each of the table's four legs: Faith, Courage, Growth, and Love. The leg of faith was the weakest part of my table. And it continues to be the primary focus of my path forward. My daily mantra is "Surrender and relax into the mystery." Before Eric's death, my concept of reality had been that I was responsible for everything that happened, past, present, and future. But afterwards, I recognized that this could not be true. Even though I had dedicated my entire life to securing my family's well-being, I had been unable to do so. And so, I dedicated myself now to having faith in life, no matter what happened. My attempts to climb back onto the table were often met with silence and, at times, with contempt, especially from my son Ryan, whose loss of an identical twin brother was something none of us could truly comprehend. But my concepts and sketches gave me a place to hang my thoughts.

One day I sketched a table on a napkin in a restaurant while talking with a friend. I didn't notice that he slipped it in his pocket as we left, but the next week he stopped by the house and gave me a watercolor painting of my "table." As I write these words, I look above my computer screen at that painting. It is written upon and surrounded by clippings of words and other pictures, pieces of my broken soul, pieced together like an incomplete puzzle. Pieces missing, amputated, never to be replaced, rough and tattered, but treasured, not for its artistic beauty but for what it represents. It is a model of our faith, our courage, our growth, and our love. Our survival.

Six months after Eric's death, after twenty-three years with the company and following long discussions with my family, I quit my job. It wasn't any great act of courage. My family was faltering. I chose family over career. It felt right. After so many years of making decisions based upon my logical, cognitive mind, I felt an incredible euphoria following my intuition, my heart.

We rented a secluded cottage on the lake for the summer. As Eric Clapton said after the death of his young son, "For a while I just went off the edge of the world." At times we feared the grief would twist us up so badly that we could not hope for healing. We chose to walk into the darkness and to trust that we would be led back out. We read, we sailed, we rested. We ate well, took long walks and canoe rides in the moonlight, we cried a million tears.

By September we felt ready to begin again. Katie went back to school and a new soccer season. Ryan enrolled at the University of Maine for another semester of mechanical engineering. Connie enrolled in an intensive hospice volunteer training program, and taught elementary school half-time. We bought two wonderful little dogs. I painted the house.

I started to think about what I wanted to do with the rest of my life. When I was ready, I accepted a vice president's position with a small non-profit fifteen miles from my home. It is a meaningful job, and I have a real passion for the company's mission. It is so delightful to look forward to Monday morning after so many years of dreading the arrival of a new week of work. I have also accepted board positions on two local community organizations—one for hospice volunteers, and the other an agency that provides social services and transitional employment opportunities for the mentally ill. I seem to possess life skills that these groups value, and I am pleased to be able to contribute where I can.

Ryan is entering his last year of college and is coaching a ten- to twelve-year-old Little League team. He plays his saxophone at every opportunity, and you can feel his beautiful soul when he blows his horn. Katie went to Bolivia last summer to work with homeless children and the poor. Since then she has been accepted at Boston College in nursing. Her excitement is boundless.

Connie is now a hospice volunteer instructor and just completed teaching a sixteen-week program preparing new volunteers to assist the dying and those left behind. She is loved by her five- and six-year-old students and fellow teachers, and adored by her own children and husband.

Eric is always near. We see him in nature: birds, butterflies, rainbows, and sunsets. But mostly we feel him. We are, each of us, Spiritual Warriors. We are awake, and nothing can break our circle. Nothing will ever be the same again.

A Broken Heart
Is an Open Heart

Yehudah Fine is a rabbi and family therapist who lives near me and whose first book, *Times Square Rabbi: Finding Hope in Lost Kids' Lives,* became a classic in the recovery field. In it he showed young adults struggling with addiction how to use their suffering as a ladder up. His message to them was that, even in the black depths of pain and despair, their struggles could give birth to their better natures. After writing that book, touring the country, and lecturing at schools, universities, and mental health facilities, Yehudah found himself on the receiving end of his own advice. He writes:

Last year, on a lonely section of a rural highway in the Catskill Mountains, I nearly died. I was running errands in the early morning when a car coming in the opposite direction swerved into my lane at forty-five miles per hour and hit me head-on. It was on that road where my life changed forever. It was on that road where I learned to deal with daily, severe pain, and reclaim my life from the broken glass and twisted metal that lay strewn over the blacktop. It was on that road where I took spiritual wisdom off the bookshelf and downloaded it into my life. If ever there was a time to find out what sustained my inner core, this was it.

I vividly remember lying in the local emergency room before being helicoptered to a big medical center. I wasn't a pretty picture. Firemen had pried me out of the car with the Jaws of Life. Blood covered my face, teeth, and lips, the result of the impact with the air bag that saved my life. A torn pants leg revealed a smeared mixture of dirt and blood oozing out of a deep gash in my knee. The force of the collision had rammed my femur out of its socket. My pelvis was shattered into nine pieces; I was broken in half. I had not yet received any painkillers and was suffering mind-bending pain. I prayed to pass out, like the guys who got shot in the Westerns I used to watch as a kid. But this was no movie.

Before I was flown to the medical center, the emergency room doctor told me that they could not transport me until they repositioned my femur bone. I gritted my teeth and said, "Doc, isn't the pain going to kill me? What if it doesn't go right back in?" He simply said, "For your survival, I have to get it back in right now." Without warning, the doctor jumped on my gurney, grabbed my leg, and shoved it toward what was left of my pelvis. The pain slammed into me so hard that I screamed in horror. The femur didn't go back in. Between crying and moaning, I whimpered, "Doc, I thought you'd give me painkillers before doing something like that."

The doctor looked at me in astonishment. "You haven't been given any pain medication?" They quickly shot me up with Valium and Demerol and repeated the procedure. This time my leg went back in with a loud pop. At that moment, although I was angry at the doctor's insensitivity, I was also grateful for his fearless skill in taking the first step toward putting me back together. I took his hand and said, "I want you to know how grateful I am for your skill and courage. But damn it, don't ever do that to another patient."

Right there, in that emergency room, I decided that, no matter what struggles lay ahead, I would give thanks to every person who attended my broken body. I was going to honor every act of kindness with words from my heart. Before I went under the knife, I told my wife how much I loved her and our kids. I also asked her to forgive me for any stone left unturned and to tell the kids the same. When we said good-bye, I did not know if I was going to survive. The doctor had told me, "In all my years as the main trauma physician, I have never seen anyone as badly shattered as you. I think you'll make it, but it will be touch and go."

So I told my wife how much I loved her. From the moment we met, I knew she was what the Talmud calls my *zivug rishon*, my soul mate. If I was going to die, I wanted my last message to affirm our love. The Talmud hints that the love of a soul mate is something that goes beyond personal identities. As I emerged from surgery nine hours later, she was there waiting for me, waiting to hold my hand. The sages got that one right.

In the ensuing weeks I was totally helpless and in excruciating pain. I had lost so much blood I looked like Count Dracula was my nightly visitor. My stitched and stapled wound stretched twenty-three inches from the top of my hip down my thigh. At the bottom was a big drainage hole dug out of my flesh, open and oozing. Nine three-inch screws had been drilled into my pelvic bones. Metal plates held me together. I would spend the next seven months lying flat on my back. The morphine drip kept me in a perpetual fog as I lay catheterized and unable to turn in any direction. I couldn't sit up or wash myself without assistance. It took four people to move and bathe me. I needed someone to help me do everything. And all the time I was fighting incredible pain. Worst of all, I didn't know if I would ever walk again.

My total helplessness brought moments of spiritual vision. I took comfort in knowing that others who faced great challenges down through the ages had held fast and not given up. But I won't kid you; I often heard the voice of despair. It would whisper that the pain was too much, that I couldn't and wouldn't go on. And so I made up my mind to listen to other whispers. Old teachings took on new meaning. The more I lived in the moment, the less I worried and the less I cried. I particularly savored a saying from two great sages, Rabbi Yochanan and Rabbi Eleazer: "Even if the sword is on your neck, do not stop yourself from praying for compassion and mercy." Calling on mercy and compassion when I was in the worst of my suffering was very comforting. In my prison of pain I rarely felt alone.

There were times late at night when I found myself quietly marveling at my predicament. For years I had given advice about these kinds of matters, and now I was finding out if I could take my own advice. It was a wonderful role reversal. I was no longer the caregiver; now I was the one getting the care.

The postoperative rehab room is the first stop for the severely wounded. This became my new world, and its inhabitants my new community. Some of my companions were amputees. Others were literally gutted and resewn, with scars that beat my huge wound. There were head-trauma folks, and crushed-limb people like me. My new teachers were Pain and Suffering. Let me report to you that in the heat of a crisis there is no such thing as transcendence. Anyone who tells you different is playing a huge joke on you. Suffering is very real, and fear is its sidekick. Fear is a sneaky thief, stealing away precious moments of your life. Much of my time was spent devising ways to deal with it more effectively. After weeks of work, I finally tossed fear away into a corner. The secret was not to fight the pain but to embrace it. Once I did that I started finding my strength.

If I could distill all the great writings on suffering down to a few words, I would simply say that suffering and crisis transform us, humble us, and bring out what matters most in life. Accidents open us to a world of meaning. Still, it is a hell of a way to be blessed. But that is why these things are called "accidents," because no one in his right mind would ever order up a serving of blessings and meaning this way! The Talmud points out that, just as we bless the good, so too should we bless the bad. I always found that a profound concept. But it is only now that I really understand how important it is to surrender to all of life's blessings—the "good" and the "bad." Nothing that happens is to be ignored. Everything requires attention and mindfulness. There are spiritual gems to be recovered from the difficult challenges. Or as the great Hassidic master Reb Dov Ber of Mezrich once said, "Sometimes we have to sift through the ashes to find a single spark."

How strange it was to have something so brutal bring out so many deep changes in my life. There is, of course, a deep mystery at work here, which the words of Chesbon Hanefesh helped to make clear: "By failing to accept your suffering, the pain you feel will be much more acute and harsh." From the beginning I tried to accept that where I was, was exactly where I was meant to be. This freed my mind up to pursue my healing. It opened new doors to the spiritual realms, new doors to contemplation and meditation. There is a deep connection between brokenness and Spirit.

As I lay in the hospital and later in my hospital bed set up in our living room, everything I was accustomed to was gone. No plans, no dreams, no visions of what I was going to do and be next. Believe me, I am a very driven person, and to have all of that just pulled away was startling. To heal, I knew I had to be fully in the present and to drop everything I thought I was, everything I thought I was going to do with my life. Letting go was poignantly sad. But it was not depressing. Rabbi Scnhuer Zalman said it clearly when he wrote: *"A broken heart is not the same as sadness. Sadness occurs when the heart is stone cold and lifeless. On the contrary, there is an unbelievable amount of vitality in a broken heart."* In the middle of the mystery of pain, I harvested this precious jewel. I also harvested the love and beauty right here, in this world. I may have been dealt a broken body and heart, but I also can tell you I have had more love and compassion poured over me, through me, and around me than I ever knew existed.

The hospital staff often asked me why I seemed to be happy most of the time. They would say, "Look at what happened to you. How come you still smile?" In reality, their question was directed not at me but at themselves. They were asking, "Would it be possible for me to be happy if I were in Yehudah's shoes?" I suspect that everyone harbors such doubts. We all wonder how we are going to respond to a crushing crisis. We all wonder if it will break us. How will we handle pain? And beyond that, we wonder if we really will be able to make amends and straighten out our lives if we are caught in the middle of a buzz saw.

There are three major hurdles to overcome in crisis: dealing with pain; working with your attitude; and using the crisis as a wake-up and a clean-up call.

Pain:

Pain management is a huge issue in the hospital or for anyone who suffers from chronic, debilitating pain. If you do not get proper pain management, it is extremely difficult to heal or keep your wits about you. However, I don't want to imply that if your pain is managed your life will come together. Nothing could be farther from the truth. Sadly, we live in a world where we are so afraid of suffering's teachings that we organize our lives around anesthetizing the messages of our anxiety and pain. Many of the folks I got to know on the trauma ward ran back into their caves of denial as soon as they got their medication and the pain went away. There is physical pain and there is psychic pain. Don't confuse the two and think that when the physical pain goes away you will be all right psychically. The longer we avoid dealing with our lives, the more trouble we find at the end. Issues not attended to can come roaring out like devouring monsters.

Attitude:

Where your attitude is, so be you. Where your attitude is, so be your consciousness. No matter what has happened in life, you have the capacity to choose how you want to be. Allowing yourself to be guided by your core values unlocks a profound spiritual blessing—the blessing of living in the moment with grace, dignity, warmth, kindness, and compassion. But I would never want anyone to think that attitude equals perfection or transcendence or any of the other sentimental stuff that often passes for spirituality. Know that there will be times in crisis when you literally break down. I certainly have, and I am not ashamed to say so. I belong, after all, to the school of imperfection.

Wake up and Clean up:

Through my crisis, I abandoned spiritual practice and embraced real life. My spiritual practice became the real changes I needed to make in my own heart. The thought of really changing is downright scary. When you are caught up in one of those chain-saw massacre cycles of life, you come face-to-face with some important questions: What really matters to me in life? What precisely do I need to learn, change, and transform within myself? From whom or what will I take my direction and motivation?

In my case, I made a conscious decision to stay with my core, to let its inner light be my beacon. And most of all, I was motivated by my children. I wanted them to see what was possible in a time of crisis. I wanted them to know that their father deemed it worthwhile, even in the middle of hell, to be a person who does not let go of what is precious in life. My daily practice now is to continually clean the chambers of my heart—to give and receive love, to stay present to myself and to others, to no longer flee, or worry, or procrastinate. I may act imperfectly, but I try to act boldly from my core values.

Don't fool yourself and think that Spirit is somewhere else, in otherworldly experiences, in great rushes or ecstatic visions. Life's deepest experience is the joy that fills our hearts when we love and give to others. Ask anyone in the middle of battling a catastrophic illness. Or survey all my friends from the acute trauma ward, and they will tell you that they live to give a halting hug, or to speak a word of grace to another. The irony can no longer be lost on me. When crisis exploded in my life, the best in me was born. I found out what I was really capable of. I discovered who I really am.

September 11th

There is a beautiful hotel near where I live that calls itself "The Oldest Inn in America." George Washington was an early guest, and one can imagine him at supper, sitting with friends in the back room, where the ceiling is so low that even short people must duck as they enter. I went to dinner there on a mid-September evening, just a few days after two hijacked airplanes struck and destroyed the twin towers of the World Trade Center. New York City lies less than ninety miles south of the inn, straight down the Hudson River. There's a good chance that one of the airplanes traveling from Boston on that fateful day flew right over the oldest inn in America, where George Washington stayed almost 250 years ago.

Before coming to dinner, I spent most of the day alone, sitting outside in the ironically sweet September sunshine. Watching the yellow bees swarming in the late-blooming asters, I could not keep myself from thinking of those planes and the people on them. A strange brew of love and sorrow flowed in and out of my broken heart, mixing with my tears. Though alone, I felt the presence of millions of other people spread out across a continent. It was as if we had been together all day, drinking from the same cup. It was as if we had been at the funeral for 3,000 people and the naïveté of our nation. By the end of the afternoon, as the low-slanting sun illuminated the first golden colors of the autumn leaves, I had cried myself into a stunned silence.

By the time my husband and I arrived at the inn to meet our friends for dinner, I was emotionally wrung out, as raw and open as I have ever been. Maybe after childbirth I was that raw, or when my father died; then too I touched that mysterious place where pain and love intersect and break open the heart. In such a state, the last thing I wanted to do was go out to dinner with a large group of talkative people, but our party had been planned for weeks, and several out-of-town guests were expected.

We gathered around a large old table in the inn's low-ceilinged back room. I sat next to my husband, who since September 11 had assumed the role of my guardian angel. Or rather, I had assigned him that role. Or maybe I had just finally noticed who he really was. In fact, since September 11, I was painfully aware of the meagerness of my perception of most people: how little of their souls I normally allow to touch my own; how quickly I judge, and therefore diminish, their humanity. Whether it was my husband, or my friends, or the president of the United States, I had been asleep to the truth of who they really are. I had been sleepwalking next to other sleepwalkers. In the smug complacency of daily living, we all had been asleep, almost drugged into a stupor, dumb to the better dreams and goodwill of each person. Could it be that we were waking up a little?

In fact, I had found myself praying for the president that day, a man for whom I would never have prayed unless it was for God to find him another job. But now I was keeping him and his wife close in my heart. I imagined them going to bed at night, holding each other in the dark, talking about their fears and plans. Instead of fixating on my hardened disdain for the president—and on what I perceived as his peculiar blend of overconfidence and ineptitude—I now wanted to pray for him to grow in wisdom and humility. I prayed that he would use this catastrophe to lead our nation in a process of self-examination. Even if my prayers made no difference in the president's transformation, they would surely make a difference in mine. I would be trading bitterness for hope, and a closed heart for one with more room.

This was new for me. I normally watched the evening news as if it were a sporting event and I an agitated fan in the stands, rooting for one team to fumble and lose. But now my allegiance was widening. I didn't want anyone to drop the ball. I was rooting for all of the teams—for what Martin Luther King, Jr., called a "double victory." I no longer wanted my myopic point of view to prevail. Where there were gaps in my own understanding, I wanted to be won over by those who knew more than I did. And where my own wisdom could shed light, I wanted to find an effective way to communicate. I suddenly saw what a colossal waste of energy and creativity it is to harden one's heart, and what an act of courage to admit one's own overconfidence and ineptitude.

My prayer was this:

*Please help me put aside my aversion toward those with different opinions
and belief systems—the president, for example. Please help the president
and his team do the same. Help us all aim for the kind of victory where we
come away enlarged in our perspectives and part of a lasting solution. Please
help us focus less on changing each other and more on seeing each other, on
helping each other.*

I looked around the dinner table, first at my husband, the guardian angel, whose sheltering spirit I so often overlooked while I ran my racket of complaints and demands. Next to my husband was a well-known author, chatting with the people around her, looking more like a bewildered girl than the fierce authority she had become. Across the table were two old and reliable friends, guys whom I could depend on to reinforce my opinions about a lot of things: politics, art, culture. They were both writers and cultural mavens—deep thinkers who had spent a lifetime working for political causes. Next to my friends were colleagues from work, a pair whose normal party demeanor was loud and humorous banter. Tonight they looked like a couple of sad sacks. It seemed to me that we were all barely coping, all reaching for some kind of anchor in a new sea of helplessness.

Waiting for our meals to be served, I was overpowered by images of the people on the airplane that had plunged into the Pentagon—as if an emotional weather pattern had made its way into the back room of the inn. I had to excuse myself and go to the bathroom, just to sit in a stall and cry. Some of the people on that flight must have understood that they were part of a terrorist plot, even as their plane hurtled toward its target. Some had called family members before the plane went down. What would it have been like to be aware not only of the immediacy of your impending death but also of its grave significance?

Sitting in the bathroom stall, I reached across the mystery that separates souls in time and space, and I thanked those passengers. I don't know what I thanked them for—maybe for their dignity, because I sensed that they had died with courage, and with tenderness toward each other. For some reason that we would never understand, these particular people had been on that plane. They had fulfilled their destinies, just as we would fulfill our own. All I could do now was bear witness and have faith that each one of us is part of the same story— a myth with a complicated plot and an underlying theme of birth and death, and redemption and evolution.

When I came back to the table, my two writer friends were talking about Barbara Olson, the conservative television commentator, whose husband, Theodore Olson, argued George W. Bush's case to the Supreme Court during the controversial presidential election of 2000. Barbara Olson had been on the plane that hit the Pentagon. She had called her husband from her cell phone to ask him what to do, to say good-bye, to tell him that she loved him. Her destiny seemed particularly poignant to me—she had delayed her flight by a day in order to spend time with her husband on his birthday. She was one of those whom I had just thanked, with whom I had just been speaking.

"Don't you think it was entirely inappropriate for Supreme Court Justice Clarence Thomas to give the eulogy at Olson's memorial today?" asked one of my friends.

"Yeah, it just burned me up seeing him there," said the other one. Being the political animal that I am, I knew that Justice Thomas was a close family friend of the Olsons. I knew this because during the 2000 election I was glued to the television set; I read two newspapers a day; I wanted to learn as much about the "enemy" as I could. The fact that Thomas was at the funeral should have felt like bitter proof of the Supreme Court's complicity in choosing the president. But at that moment, I believed that Clarence Thomas was merely Ted Olson's friend, a man on whom Ted needed to lean. In lifting the veils from the eyes of my heart, I had also dropped the fighter's gloves from my fists.

But the discussion at the table was going in another direction. The usual camps had been established, the predictable blame bestowed. I felt suddenly weary, and dangerously so. I was like a live wire, snapped during a storm, lying exposed on the ground, just praying that no one would touch me, sure that I was capable of sending shocks of electrical energy into the body of any fool who got too close to my frayed ends. Hoping to shift the tone of the conversation, I turned to my friend and asked him, "Can't we let Ted and Clarence be people today? Just for one day? Maybe even a week? Can't we grant them their humanity in their time of loss?"

"No, sorry, I can't," said my friend, looking betrayed by my sudden defection from party politics. "Not after their dirty tricks. Not after that election. They're hypocrites and criminals." Others at the table agreed, and as the meal progressed the conversation veered back into the months and years before September 11, when we had enjoyed the luxury of having obstinate opinions. Now closed-minded convictions troubled me. What was the difference between that kind of bullheadedness and the unyielding self-righteousness of the terrorists? Surprising myself, I stood up.

"I don't know what I think anymore," I said. "All I know is that a lot of people are in pain today. A lot of people are often in pain. Whether they're Republicans or Democrats, or Muslims or Christians, or men or women, it doesn't matter. If we can't feel compassion now, when will we ever be able to? Don't you see how important it is to see each other as human beings first? Don't you see what happens when we put each other out of our hearts? Don't you see?" By now I was weeping and creating a spectacle.

Our waitress came over. She had been quietly listening, frozen in her tasks at a nearby table. She was crying too. She put her arm around me. "I work during the week at Windows on the World," she said, referring to the restaurant on the top floor of the World Trade Center. "I lost fifty friends on Tuesday. They were serving breakfast." A silence fell over the table, like rain on a dry field. "The only thing you should be talking about tonight is how precious your life is. How lucky you are to be alive. How important it is to love each other." She stood with her arm around me. "How lucky you are," she repeated in a whisper, tears rolling down her face. Then she wiped her eyes on her apron and briskly started clearing the table.

We passed our plates to the waitress like children at the end of a meal. We said nothing. A quiet sadness—almost a sacredness—had settled around the big table in the little room in the oldest inn in America. In this same room Americans had dined and argued and grown through two and a half centuries of war and peace. We were next in line in the great experiment. Could we help our country and our world transform terror into understanding, hatred into compassion, loss into change? Could we bring the best out of each other, instead of driving our fellow citizens into defensive corners?

We sat in contemplation until my friend said, "I stand corrected. Corrected by a wild woman and a waitress." We all laughed, even the waitress, but the dinner was over, and we were ready to leave.

Driving home in the warm September night, I found my thoughts returning to the people on the airplanes, and to that moment when they realized they were speeding through space toward their death. I let my grip on life loosen, until I was with those people, sharing the awe, finally understanding the secret—the same secret we will all know when death is just a breath away: In the end, what will matter is how much we loved—our children, our mates, our families, our friends, everyone we knew, everyone who traveled with us during our brief visit to this unbearably lovely place. What will matter is the good *we* did, not the good we expected others to do.

Six hundred years before the birth of Christ, the Chinese wise man Lao Tzu counseled, In times of adversity, make energetic progress in the good. This is still the real work at hand: for each one of us to meet the bad in the world with the good in our own hearts. To energetically rouse ourselves out of tired habits and worn-out loyalties and replace them with bigger and broader circles of inclusion. It was time for me to let as many into the circle of family and tribe as I could: the president; the poverty-stricken people of the world hardened by years of war; the shortsighted corporate crusaders, gobbling up the resources of the world; the intolerant religious fanatics, clinging to simplistic answers in a mysterious universe. In widening the circle, I could still hold to my convictions. What I needed to surrender was anger and judgment. What I needed to adopt was vision and humility.

Sitting still in the dark closeness of the car, letting my guardian angel steer us through the night, I felt the hand of God changing the way I thought about everything; as if God was a waitress, late at night, in the dim light of the bar, and I was a wineglass she was drying, holding me by the stem of my heart, turning me around and around, cleansing the film from the lens of my vision, so that one day I might see the world as she does.

Crooked Hearts

I met Sharon when she took one of my first workshops at Omega. Although she said very little, something about her touched me, and I remembered her immediately when she wrote me a letter soon afterward. Although she was older than I, and was a successful family therapist, she trusted me with her heart. We started a correspondence that has lasted through the years. In a recent letter, I asked her to sum up the journey she made since we first met. This was her response:

I was forty-five years old then—forty-five yet lost. On the outside I was the wife of a doctor, the mother of two sons, a respected professional. But on the inside, my marriage was in a terrible state, my work had lost its sense of meaning, my kids had grown up. I felt as if I was treading water in a stagnant pond. I did not really know how to go on.

And then we got the call. My twenty-year-old son, Geoff, who was studying abroad in Italy, had been found dead in Rome, lying by the Tiber. No one knew what had happened. Forever a mystery. Asthma attack, most likely, while sitting on the wall, falling at night, no one heard him scream. They say he had a branch in his hand. I could not bear to think of that, but for the next year I was haunted by images of him falling, grabbing, holding on to the branch, falling, suffering. That was truly the darkest imaginable time. I wanted to die because living was so painful. It had never occurred to me that either of my beloved children could die before me. I loved Geoff more than I can say. I needed him. I didn't know that then. I didn't know anything. This was the beginning of the next life.

Geoff's death was the event that rocked Sharon's inner world. It was the tipping point from which she made major changes in her marriage, work, and her deepest sense of self. For a while, Sharon spiraled down into her grief, and once there she was confronted by the deadness in her sexuality, the pain in her marriage, and the fear she felt about life itself. It looked to her as if her own life would not survive the death of Geoff. "His death held up the mirror to my pain," Sharon writes, "in a way that nothing else could have. A mirror of pain that reflected more pain—like a fun-house mirror, distorting everything, making it bigger, scarier."

In one way, Geoff's death was Sharon's death. But it also was her rebirth. It brought her into the shadows, where she retrieved the parts of herself she needed in order to live again. While some people recover from a Phoenix Process in a matter of months or a couple of years, it takes others a long, long time. I honor those people who stick with the process for as long as it takes to reemerge healed and whole. I admire those who buck the cultural expectations that we should move on quickly after a loss as huge as the death of a child, or the end of a marriage, or the demise of a career. If we do not suffer a loss all the way to the end, it will wait for us. It won't just dissipate and disappear. Rather, it will fester, and we will experience its sorrow later, in stranger forms.

For a while Sharon left her husband and experimented with a life without him. Her courageous journey took many years. It brought her to places she had never explored, and ultimately gave her back not only her marriage but also a strong sense of who she is, what she loves, and what she can give to the world. Today she is an award-winning poet, a teacher of young women in prison, a grateful wife, and a proud and loving grandmother to the children of her surviving son. She writes:

Make no mistake, I still struggle. But the rewards are clear: I'm all here. I'm aware of what is happening in me, in my life. It's not hidden anymore, so I have choices. I don't have to be pulled into the darkness again to be born. I choose to be married to my husband now; I have put both feet into the relationship, something I was never able to do before. I love all of who my husband is with all of myself. Tomorrow is Geoff's thirty-fourth birthday, and, after all of these years, I don't find myself longing for him to be alive the way I used to. I am filled with tremendous sadness at times for all my losses, for the loss of him, for the loss of my youth, for lost chances.

But more than that, I know that this is my path and the particular difficulties given to me are my teachers. I guess what I am saying is that the end
result of all this is that I can deal with life's impermanence oh so much better than I could before my "spiritual" death. I am really here.

I remember another woman in one of my workshops who was unable to
consecrate a big loss to an equally big inner change. Her husband had recently
died, leaving her and his grown children from a previous marriage behind.
During the workshop this woman cried bitterly and shared with the group that
she would never be able to forgive herself for not being as kind to her husband
as she could have been during their years of marriage. He had always wanted
her to accept his children, but she had not been able to. It was just too hard.
Now he was gone and it was too late. She had let him down. I told her that she
still had the chance to make it up to him by accepting and loving her stepchil-
dren now. But she said that was out of the question—they were demanding
money from her and making her life miserable. Yet throughout the workshop
she wept every time she recalled how she had treated her husband and his
family.

If we are not willing to confront the truth about ourselves that a loss un-
earths, we squander a rare and precious opportunity for transformation. Our
grief, while deeply felt, runs the risk of becoming a sentimental escape from
the most meaningful part of the journey. If we do the hard work of a Phoenix
Process, when we lose someone we love then we find ourselves blessed with
more love than we ever knew existed. In a beautiful poem called "As I Walked
Out One Evening," W. H. Auden expresses in a few lines what to me is the
essence of the Phoenix Process:

> O stand, stand at the window
> As the tears scald and start;
> You shall love your crooked neighbour
> With your crooked heart.

A heart made crooked through loss and change is a heart that can love the
world and its less than perfect people. A woman who lost her brother in 1995,
when the Murrah Federal Building was bombed in Oklahoma City, writes, "It

is so awful what happened, but it's a different life for me now. It's a deeper life. A life of connection to people on a more real level." Sharon would agree with that, as would the other people whose stories I have shared in this part of the book. The next part is the story of my own Phoenix Process, one that reshaped my heart and led me into a deeper life.

PART III

The
Shaman Lover

Surviving the Holocaust, enduring the loss of one's child, learning to live with an incurable illness, witnessing terror, or experiencing trauma—these are Phoenix Processes of the tallest order. Come through one of them with an open heart and you light a path through the woods for all of us.

My own big Phoenix Process was hardly as grave. And yet, to date, the end of my marriage and the dissolution of my family are the events that changed me as no other life experiences have. I do not think I am alone in viewing intimate relationship as a powerful catalyst for personal growth and transformation. While I have been broken open through travails at work and in the world, nothing has awakened my heart as much as the pain of a broken family. Nothing has given me as much strength as the time I spent alone in the ruined aftermath of a marriage. And nothing has stirred my passion for life more than the awakening of my womanhood. No surprise here: The greatest stories ever told trace a path through the charred and exalted landscapes of romantic love.

For many, many people, a tested or failed relationship is the gateway into their most formative Phoenix Process. There is something primal—even dangerous—about this kind of experience. Passion, sex, and the dark side of a love affair can ignite a parched heart and burn a life to ashes. At the same time, the stirring of Eros in the body and heart revives the soul's water and nourishes rebirth. This is the classic descent and resurrection process—where life arises out of death.

The outcome of my own Phoenix Process was the end of my marriage and the beginning of a new life. I know just as many couples, though, whose relationship survived the process, and together the partners began a new life. What burns and dies in a Phoenix Process is not necessarily the relationship itself but the untested ideals, the unexpressed truths, and the repressed energy of the lovers. What rises from the ashes are more vital and mature individuals who have learned how to give and receive the gift of love.

I doubt there is a clean and easy way to break open through the pain of intimate relationship. Heartache is a messy affair, and it often drags whole families into its drama. For this reason, many people choose the stability of a shrunken relationship over the chaos that might ensue should one or both of the lovers confront what wants to live. Sometimes people look elsewhere—to their work or children or art—for the vitality they crave. I make no judgments here; I only tell my story, which is the tale of a woman whose heart was wrapped around itself, until it broke and blossomed.

Leaving My Father's House

There is some kiss
we want
with our whole lives.
—Rumi

I have three sisters, and three sons. I grew up in a family of women, and created a family of men. Now my house and office are populated primarily by men. But when I was a child, my world revolved around girls and women. Our house was full of them—my mother, my sisters, our girlfriends, and my grandmother and great-aunt. And one man: my father. Outnumbered, yet still the sun in our galaxy, my father kept his distance. His will prevailed, but it was filtered through a female atmosphere and was obeyed with a combustible combination of respect and resentment.

My father was a man of maverick passions. He worshiped nature, loved to read, argued politics, collected junk, and fixed things around the house in imaginative and harebrained ways. Given a choice, he was a lone wolf. But given reality (husband, father, creative director at a New York City advertising agency), he tolerated the inconvenience of a family and turned on the charm in social situations. He managed relationships by being in control.

My mother explained away my father's aggressively self-centered behavior by telling us that he had been an only child, as if this fact condoned his lordly ways. When he was home, it was his way or no way. There was no sleeping late, no idle afternoons, no gabbing on the telephone, and no "girl talk" at the table.

On weekends we became the members of his regiment and he, the captain. If he wanted to climb a mountain in New Hampshire, he would deploy his wife and four daughters, drive north for five hours, and march all of us up and down the White Mountains for a few days. No one was asked if she wanted to accompany my father; it was assumed that what he did, we did, no questions asked, no complaints registered. It made no difference to him if we had a cold or homework or a social event. If he was going, we were going.

This is how I spent my childhood, although sometimes, instead of climbing, skiing, or hiking mountains, we would help our father in his vegetable and flower gardens, or trudge for miles through the dunes to find the one spot on the Atlantic seacoast where no one else could be seen in either direction. Us girls (as the rest of the brigade was called) would grumble to our mother about leaving home almost every weekend, missing birthday parties and school plays, and being exposed to foul weather in every season. But we also admired our father's dauntless eccentricities. We grew to love the great outdoors; we weren't as clear about our feelings toward him.

I was more sure about what I felt toward the female members of the family. My mother was an unusual woman for her times, with many interests in and outside of the home. She created a rich and eclectic world for her daughters. She taught us how to make a house into a home, how to sing and draw and write, and how to raise a family while pursuing meaningful work. She went back to school and got her master's degree as she mothered four daughters and taught high school English. She was politically and socially active in our town. She opened our minds to the world and encouraged us to be curious people. But still, my father's priorities came first. My mother would drop her plans to facilitate his and suppress her needs to attend to his.

From my sisters I learned about living with women—how to laugh and cry and fight with them, joke around with them, help them when they were down, and take pleasure in their happiness. From my grandmother and great-aunt I learned some of the old skills: cooking, sewing, gossiping. But there was no one to teach me about being with men. Because of my father's elevated position and emotional distance, I did not regard men as fellow earthlings. Rather, I saw the entire lot of them as a mysterious solar system with which I longed to make meaningful contact.

When I left the pull of my father's gravitational force, I was completely untutored in the ways of the opposite sex. In retrospect, I am impressed by the choreography of my awkward dance away from my father's house and into the world of other men. I can see how the painful trip-ups were balanced by the impressive leaps forward. But nothing felt well-scripted when I was dancing away from home. Nothing about my journey from unconscious girl to full-fledged woman felt particularly graceful. In fact, it has been the gracelessness of my relationships with men that has broken, changed, and transformed me more than any other life experience.

There is some kiss we want with our whole lives, Rumi says. I went searching for that kiss after leaving my father's house. How I knew that it even existed is a mystery to me. My mother told us girls that being in love was a romantic fantasy, and that the life of the mind was the one to trust. My father was mute on the subject of love, as he was on most subjects that he called "girl talk." But I was born with a longing inside of me; I wanted that kiss—that sense of merging body and soul with another being, whether mate or friend or God. I wanted it, but I was too ashamed to want it with my *whole life.* I followed it haphazardly and halfheartedly, and I felt foolish doing so. In private I wrote poetry, read novels, and prayed fervently to gods who were outlawed in our family. My parents perceived religion as a lower form of human intelligence. Although my mother did read us passages from the Bible, she made sure we understood that these stories were myths to be mined for a few relevant gems of wisdom. But that's not how I heard them. I was smitten with Jesus; I wanted to go to church.

For a while, I tagged along to Catholic mass with my best friend's family. I went looking for the kiss. Perhaps it was in the wine and the wafer at the altar; perhaps it was behind the black screen of the confessional. I dreamed of becoming a nun, marrying Jesus, devoting my life to God. When I came home from church on Ash Wednesday with a black smudge on my forehead, my sisters nearly died laughing.

One day, as I was sitting next to my friend on the school bus, she whispered to me that even if I went to mass every Sunday for the rest of my life I would still go to hell since I wasn't a Catholic girl. After that I stopped going to church. Instead, I prayed alone to a picture of John F. Kennedy that I hung in my bedroom after his assassination.

There is some kiss we want with our whole lives. When I couldn't find the kiss in church, I went looking for it in books, and then in parties, politics, and pot. By the time I got to college, I was marching in antiwar demonstrations and staying up all night at rock concerts. For a while the excitement of being on my own at college in New York City was a channel for my longing. I threw myself into the wildness of the times in all areas except one. Some girls on my dorm floor posted a list that we were supposed to mark each time we had sex with another guy. My name was never on it. Although I had a boyfriend or two, I was shy to admit it. And although I lost my virginity, I never lost my heart. Sex never felt like the kiss I wanted with my whole life.

When I began the journey with the man who would become my first husband, I arrived carrying one big bag stuffed with longing. I brought with me nothing else—no experience, no training, no wise advice, no honed instincts. I was a babe in the woods of intimacy. And so was the brilliant young man who came into my life exactly when I needed him, and when he needed me. We were delivered to each other by fate, like two refugees fresh off the boat from childhood. Neither of us had yet taken up residence in our sensual body. Neither of us knew much about the opposite sex. We didn't know how to transform the tension between men and women into passion, or how to span the gulf of our differences with communication. Instead, we sparked off each other's similarities—our questing spirits, our open minds, our maverick streaks. We were like a brother and a sister gone out into the wide world. Whole big chunks of us went underground. And there they stayed for many years, until both of us, in our own ways, began to want the kiss with our whole lives.

Marriage Math

What is not brought to consciousness,
comes to us as fate.
—CARL JUNG

My first husband and I did what many young couples do. We unconsciously re-created our parents' marriages. We found in each other qualities that seemed safe because they were familiar, and we fell into patterns that we had learned through osmosis in the presence of our parents' relationships. Although, like my mother, I was aware that a woman is as *capable* as a man, I was also like my mother in another way. Without knowing it, I had absorbed our culture's silent yet pervasive message that a woman is not as *valuable* as a man. I did not respect my own voice; I could barely hear my own voice. All I knew was that sometimes my values differed from my husband's, and that I believed them to be less credible than his. What I wanted for us as a couple, and later as a family, was deemed less important, less impressive, less *real*. My husband's values seemed eminently real and worthy, just like his father's had, and my father's had.

Early in our relationship, in rare moments of self-confidence, I would feel a confused mixture of anger and sadness settle in my heart when I deferred to my husband if we disagreed about anything from the political to the personal. Hadn't the women's movement taught me that men and women are equally smart, equally deserving, and equally legitimate? Then why did I doubt myself so readily? When I wanted to talk and he wanted to be silent, I thought something was wrong with me. If I liked a certain place or person or movie or food and he didn't, I assumed that he was right.

For all of my smarts, I was unable to articulate what I sensed was of value for our relationship and our life plans. I yielded to him not only because he was a powerful and persuasive person but also because I did not trust my own instincts, my own heart. My feminine heart was sleeping deep down within me. That earthy, fertile, feeling, fierce, erotic, and tender part of me that some call "the feminine principle" was trapped beneath layers of culture and childhood. I needed that part of myself; my marriage needed that part of myself. But I didn't know that, and my husband didn't know that. One day our lack of consciousness would rise up, as Jung says, and *come to us as fate.*

As the years went on, I stuffed the anger and sadness about my lost feminine values underground. I turned my attention instead to the business of our life. And there was a lot of business. From the beginning my husband and I were a duo with high ideals and big plans. Within a few years of our being together, we had become serious students of a spiritual teacher, the leaders of his community, the cofounders of Omega Institute, and a doctor and midwife team with a busy practice. Metaphorically, there was always someone else in bed with us—our teacher, our work, our colleagues, and later on, our children. We made sure of that. To have been alone with each other would have exposed our uneasiness with an intimacy that neither of us knew how to nurture. And so we continued our busy lives, as if we were the bread and the rest of life was the center of the sandwich. As we added more and more filling, we grew further and further apart.

By the time I turned thirty, I had been married for ten years. I had two small children, a beautiful house, meaningful work, and a hole in my heart stuffed with unconscious and fateful longing. I adored my little boys with the kind of mother love that exists outside of all other feelings. It is as if mothers have two hearts and two bodies—one heart loves the babies, the other heart attends to the world; one body feeds the babies, the other body moves through time and space. I had those two hearts and two bodies. Over in the world of mother love, I was alive and well. That body made us a good home, cooked dinner, wiped noses, and snuggled. That heart made up bedtime stories, laughed at a five-year-old's jokes, and was overcome by the sweetness of little boys. But in the other world my heart was burdened, and my body, well, my body was yet to be born.

I would wake up each morning wondering if this was the way life was going to stay. I would do the emotional math over and over in my head, and come up with the same answer. I'd construct an equation where A represented my children or work or friends, and B stood for my marriage, and C was my life. Over in the part of the equation called A, I felt fine, at times even buoyantly alive. But if I did the math—the $A + B = C$—the equation would sink. If I left B out of the equation, I felt I could get out of bed in the morning and carry on. Excising my marriage from my life was one thing to think about in the abstract. In reality, I was not the type of person, or so I thought, who could ever unravel a family.

Certainly there were reasons why my marriage was so heavy it could sink my life. He was overwhelmed at work; I was absorbed in mothering. He was aloof; I was judgmental. Early in our relationship he had broken my trust; I couldn't forgive him—in fact I spent a lot of time blaming him for just about everything that felt wrong in my life. In mythological terms, he was Peter Pan and I was the classic nag. Our marriage became a firing range: I lobbed complaints at him, and he deflected them.

But here's the thing about marriages: Every one of them has a story that could end in divorce. That does not mean they all should. Nor does it mean that divorce will automatically raise the wreckage of the soul from the bottom of the sea. The rebirth of the soul is a much more arduous endeavor than merely getting a divorce, or changing jobs, or having a crisis crash over the flimsy structure of a life.

What matters is that we take the deadness of the soul seriously; that we pay attention to the contents of the heart; that we ask the hard questions, and fearlessly face the hidden parts of the self. What matters, Jung says, is that we shine the light of consciousness in the dark corners of our life. *What is not brought to consciousness,* he says, *comes to us as fate.*

During the last couple of years of our marriage, fate sent my husband and me several messages about the state of our union. I began to get sick with an exhaustion that no one could diagnose. He became restless in his work. We moved from the commune; we left our spiritual teacher; we relocated. None of this helped with the "marriage math." I worked the equation over and over, trying to make B as lively as A so that I could add them together and float happily through life. But floating was no longer an option. I felt something tugging at me from beneath. And then fate took over.

The Shaman Lover

*The great epochs of life come
when we gain the courage
to re-christen our evil
as what is best in us.*
—FRIEDRICH NIETZSCHE

I n some cultures, a person in the midst of a crisis or heartache will consult with the shaman—a medicine man or a healing witch who holds an exalted place in the society. The dictionary describes a shaman as "a member of certain tribal societies who acts as a medium between the visible world and an invisible spirit world, and who practices magic or sorcery for purposes of healing and divination." Shamans are on speaking terms with all of the spirits—the good and the friendly ones, and the wrathful ones too. A shaman can lead a lost soul through the darkness into the light because he knows the darkness; he spends much of his time down under, mixing the alchemical brew of transformation. He knows that a person's suffering is healed by a magical blend of dark and light.

There are shamans here in our midst. They may not look like medicine men or wise women—they may work in hospitals or office buildings—but they have the same powers. Some doctors and therapists have the shaman touch. They are comfortable with the dark realms of the mind and the heart; they don't shy away from troubles, illness, or the process of dying. I've known nurses and midwives who have strange powers, born out of years spent in the underworld of birth and sickness and death.

And there is another kind of shaman—the kind I call the Shaman Lover. The Shaman Lover is a man or a woman whose destiny is to heal the heartsick with the sweetness of love, and to give the gift of fire to those whose passion is frozen. Some call the Shaman Lover a temptress or a cad, a siren or a snake. Sometimes this is true; sometimes the Shaman Lover has bad medicine to offer. Sometimes the smartest response to the allure is to run away. But sometimes the Shaman Lover has been sent by fate to blast us open, to awaken the dead parts of our body, to deliver the kiss of life. And if we succumb, we are changed forever.

I have met indigenous shamans from the mountains and rain forests of India and South America. In their presence I have witnessed healings. I've ingested therapeutic herbs under the guidance of a Hopi medicine man and had powerful dreams and visitations from the spirit world. For several years I met weekly with a psychotherapist who practiced a modern form of healing as potent as any ancient tradition; he was a shaman of sorts. And I have had the honor of working with a veteran midwife who would have been called a witch in other eras, so powerful was her ability to harness the life force and bring babies safely from one world into another.

But it is the Shaman Lover who changed my life. It is the Shaman Lover who initiated me into womanhood through the healing power of sex, love, and passion. The Shaman Lover brought me all the way down into the underworld and left me there to find my way home. The journey down was as important as the journey up. He guided me down, and in finding my way back, I found myself.

Some will call my dance with the Shaman Lover just a clever name for an extramarital affair. Before I took the plunge with him, I would have had the same reaction. I would have been unsparing in my judgment of those who could be so deceitful, so morally lazy. I would have wondered if they knew the difference between right and wrong. Now I know that "right" without its shadow partner, "wrong," is a brittle and untested ideal. Now I know that when we show only our light side to the world, our shadow grows restless, sucking into itself much of our energy and passion. In order to release my trapped energy and awaken my best qualities, I had to engage with my shadow. I had to see how everything that I judged and feared in others was also in me. I had to be broken open so fully that my whole self was laid out before me to own and to forgive and to love. Before I could participate freely in wonders of the world, I had to taste the dark fruit and leave the garden of my innocence.

Wise people throughout the ages have talked about shadow energy, giving it the names and personalities of dark gods and goddesses, devils, and natural forces. From the Greek legends to the New Testament, we are told not to run from the evil forces that trouble our dreams or visit our lives. If we do, the exiled and dishonored shadow-self will triumph. Jung said that people tend to become what they ignore or oppose. He steered his patients away from resisting evil and toward transforming and redeeming it, or as he wrote, "putting the light of the superior functions at the service of the dark."

The philosopher Friedrich Nietzsche would call my dance with the Shaman Lover a "great epoch." He says that *the great epochs of life come when we gain the courage to re-christen our evil as what is best in us.* Your great epoch may involve a different kind of shamanic force than mine. You may be drawn to face your shadow through an engagement with a mentor or a religious leader or a counselor who abuses his or her power and betrays you. You may fall under the spell of a defiant friend and follow him or her into a way of life you never imagined for yourself. Some people fall under the spell of drugs or alcohol. One might call a drug or drink a shamanic substance—a dark elixir that teaches you about your own darkness and, one hopes, delivers you back into the light with the hard-earned gift of what is best in you.

If you are a quick learner, your time in the underworld will be brief: a vacation, a business trip, an exotic detour from everyday life. But you may need a deeper engagement, as I did. Your life may have to change. You may have to become unrecognizable to yourself and to those around you. You may have to enter into a great epoch long enough to gain the kind of courage to which Nietzsche is referring—the courage to turn and face and own all the exiled parts of the self until you can step firmly onto higher ground.

The people I have talked to about their underworld experiences all paid dearly for the journey down but were richly rewarded by what they learned and how they grew. Many people have come to my workshops struggling with the grave decisions and wounded trust that accompany affairs of the heart. If they use the dark energy wisely, they pull through as better people, better mates, better parents. I have gone with friends to AA meetings and wept at the courage of those trying to use recovery as a path to self-awareness. I have spent time with women who got mixed up with violent men. Those who found the strength to make a change and to confront their own inner demons reclaimed their lives with new power and selfhood.

Addiction, secret love affairs, journeys into the underworld of passion and sexuality—this is the stuff of myths. Persephone left the floral world of her mother (some say willingly, others say through abduction) to be with Hades, the king of the underworld. There, she found missing parts of herself and became a woman. It is said that Inanna, the Sumerian goddess of love, gained "Truth and the Art of Lovemaking" from her journey down below. Before she took the journey, many translations of the myth refer to Inanna as "the pure Inanna." The pure Inanna descended into the shadows, lost her innocence, and emerged as the Goddess of Love. Dante's pilgrim journeys through hell in search of his true love and his true life. Mark Musa, a translator and interpreter of Dante's *Inferno* writes, "The only way to escape from the dark wood is to descend into Hell; the only way up that mountain lit by the ray of the sun is to go down. Man must first descend in humility before he can raise himself to God. Before man can hope to climb the mountain of salvation, he must first know what sin is. The purpose of the Pilgrim's journey through Hell is precisely this: to learn all there is to know about sin, as a necessary preparation for the ascent to God."

I do not wish upon anyone a descent into hell. But if your life has to be turned inside out in order for you to know yourself—if the shadow of a shaman crosses your path and you turn and follow it down—I pray that you use its force wisely. I hope that you take the ultimate responsibility for your actions and that you consecrate any destruction to the rebuilding of your higher self and a more radiant life.

I followed my longing for the kiss into the underworld. I didn't know what I would find there. I didn't know that my abandoned feminine heart was there. I didn't know that my missing pieces—my passion, my body, my humility, my joy—were there. And I didn't know that I would have to confront my insensitivity, my conceit, my rage, and my sorrow there. I didn't know anything. I only followed my longing for the kiss.

The journey down cost me my marriage, my financial stability, the way I was perceived by my family and friends, and my reputation at work—a steep price to pay for a Phoenix Process. But what I bought for that price was worth it all. I bought myself, and with that purchase I came at last into the landscape of love. I became a lover. I learned how to receive love, and how to give it. I am still learning, but it started there, in the underworld with my Shaman Lover.

Initiation

Before I begin this story, I want to do justice to the real man who was my Shaman Lover. It is *I* who am giving him that title, and I who chose to travel downward on the arc of our affair. Although he led the way, he didn't make me go. I willingly tumbled, head over heels in love with him. I paid my own way in our agreed upon currency of secrets and lies. I followed him because something inside of me sensed an urgency I had never known before. I felt I would die unless I went with him into a dark and beckoning sea.

What I found in that sea was the courage to re-christen my evil, as Nietzsche says, as what is best in me. But that doesn't mean that my Shaman Lover was evil. He wasn't. His life experiences—as a child and a young man—had toughened him, and wounded him. He had a wildness that could erupt as both passion and anger. And he had a heart of gold; he had both. I loved both, and I learned from both.

What I did while I was with him—the secrets I kept, the lies I told, the heart I betrayed, the family I altered—had nothing, really, to do with him. And what we drank together in the underworld—both the bad medicine and the magic potions—came not from my Shaman Lover but from the well of wisdom that is to be found and imbibed down under, and rechristened when the journey is over.

To this day, I do not know what our relationship meant to my Shaman Lover. I do know what it meant to me. His love was one of the greatest gifts of my life. It awakened my passion, gave me my body, and softened my heart. Before my dance with the Shaman Lover, I had drifted timidly through my days, with only half of myself involved. After our dance, I lived more fully, and with more tenderness, humility, and joy. But it didn't start that way. In the beginning, I was aware only of an overpowering attraction.

When I first laid eyes on him, I knew I was in the presence of something out of my control. I read it in his glance, and in the clothes he was wearing (a woven poncho and a beret), and in the defiant way my heart opened to him. One part of me—my reasonable self—was amused by the triteness of the whole thing: A poncho and beret? Love at first sight? Come on! I was married with two little kids. I was running a large organization. This was not a good idea. The other part of me—the part that was starving, the part that was willing to die in order to live—had already started the journey down. My reasonable self told me to stay away from this man. I did the opposite.

I was drawn to him by a force stronger than any kind of will to turn away—as if his gravitational pull matched that of a planet. I've conducted research on the Shaman Lover—not in books, or in the Amazon, or the Himalayas but in the stories of ordinary men and women. Through this research, I have confirmed that the force of a Shaman Lover is indeed of planetary proportion. I have heard about a chance meeting on an airplane, a voice on the phone, a glance in the office. And like those near-death experiences where every patient notes the same landmarks (the floating feeling, the long tunnel, the light), the experience of meeting the Shaman Lover has its common markers. You will know you are on a journey with a Shaman Lover if you feel a sudden loss of control, a fearsome sense of abandon, and especially an air of foreignness. The Shaman Lover is not the one you thought could turn the large ship of your life around. If you thought you would be attracted to someone with money, he is broke; if you wanted respectability, she's a gypsy; if you longed for sweet romance, he's mean; if you wanted deep peace, she's trouble.

I met my Shaman Lover through my work. He was funny, feral, and as fluid as a water snake. Whenever I was around him, a primitive force overtook me. I had always prided myself on my good sense. But now I made a string of irrational and doomed decisions. The first was to begin a secret love affair at all. If you have never lived a lie, you can barely imagine the terror of digging yourself deeper and deeper, day by day, into the kind of deceit that will eventually end in disaster. The next risky choice I made was to mix up my personal life with my work life. But the most troublesome aspect of my behavior was that it had the possibility of affecting my children. I was a mother who had always put her children first. Suddenly my own needs were competing with theirs. What I thought was the best of me—devoted mother, faithful wife, public leader—gave in to the demands of an irrational force. What was I doing?

Years later I can see exactly what I was doing. Now I know that the "good

wife" and the "social servant" I tried to be were pale versions of my real capa-
bilities. I now understand that a frozen and frightened girl cannot be a good
wife or a mature mother, that a person who has never been wounded cannot
heal, and that a leader is worth following only if she can follow her own heart.
But I never would have known any of this had I not fallen for my Shaman
Lover.

After we acknowledged our feelings for each other, he gave me these lines
from the Japanese poet Fujiwara no Teika:

> *From the beginning*
> *I knew meeting could only*
> *End in parting, yet*
> *I ignored the coming dawn*
> *And I gave myself to you.*

While I had never felt anything like this before, my Shaman Lover was
practiced in the art of falling in love. He saw the end coming even before we
started; I danced into the flames like a silly moth, drunk on the fire, drunk on
the kiss. This was the kiss, and suddenly I wanted it with my whole life.

My affair lasted for more than a year. All during it, I never told my husband. I never told another living soul. It was as if my Shaman Lover and I met
on an island at the far end of the world. Nothing else mattered except what
happened there. It was there that I finally surrendered to another's body, and
in doing so found my own. I remember running my hands over my own neck
and shoulders and breasts in the same adoring way I would have touched my
babies. I remember tracing with my fingers the little valley between my hip
bone and my belly as I lay naked on the bed, loving what I felt for the first time
in my life—the softness of the flesh, the tightness of the muscles, the hardness
of the bones. I was being born again—this time with awareness and gratitude—
into my human body. And now, because I had come home to my body, I could
make love to another body.

The ancient Greeks had a name for this kind of awakened, embodied passion. They called it Eros. In Greek mythology, Eros, the son of Aphrodite, was
the golden god of love and the personification of passion and sexual relationship. For many people, an awakened sense of Eros in the body probably comes
as part of the standard operating system. I remember those girls in high school

who seemed to make a graceful leap from childhood to womanhood—the ones all the boys loved, the ones who lived in their bodies. But I had to earn my Eros. I had to go through a rite of passage—an initiation into womanhood.

For a few months the sheer joy of being in the grip of Eros overrode the furtiveness of my affair. Even though we were careful not to be seen in public, and our times together were brief, my Shaman Lover and I had a whole life of our own. We talked and played and cooked and read to each other. We behaved as if we were from another age. We exchanged handmade gifts, wrote each other letters and poems, and sang our favorite songs as we lay in bed in the dark. I loved my Shaman Lover to the exclusion of the rest of my life. As I neglected everything else around me, my heart awakened and my body healed.

But after a while the secrecy began to take its toll—on my nervous system and on the climate at work and at home. Something else changed as well. My Shaman Lover and I began to fight. The dark passion of our fighting was as new to me as the sweet passion of our loving. We yelled, we threw things, we slammed doors and wrote each other angry letters. Then we made up. Then we fought again. I felt as if I was living in a romance novel. Soon we were fighting more and more. We had unleashed not only Eros but also the Furies. We had trapped ourselves in an untenable situation, and I began to understand that this story would not have a happy ending.

Jung wrote, "Eros is a questionable fellow and will always remain so. . . . He belongs on one side to man's primordial animal nature, which will endure as long as man has an animal body. On the other side he is related to the highest forms of the spirit. But he thrives only when spirit and instinct are in right harmony." My spirit and my instinct became less and less harmonious in my relationship with my Shaman Lover. Spirit does not fare well when lies are told and when children are in need of their mother's attention. A longing for honesty—like rays of light poking through a thick cloud cover—started seeping into the underworld where I had been living. I began to feel a pull toward the light as urgently as I had felt the pull toward the darkness. I wanted to come clean. I wanted to bring what I had found below into the light of day. Like Persephone, I had to find a way to bridge the two worlds.

The Crossroads

On one side of my kitchen table sits an antique bench made of splintering, rough-hewn pine. It really should be replaced. The bench is so unstable that it is more like a seesaw in a playground than a piece of furniture in a house. More than a few friends and family members have been dumped on the floor when the person on the other end stood up abruptly. At my father's eightieth birthday party, his aged secretary from earlier days was tossed from the bench when another party guest arose from the other end. Food and wine spilled all over her dress as she landed in a heap. "Oh, that bench!" I exclaimed in apology to the woman, who was shaken yet fortunately unharmed. "I should really get rid of that bench."

But I cannot bear to let go of the bench, because when I sit on it I remember the moment when my underworld journey reached the Crossroads. Marion Woodman—the great Jungian analyst and author—says that we come to the mythic Crossroads during "moments in our lives where the unconscious crosses consciousness; where the eternal crosses the transitory; where a higher will demands the surrender of our egos."

It was on the bench in my kitchen that my unconscious behavior crossed my conscious awareness and I knew I had to end the affair. I can recall that moment as if it were this morning, even though it was years ago. Often when I sit down to a meal, and I feel the splintery wood and the wobbly legs of the bench beneath me, I am drawn back to the Crossroads. I remember the stillness in the empty house and the contractions of my heart as I sat on the bench and wept from a kind of sorrow and terror I had never known before. I don't remember the season, or the day of the week, or the hour of the day; I do remember a moment when I finally understood, as if a guillotine was about to cut off my head, that my life as I had known it was over.

I had just returned from Santa Fe—from the trip where I met with the psychic in the trailer park. Tired from the traveling, and stunned by what the psychic had told me, I sat on the bench after getting the kids off to school. The words of the psychic rang in my ears. I heard her asking me what my soul wanted. And for the first time, I let myself understand that my soul wanted the truth. "What is the truth?" I asked, ready to let the lid off what I already knew. And as if the psychic was there on the other side of the bench, the answer came right back: The truth was that my marriage had been over for several years now, and that my Shaman Lover would never want to commit his life to my children and me. Both relationships could not survive the truth of who I had become. For my sake, for my husband's sake, for my children's sake, and for my Shaman Lover's sake, it was time to tell the truth. A raw and desperate longing for the light of day—the twin of the longing that had got me into this mess—took hold of me. A new kind of courage took my arm and led me to the telephone. I made two calls. The first was to my husband. The second was to my Shaman Lover.

And then I sat back down on the bench, marooned by the truth. I cried months and months of tears—tears of shame, of fear, of surrender, and of relief. I knew that in giving up my marriage I was giving up a precious union I would never be able to re-create. I would never mate or marry again with such innocence. The novelist Robertson Davies says, "One always learns one's mystery, at the price of one's innocence." I was learning my mystery—the mystery of myself—and paying with my innocence and my marriage. But the time had come.

I also knew, in walking away from my Shaman Lover, that I would never again fall in love with such wild abandon and blind determination. I was terrified to give up a love that had saved me. But I knew further that what I had found with my Shaman Lover was mine to keep. Even if I never fell in love again, once would have been enough. Because once we have given ourselves to another, we are able to fall in love with life itself. And that can last forever.

While I was in Santa Fe, a few days before visiting the psychic, a friend took me to a natural hot springs in the mountains. After we soaked in the sulfury water, a Mexican woman wrapped us in wool blankets and settled us on cots, in a courtyard, in the sun. I don't know how long we lay there, and I don't know if what I experienced was a dream or a vision. Whatever it was, it was not a normal nocturnal dream. It seemed real—almost more real than life.

I am walking in a desert toward a dark shape—the only shape on the flat landscape. As I near the blackened shape, I see that it is a burnt tree trunk, standing alone amidst the desert rocks and stubble. Out from behind the dark mass steps a dear friend who has recently died from leukemia. I go to her, and as I do, I become her, standing alone and dead, by the gloomy tree. I feel a great weight of sadness crushing my heart. I am dead, the desert is dead, the tree is burned and dead. I sit by the tree and wait. And then my Shaman Lover appears. He reaches his hand into a hole in the tree trunk and pulls out rough desert rocks encrusted with gems—turquoise, coral, quartz. He turns to me and feeds me the gemstones. They fill me with warmth and joy. And as suddenly as he appeared, he is gone. I am left there, no longer dead, but alive with something luminous and solid burning in my core.

A journey into the underworld never turns out to be what we feared, and at its core the darkness becomes the light. My dance with the Shaman Lover took me into the darkness. Our relationship showed me hidden aspects of myself that I never would have seen without him—marvelous, passionate, and loving aspects, and horrible, destructive, and deceitful aspects. When I arrived at the Crossroads—starting on that bench in the kitchen—and when the spinning plates of my marriage and my affair crashed to the ground, I was left with nothing but my most human self. There was no more pretending that I could have a perfect life. I knew now that I was a flawed being, capable of both sin and love. From now on I could blame no one else for what happened in my life, nor could I look to anyone to save me. My life was my own. It was up to me to rechristen my evil with what was best in me.

As I ascended from the underworld, I vowed to leave my idealized version of the world behind. I vowed to work every day to transform my fear into openness, my blame into responsibility, my hubris into humility. I wanted to trade my shame—my embarrassment at being human—for the kind of wisdom that makes for a happy, kind, and courageous life. That is what I decided at the Crossroads. I chose a different path that day. I took a new road: the Road of Truth, as the psychic called it. It's not an easy road to travel, but it leads ever onward into landscapes of freedom.

It took me a long time to repair the damage done during my descent. Separating from my Shaman Lover was painful for both of us. My ex-husband and

I struggled to leave each other with dignity and fairness, and still our divorce was wrenching and messy. My role at work changed forever—for better and for worse. I was set back financially for years, but I was also set free to explore other creative aspects of myself. My family, my children, and my role as a mother also went through big changes, which I write about in the next part of the book. There is no getting around the fact that a Phoenix Process is both wounding and liberating. But wounds can heal, while liberation is without end. When I emerged from my journey in the underworld, I was cracked and battered, but I was also strangely at peace. I had broken open. I was no longer a tight little bud. I had risked everything and had blossomed.

Goethe's Chain Letter

And so long as you haven't experienced
this: to die and so to grow,
you are only a troubled guest
on the dark earth.
—Johann Wolfgang von Goethe

When I was first getting to know Tom—the man the psychic in the trailer park called the "name vibration," the man I would marry—he sent me "The Holy Longing," a poem by Goethe that ends with the lines above. At the bottom of the poem was a note that said, "I only want to be with someone who has died." Fortunately I knew what he was talking about; someone else may have turned him in to the police. Perhaps it is strange to find a poem about death romantic, but I was attracted to the kind of man who would use a melancholy Goethe poem to seduce a woman.

Tom was a few years ahead of me in the divorce process. He and his wife of fourteen years had been divorced for several years when we first met. He was a devoted single father of a six-year-old boy, a lapsed lawyer, a real estate investor, an exceptionally funny man, and a Texan—which to a New Englander was more foreign than someone from France or Thailand or Mars. He was not like other men I knew. He had been raised on a cattle ranch and was his high school's star athlete and valedictorian. He played basketball in college. He was an all-American sort of guy. I was a New Yorker; my parents came from Brooklyn; I'd lived on a commune. But the differences in our backgrounds paled in comparison to what we had in common. We shared what Goethe called the "holy longing," and that made me feel as if I had finally come home, that I was safe at home with Tom. I felt that the minute I saw him, and I had it confirmed when he sent me the poem:

The Holy Longing
Johann Wolfgang von Goethe

Tell a wise person, or else keep silent.
Because the massman will mock it right away.
I praise what is truly alive,
what longs to be burned to death.

In the calm water of the love-nights,
where you were begotten, where you have begotten,
a strange feeling comes over you
when you see the silent candle burning.

Now you are no longer caught
in the obsession with darkness,
and a desire for higher lovemaking
sweeps you upward.

Distance does not make you falter,
now, arriving in magic, flying,
and finally, insane for the light,
you are the butterfly and you are gone.

And so long as you haven't experienced
this: to die and so to grow,
you are only a troubled guest
on the dark earth.

Tom had "died and grown" through the loss of his marriage. We both had felt the heat of the flame; we both had been hurt deeply by divorce; and we both were changing from the experience. While I was discovering a new kind of power and courage through my Phoenix Process, Tom had come away from his with an awakened sense of empathy and a softer heart. Both of us wanted to use our past mistakes to tame the jagged parts of our egos, to learn how to love, to become whole. We felt ready to try for a different sort of relationship than either of us had known before.

Goethe's poem is the bedrock of our marriage. When things get touchy between us, when I wonder what in the world I am doing with a Texas boy and he wonders how he ended up in New York living with me, we remember the poem. During the most stressful years of our relationship, when we combined our families and devoted ourselves to raising our sons, we were often saved by Goethe. We had sworn our hearts not only to each other but also to our faith in the Phoenix Process. Our first commitment was to spiritual growth—his, mine, and ours. If we could remember that when we wanted to throw in the towel, we would make it. And we have.

When my closest friend at work was teetering on the edge of a Phoenix Process, I gave him Goethe's "The Holy Longing." It sent him over the cliff and into the flames. Fortunately, he was ready. But I realized then that I would have to be careful; I could give Goethe's poem only to those willing *to die and so to grow.* The poem was like one of those chain letters I used to get in the mail when I was a girl—the kind that ended with dire warnings of what would happen if, on the one hand, you kept the letter or, on the other hand, you mailed it to the wrong sort of person—the sort of person who would not do what it says to do.

Every now and then when I am teaching, people in a workshop will share a story that reveals a readiness to take the plunge into a Phoenix Process. I will sense in their story a sincere longing to move beyond being *a troubled guest on the dark earth.* I will note in their eyes *insanity for the light,* and I'll hand them the poem.

The Joy of Being Wrong

Tale as old as time,
Tune as old as song.
Bittersweet and strange,
Finding you can change,
Learning you were wrong.
—HOWARD ASHMAN AND ALAN MENKEN
FROM *BEAUTY AND THE BEAST*

I sit across the table from my old college roommate. I recognize a dark shadow on her shoulder; I see fear in her eyes. She doesn't know that the heavy hand on her shoulder is the wing of the Phoenix. She just feels the force of something turning her—away from the life she has tried so hard to control and toward the pain of its undoing. Should I tell her to follow that dark force? Should I warn her of the arduous length of the journey? I don't want to do that. She must enter a Phoenix Process willingly, of her own accord. She must take the journey all on her own, from the beginning to the end, because its very purpose is that: to go *alone* into the flames, to burn away the illusions, and to arise from the ashes with the prize of one's true self.

My friend has recently discovered that her husband is having an affair. This friend, whose life appears so perfect to the casual observer, and whose fifteen-year marriage, two happy children, and lovely home stirs envy in the minds of many, has been brought to her knees. She is done with trying to appear perfect. That game is over. She sits at my kitchen table with a lifetime of being one way behind her, and a mysterious force pulling her into the unknown future. When she found out about the affair, she felt she had choices in how to deal with it: She could freeze and forgive him, stay with what they had, hope it would never happen again, make a few demands, and then forget the whole thing. Or she could rage and punish and make him feel so awful about what he had done that he would resume his role of the upright, superior, brilliant man she had married, and then things would go back to normal. But now she feels she has no choice at all. There is only the weight of the wing on her shoulder, and the urge to turn and face what has been hidden for years. She feels instinctual, ignorant, intent on something, but she doesn't know what.

All she knows now is that she was wrong—wrong to idolize her husband and doubt her own intelligence and power for so many years; wrong to restrain her inner music in deference to her husband's one willful note; wrong not to sing her own song, whether or not it was in harmony with his. Suddenly, to know how wrong she has been is her only salvation. She wants to go there—into the deceit of the game they have been playing. She wants to explore every wrong note, every illusion, every misstep. She doesn't even care anymore if he wants to go with her as she journeys down—down beyond even death, down into the place where new life is waiting.

Since feeling the wing of the Phoenix on my own shoulder, I can sometimes sense its weight on other people long before they can name its presence. Over the years I have watched friends, family members, and people in my workshops turn either toward or away from the beckoning force. Sometimes I give them Goethe's chain letter, or tell them a story from my own life, if I think they can handle a push over the edge. But most of the time I just watch. I pray that they find the courage to go into the flames. I do not pray that they turn away from a Phoenix Process. Although the fire burns hot, it seems more painful to me to remain frozen in an unexamined relationship (or a soul-killing job, or a difficult loss, or an impending change) than to go into the unknown, through the fire, into the ashes, and out again into new life.

A young woman came to one of my workshops because she wanted to learn how to slow down and relax. Her life was so busy, she said, that she rarely had a minute to think her own thoughts. During the weekend, every time I led a deep relaxation exercise, she would cry. When I asked her about her tears, she said she was surprised by them herself. She spoke with great enthusiasm about her life. She loved her work. She lived in Southern California and was a surfer.

She was married to "the most wonderful man in the world." She said that she and her husband just could not understand why so many people were depressed. She had no tolerance for complainers. As we chatted during a break, she told me with a naïve and even self-righteous tone that "life is what you make it." And then, as I led the class in a meditation, and as the others slipped in a silent reverie, she once again began to cry.

A few years later, I heard from the young woman. She was in the midst of a Phoenix Process. I asked her to write about it. These are her words:

All during my thirties I was happy, happy, happy: surfing, working, and well, perhaps thinking I was pulling things off better than other people. I loved my husband. I loved my life. I couldn't really understand why people complained so much. It seemed to me happiness was a function of staying cheerful and making sure other people in my life were happy too. Sometimes I would feel this emotional cloud descend, and with it a sense that there was something deeper, greater, something that wanted me to listen to it. But I didn't want to give energy to that cloud—I called it my cloud of dissatisfaction.

Sometimes I would find myself crying for no reason. Like at the end of yoga class, lying in deep relaxation, I would sob. But it was really important for me to keep my life going at full speed, to keep my relationship alive, to continue to make it "the best." This created anxiety and conciliatory behavior with my husband, but I just thought that's what it took.

Then, my "perfect" husband, who always told me how much he adored me, had an affair. This was after thirteen years of bragging to friends that my husband would never do something like that. And why should he? I was such a nice and smart woman; we had sex whenever he wanted to; I never put too many demands on his time. When he told me that he was involved with a mutual (and younger) friend, I felt deeply ashamed and humiliated. The force of the betrayal and the sudden distance between us left a hole so large that I felt the whole world disappear into it.

I decided to file for divorce, even though I knew that would plunge me into the dark night of the soul. But the prospect of riding things out while he continued his affair scared me even more. I also knew that it would take so long to heal that I had better get started. This was such an important time for me, and boy did I need help. I had the incredible fortune of having a wonderful therapist, who helped me deal with everything from my inability to eat and sleep to my almost constant tears. I also had good friends who understood me and accepted the huge changes that I was going through. My yoga and meditation practice were crucial to me during that time. All of the above helped me stop blaming myself and give myself over to the process of healing, even if it took years. I had been in the relationship for thirteen years. I couldn't expect to get over it in a few weeks.

Several years later, I am still in the process, but I feel a self-reliance, a sense of freedom that I have never known before. A compassion for others is emerging from my huge broken heart. I guess it had to open fully to the pain of this life, because things are—in a strange way—better for me now. Loss and change seem easier. I still get hurt, cry a lot, but there's a sense of strength and equanimity for having survived. There was no other option for me than to move toward my true nature. How strange to find in the midst of life's drama the springboard to who I really am. How strange to discover that I had been so wrong about so many things—me, who thought she knew everything! And how great to discover that it is better to be honest and free than it is to be right and trapped.

I once saw a bumper sticker that read, "Would you rather be right, or would you rather be happy?" There is a great joy in discovering our ignorance, and a great freedom in realizing how defended from the truth we have been—how what we think is so, often not so at all. The young woman in my workshop now understands this. And so does my college friend who felt the weight of the Phoenix's wing on her shoulder. She turned and faced the unknown. For several years she lived in a dark world where right became wrong and wrong became right. She and her husband were like stones in a vibrating tumbler—they rubbed up against each other, chipping away the rough edges and the protective layers until their hearts were polished by the truth. Their marriage is less innocent now but also less smug, less blind, less "right." My friend is learning how to love and respect herself, and how to forgive and accept her husband. As she takes responsibility for her part in what went wrong, she is also claiming her own power and taking her husband down from the pedestal. And her husband is helping her in the process. He has been humbled by his fall from grace; he has been broken, opened, and changed.

In the European folktale "Beauty and the Beast"—a story about true love surviving false identities—Beauty stays with the Beast because she sees who he really is, beneath his deceptive and fearsome veneer. This story has been told and retold through the centuries. In our times, in the Disney version of the tale, when the Beast and Beauty awaken into who they really are, they sing this song to each other:

> Tale as old as time,
> Tune as old as song.
> Bittersweet and strange,
> Finding you can change,
> Learning you were wrong.

Whether a marriage or relationship survives the heat of a Phoenix Process is not really the issue here. Something much greater is at stake when we choose to learn and grow in the crucible of love. When trouble visits a relationship— a dance with a Shaman Lover, a long period of deadness, a shift in roles, a change in expectations—we are faced with weighty choices: Will we turn away and go back to sleep? Will we fall unconsciously into meaningless destruction, vengeance, or acting out? Or will we use the dangerous force of the heart's longing wisely, and put it in service of our spiritual growth? Will the pain make us better, stronger, kinder, bigger? Will we learn from a betrayed devotion or a broken family, so that our mistakes are not repeated over and over again? These are the challenges put to those of us whose Phoenix Processes occur through the ordeal of relationship.

For your sake, for your partner's sake, and for the sake of the children, who learn from us how to change and how to grow, I pray that your bittersweet and strange adventure leads you into the landscape of love. I pray that the new relationship you build, with your old partner or with a new one, is a marriage between two whole people—two people who have married the shadow and the light within themselves, and who love the truth as much as they love each other.

PART IV

Children

I F YOU WOULD LIKE TO BE BROKEN OPEN—if you want to pursue a Phoenix Process of the highest order—I would recommend raising children. Parenthood is a clumsy yet majestic dance in the flames. When you parent you fall in love with a person who is always changing into someone else, and who you know will leave you. Yet most parents will say that they have never given themselves to anyone as fully as they have to their children. The stories in this part of the book are about the work and the wonder of being a parent—a career with the crazy-making job requirement of simultaneously surrendering to and letting go of someone you love, over and over and over again.

Parenthood is a never-ending journey down a wide river of worry and love. You get in that boat with your kids and you never get out. They get out—they build their own boats and row into their own destinies—but you stay in the original boat, always their parent, forever caring and forever kvelling (a useful Yiddish word that describes how parents express pride in their children).

Sometimes the act of parenting is an awe-inspiring adventure. Your heart expands to accommodate a vastness of feelings so tender and unselfish that you step boldly into the nobility of your true character. And sometimes parenthood is tedious yet unpredictable, demanding yet ever-changing: Just when you get the hang of sleeping upright in a rocking chair and changing dirty diapers, your child sleeps through the night and poops in the potty, and the job description changes. It's a lot like the comedian George Carlin's complaint, "Just when I found out the meaning of life, they changed it."

So you go back into on-the-job training. By the time you have mastered communication with a tantrum-throwing toddler and become addicted to the warm, wet smell of your little one after a bath, he squirms away and goes to kindergarten. Now you have to learn to deal with play dates and social studies reports and parent-teacher conferences. And then school plays and Little League games, friends and hurt feelings, and that shifting boundary between granting them freedom and giving them direction. Soon they are teenagers, and there is no manual for that, so you take it one day at a time, difficult decision by difficult decision, and finally, if things go the way they ought to, your children leave home, they leave you, and they push off into the future.

Parenting in all of its stages is a spiritual path with mythic twists and turns. If your spiritual goal is to embrace life, moment by moment, in both its rapture and its pain, then parenting offers you that opportunity every day. Holy texts throughout the ages tell us that the truth is to be found between the seeming opposites in life—between your own will and a greater will; between limits and liberty; between the call to care for others and the need to care for yourself. In the parent-child relationship, these concepts become supremely real. And you get excellent feedback all the time from a pint-sized spiritual master—your own kid—whose specialty lies in teaching you how to keep on loving even when you are tired, scared, confused, or pissed off. Isn't that what every seeker is after?

At each stage of your child's growth, you are given ample opportunities to use parenthood as a mirror. You get to see exactly where you fall short in the most graphic ways: Are you self-absorbed? Do you resist putting the needs of others first? Or do you err in the other direction—are you a martyr, a guilt-tripper, a codependent smotherer? Do you fear change? Are you impatient? Jealous? Comparative? Whatever it is that wants to be transformed in your psyche will be revealed as you parent. If you accept the challenge, parenting becomes a perpetual process of change and transformation—a dynamic experience of being broken open by love.

Firstborn

My children and I grew up together. I was twenty-two when my first son took up residence in my womb. I was really just a kid—a big kid having a little kid. I remember the first moment I became a parent, when I let the mind-boggling reality of being a mother overtake the whimsy of being a girl. I can recall that moment all the way down to the tiny speck that was my baby growing within me.

It was an unusually warm late autumn day. The baby was due in May. I was on kitchen duty at the commune, preparing lunch for a hundred and fifty. Morning sickness—a real misnomer, since I was plagued by nausea morning, noon, and night—was so severe that I vomited most everything I ate. The smells from the stove suddenly got the better of me, and I ran out of the kitchen building, down the stone steps, and up the dirt road. By the old Shaker barn I sank to my knees and coughed up half of a cracker. Throwing up is something children do, I thought. And then it hit me: How could I have a child? I had just finished being one myself! What in the world was I doing? I was giving up my entire life! Would I be able to do this? Would I know how to be a mother?

There, on my knees in the fallen leaves by the side of the road, I became conscious of the transition I was making. My childhood was over; my baby's childhood was about to begin; and I had no idea what I was doing. I was terrified, yet at the same time strangely confident, as if a dormant animal mother was awakening within me. That was my first glimpse of the true nature of parenthood—my first step on a long journey of self-doubt and innate wisdom.

In one way, my pregnancy had been an impulsive, improbable act. My friends from college were deferring motherhood in favor of more politically correct job descriptions. They were going to graduate school, traveling the world, or climbing career ladders. For them, having a baby would have to wait. But I had chosen a different path. I was living in a rural commune in an old Shaker village with a group of utopian dreamers. We had not only gone back to the land but also gone back in time. We were bent on the old-fashioned way. We might have looked like college-educated baby boomers, but we lived like our pioneer predecessors—growing our own food, fixing our own buildings, and birthing our own babies.

In another way, my pregnancy was not improbable at all. I had been planning on having a baby for a long time—since I was about four or five. I was one of those little girls whose greatest joy was to cradle a doll, sing to it, and tuck it into its crib. I would never go to school without arranging the babies and stuffed animals comfortably on my bed, making sure they were warm in the winter and cool in the summer, and grouped according to their current likes and dislikes of each other. I had already caught the motherhood bug: I could feel what my dolls were feeling; I wanted them to be happy and safe; I worried about their well-being. My sisters found a reliable way to antagonize me in my devotion to my dolls. I once found a baby doll hanging in my room like a lynch-mob victim, the pull string of the window shade wrapped around her pudgy plastic neck.

For months after this incident, I paid extra attention to the doll, hoping her little psyche had not been traumatized. If therapy had been in vogue, I would have found a doll therapist and spent my allowance on the baby's recovery. Even after I stopped playing with them, I never banished my dolls to a box in a closet. I knew that would hurt their feelings. I still have them; they sit silently on a shelf in my grown-up bedroom. I rearrange their seating every now and then.

The devotion I displayed toward my dolls should have tipped me off to the kind of mother I was going to be. From the moment I looked at my son, I was like the first parents in a myth that Joseph Campbell retells: "There is a Persian myth of the first two parents, who loved their children so much that they ate them up. God thought, 'Well, this can't go on.' So he reduced parental love by something like ninety-nine and nine-tenths percent, so parents wouldn't eat up their children." I was a goner for this little boy. I came close to eating him up several times. All of my fears of not knowing what to do, or not being ready or able to take care of a child, disappeared when I held my baby and looked at his amazing face. I loved him with an all-consuming, fierce, and wild kind of love. I was a lion and he was my cub.

Most of us start out like this with our children. When they are helpless infants, wild parenting is an appropriate style of care. But as they grow, and become their own people, it becomes an imperative to "reduce parental love by something like ninety-nine and nine-tenths percent," so as not to consume the poor things with excessive coddling. I must admit that I am still working on reducing my parental love to a reasonable percentage, although this may be a moot point, since my children are now men who will soon be spoon-feeding lavish percentages of love to their own unsuspecting little ones.

We chose our firstborn's name from the Bible: Rahmiel, the angel of mercy. Even though he cried from colic for months, rarely slept, and showed us little mercy night or day, I could see who this little one was. Some infants enter the world looking like the archetypal baby: fat, sweet, and sleepy. Some babies resemble old people, tiny versions of who they will grow up to be. My first baby looked neither new nor old. He was otherworldly, like a pure ray of intelligence, like an innocent visitor from a more benevolent planet. I saw this in Rahmiel's face.

It was a good thing I saw it, and it was a good thing I had no previous experience with babies when my first was born—I assumed they all cried all the time, and so I walked him around, day and night, until we were both dizzy and wrapped tightly around each other's hearts. When the crying stopped, Rahm became a sweet yet bossy toddler, and we his loyal servants. He was a careful, smart, and sensible fellow, not the kind of child who wanted a lot of toys or watched endless television. He always knew his limits. When his grandmother gave him carte blanche at F.A.O. Schwarz, the largest toy store in the world, he chose a ball. But when he wanted something and couldn't have it, his tantrums were legendary.

Once he threw a spectacular fit when a friend of mine was visiting. At that time Rahm was three, and we had yet to reduce parental love by even a few percentage points. Our toddler was the sovereign ruler of the household. He had established a law that only his favorite tape could be played in the car or the house. For several weeks we had been listening exclusively to *The Singing Rabbis,* a collection of folksy Jewish songs that somehow intrigued him. I had neglected to warn my visiting friend of the music law and was upstairs when she foolishly chose another tape and pressed the Play button. By the time I got

downstairs, the little king was revving up into royal histrionics. When I refused
to replace the unauthorized music with *The Singing Rabbis,* the tantrum escalated into the kind of sobbing that resembles choking. I had to take Rahm outside and put his bare bottom in a snowdrift just to get him to breathe. My
younger sons still love this story.

As he left the toddler stage, Rahmiel grew back into his name. He became
an unusually caring child, a protective older brother, and the family peace-
maker. As he grew up, I began to wise up. Loving one's child did not necessarily
mean giving in to his every desire. This was the kind of love that the ancients
knew must be reduced by ninety-nine and nine-tenths percent. If we don't
purge ourselves of disproportionate, neurotic caring—if we raise our little dar-
lings in a bubble of comfort; if we stay one step ahead of their every need; if we
try to shield them from the pain of the world—we deprive them of their early
Phoenix Process training. I write from experience. I tried to do this. I learned
that too much giving to children is not a gift. Rather, it's a taking away. It denies
children the skills they will need for life outside the bubble. All of my sons
taught me this as they grew. Rahmiel—the angel of mercy—was the first.
Today, Rahm is one of the more compassionate men I know. And I am still
learning how to be a parent.

Run Away, Bunny!

Once there was a little bunny who wanted to run away.
So he said to his mother, "I am running away."
"If you run away," said his mother, "I will run after you.
For you are my little bunny."
—MARGARET WISE BROWN

I read my sons *The Runaway Bunny*—Margaret Wise Brown's beloved book about a plucky little bunny with big dreams—to mixed reviews. My first-born, who appreciated order from an early age, was relieved to know that the mother in the book would always catch her little bunny, no matter how hard he tried to run away. She would become a tree if he became a bird, the wind if he became a sailboat. She would blow him back to port over and over again, no matter how far he ventured from home. This consistent and dependable love appealed to Rahm. He was the kind of child who wanted to know that he could light out for the next aisle in the grocery store and I would come and save him from his own wanderlust.

My second son came into the world marching to the beat of a different drummer, even before he could walk. He didn't like *The Runaway Bunny*. "Why doesn't the mommy let the bunny do what he wants to do?" was Daniel's response to the plot line. As we snuggled up with the book, Daniel would hatch crafty plans to help the bunny realize his dreams of freedom. "Run away, bunny!" he'd yell as I turned the pages of the book and the bunny attempted to run, or swim, or fly away from his ever-protecting mother.

I found Daniel's interpretation of the book interesting and endearing. I wasn't yet thinking of how his love of freedom would play out over the years. I had no real understanding of what happens to children and parents when the bunnies grow older and actually do run, or swim, or fly away. All I knew was that Daniel was a chubby toddler in light blue pajamas, one with an expansive and offbeat imagination, and I was his mother, reading him a picture book. Perhaps I thought he would stay a baby forever; perhaps I wasn't thinking at all. Some sort of dreamy chemical must flow through the blood of mothers, shielding us from what's around the corner, and keeping us fully engaged with our children at each stage.

Daniel was the kind of baby that everyone—adults, his brother, other kids, and especially little girls—fell in love with. He was the kind of baby who was happy to sit on the floor playing with a set of keys or a couple of spoons. He loved everything; he seemed to have a mystical appreciation of life even before he could talk. Common things, like food and baths and music, enchanted him. I can still see him, sitting like an ecstatic Buddha in the kitchen sink, eating fruit or crackers or little pieces of cheese, singing a made-up song, as I made dinner and he took his bath. He was late to talk, but his first words were lyrical harbingers of the poet that Daniel would become. He called himself Dandyboy; water was "lakey-la"; girls were "gina-kids." He was a deep baby, and became an even deeper kid. I had the kinds of conversations with Daniel at four and five that I still can't have with many grown-ups. All through his childhood we discussed his friends and family from a psychological perspective, and talked about nature and God as if we were Walt Whitman and Emily Dickinson at tea.

For a long time, Daniel's favorite song was "Light My Fire." He heard it on the radio once as I drove his older brother to school, and he liked it so much that I had to dig through a box of old stuff stored in the barn to find my 1967 Doors album. It took me a while to understand what he loved about the song. He thought the line, "Come on baby, light my fire" referred to a little kid striking a match, something he wanted to do and I wouldn't allow. Yet Daniel was also the kind of child who was afraid of the dark, of big barking dogs and scary bedtime stories. At the ripe old age of five he began to have trouble going to sleep. Night after night I would lie next to him in his little bed, scrunched in a corner against the wall, massaging his back, waiting for his eyes to close. After a few months our nightly ritual was taking up more and more time and becoming a habit I wanted to break. I tried to get to the bottom of it.

"Sometimes," I suggested to him, as we lay in his bed, "if you say what is happening to you, then it will go away."

"Really?"

"Sometimes."

"Okay, I'll tell you," he said, as eager to be released from his evening torture as I was. "I'm afraid."

"Afraid of what?" I asked.

No answer.

"The dark?"

"No."

"School?" He had recently started kindergarten, and the whole process, from taking the bus to remembering to bring home his lunch box, overwhelmed him.

"No, not school," Daniel said.

"Spending the night at Grandma's?"

"No."

"Then what?"

He rolled away from me and whispered something into his pillow.

"What?" I asked, taking the pillow from his face.

"I'm afraid of the big thing," he squeaked in a tiny voice.

"What big thing?" I asked, looking around the room.

"You know, the really big thing."

"Monsters?"

"No," he said, disgusted, "I don't believe in monsters. I mean the *big* thing . . . *dying*. I'm afraid of dying."

I was stunned, and sorry I had suggested that naming his fear would make it go away.

"Well, honey, join the crowd. Lots of people are afraid of dying," I said to the little boy with feelings and thoughts too big for his years. Early-onset fear of death must be genetic. I had it, and I had apparently passed it on to Daniel. But it was that same death obsession that drove me to search for answers to life's big questions from an early age. And Daniel too. At age ten or so, the poetry began—poetry that could have come from St. John of the Cross, or T. S. Elliot, or William Blake. Every few days we'd have a new poem to discuss, a new aspect of the human dilemma to ponder. All through his childhood, and into his teen years, Daniel and I engaged in the perennial dialogues about wisdom and suffering, art and religion. I didn't care if he was a dreamer in school; I didn't mind that his grades were mediocre. I probably should have, but I didn't. We joked in the family that he was from another planet, but I knew that he was after the things of the soul, and as far as I could tell, he was right on track.

To trust who our child is, and not who we think he should be or what the world wants him to be—that perhaps is the single greatest gift a parent can give. Faith in our child's own destiny, in the destiny of her soul—that's the one ingredient that will make the biggest difference in our parenting.

But, of course, it never takes only one ingredient to bake a cake or build a bridge or raise a child. We must also hone other essential parenting skills as we try to steer our kids safely and sanely through their childhoods. Even as we notice and respect who this baby or toddler or little boy or girl is, we must also assume the difficult role of naysayer, rule maker, and cop. It is not enough just to value who they are; we must also get in their way when they don't want us to, and get out of their way when *we* don't want to. We must fumble around with that delicate balance between control and leniency, fear and trust, holding on and letting go, until the parenting adventure is over. The good news and the bad news is that it's never over.

The Great Movement
of the Couch

Normal is someone you don't know very well.
—ANONYMOUS

One of Rahm's childhood friends, Jonah, began directing and shooting films when he was still in elementary school. This was fortunate, because I have an aversion to using cameras. My picture albums are filled with photos taken by my mother, and the only video footage I have of my children was made by Jonah—fully scripted theatrical pieces involving large casts and well-rehearsed scenes. At a recent Thanksgiving gathering, my whole family watched a couple of these videos. One in particular helped me retrieve some lost memories from an important time in my parenting journey—the three years between my first and second marriages when I was a single mother. The film, entitled *Slam Ball,* is a hilarious how-to sports documentary about a complex and wildly imaginative game that the boys had invented. Slam ball had its heyday during a long and snowy winter, when my kids and their friends would congregate almost every afternoon in my living room.

When we watched the slam ball instructional video, my sisters were astonished by the mess I had allowed to overtake the house. "I never let my kids be so wild in my house," one of my sisters said. "Or rearrange the living room into a sports arena," said another. Looking around the same house now—at the carefully arranged furniture and objects of art—it is hard to believe that I ever let a gang of boys shanghai the living room, push the couch against the French doors, duct-tape the boundaries of the court on the wide-board pine floor, and use the center pattern of a Persian rug as the circle from which a large rubber ball would be slammed with great force by the server's fist.

The video features my sons and their friends playing a rousing game of slam ball, which is a cross between squash and professional wrestling. At one point, as the players hurl themselves at each other, the ball ricochets off the ceiling and smashes into the television set. But while it shocked my sisters, watching the film was a nostalgic experience for me. It brought me back to a few months christened the Winter of Slam Ball by Jonah and Rahm. During that entire winter I left the slam ball arena intact. I was too overwhelmed by single motherhood, work, and life in general even to remember that living rooms can also be used for lounging quietly on a couch or entertaining people who prefer talking to slamming into each other.

I look back on the Winter of Slam Ball with a certain sense of pride. Pride that this girl raised in a family of girls acquired a taste for the wildness of boys, and took pleasure in hosting their wacky experiments. I was genuinely happy to be sharing my life with a whole village of kids—feeding them, listening to them, hitching a ride on their exuberant energy. But I also see in my permissiveness a desperation to make a happy home for my sons. As a single mother I lived with a nagging sense of shame—shame that my family wasn't a "real" family, and that I wasn't providing for my kids the normal life they were supposed to have. And since I had destroyed the possibility of normalcy, I was going to knock myself out making sure they were happy. If they wanted to use the living room as a gym, then I'd let them. And so I allowed my house to double as a slam ball arena week after week as the winter dragged on.

The video does not include an important slam ball moment, dubbed by Rahm and Jonah the Great Movement of the Couch. Toward the end of the winter, when the melting snow and heavy mud of March were being brought into the living room on the kids' boots, I had an epiphany about slam ball, parenting, and families. It began in the late afternoon, as I stood in the kitchen watching my boys and their friends troop through the woods from the school bus, laughing and shoving each other, getting louder as they approached the house. I had the sudden urge to lock all the doors. The prospect of another afternoon of slam ball had lost any appeal. I hated slam ball. Things had gone too far. I wanted my living room back. It was as simple as that. If not, I wanted these boys to go away; all of them, even my own kids. My heart sank. I was mortified to feel like this, but there was no denying it: Something had to change.

As the kids descended on the house, kicking off their muddy boots in the living room, draping their coats and bags wherever they wanted, raiding the refrigerator, and bringing food and drinks into the slam ball arena, I secretly decided that this was the last time I would allow the game to be played in my living room. If I didn't put an end to slam ball, I would have to bar the players from the house, and that wouldn't do, since two of them belonged to me. As I watched them clear away stray items from the court and set up for another raucous game, I knew that it was time for me to step back into the role of the adult and set some guidelines for civilization.

The afternoon dragged on; the slam ball volleys were as wild as ever, but I was calm. I had made up my mind. The game came to its natural end as it was getting dark. Several kids left, others put on their coats and boots and waited for their parents to pick them up. Finally, only Rahm and Daniel and Jonah were left.

"Boys," I said, coming into the living room, "I want you to help me rearrange the room."

"But, Mom," Rahm said, "we're just going to have to put it back the same way tomorrow."

"No," I said, with a sad firmness in my voice. "I don't think so. I don't want you to use the living room for slam ball anymore."

The three kids looked at me as if I had announced the end of the world.

"I want to move the couch here," I said, pointing to the middle of the room.

"But, Elizabeth," Jonah protested, "that's the *middle* of the slam ball court!"

"I know, Jonah," I said, putting my arm around his shoulder. "I just cannot have slam ball in my living room anymore. It's time for you guys to invent a different game, in a different room, or go outside, or find another house where the parents are as crazy as I am."

"You're not crazy, Mom," said Daniel. "You're nice." Being the little brother, Daniel had never been allowed to participate fully in slam ball games and so had less to lose, but I took it as a compliment anyway.

"Thank you, sweetie," I said, choking up. "But I think I've been a little too nice. Let's move the couch, okay?"

So the two older boys got on one side of the couch, complaining and bargaining with me as they lifted and pushed, and I took the other side with Daniel, and we placed the heavy piece of furniture smack in the middle of the slam ball court. Later, when Jonah had gone home and the boys had gone to bed, I vacuumed the rug, unstacked the chairs, and arranged the room to look like the kind of place where people chat and read. I lit a fire in the fireplace, sat on the rug with a glass of wine, and tried to pretend that everything was normal, now that the couch was back in place and order had been restored.

But who was I fooling? My life was *not* normal; things were seriously out of order. I was divorced. My kids went back and forth between my house and their father's. This was not the way things were supposed to be. During the divorce I had hung on to Carl Jung's words that "nothing has a more disturbing influence psychologically on children than the unlived life of the parent." That sounded right to me: I hoped the divorce could bestow on the boys the gift of parents with full and happy lives. But now I was so racked with guilt that I was unable to really believe anything.

I sat there, letting these cold facts chill my heart as the fire warmed my face. In the stillness, with nothing to distract me, an all too familiar feeling of despair descended and hijacked my heart. But instead of getting up, washing the dishes, or calling a friend, I let myself sink into the thick soup of shame and sadness. Tears pooled in my eyes and fell down my cheeks. "How long do I have to feel like this?" I asked the flames. "How long does it take to get back to normal?"

As the fire crackled and I cried and sipped my wine, I remembered a funny thing someone had recently said to me, and I said it out loud: *"Normal is someone you don't know very well."* And then, staring at the flames, I laughed, and I threw my hands up and announced, "I give up. I am not normal. I'll never be normal again."

Was it the wine? The flames? The end of slam ball? I don't know. But in that moment I sensed it was time to let normal die. I saw clearly how some of my freewheeling mothering style came from a respect for the natural spunkiness of children. I liked that part of the way I mothered. I decided to hold on to that part. But some of my leniency came from my guilt over the divorce, and from my mistaken notion that normal homes are always happy homes. It was time to let that part go.

"May I toss my yearning for normal into the flames?" I asked the Phoenix in the fire. "Will you burn it to bits and show me a new way?" I thought of my boys asleep upstairs, of Jonah at his house up the road, of children everywhere in all kinds of families. And I said a prayer to the Phoenix, to the goddesses and gods of all parents, to whoever was listening: "Please help us raise our children with grace and wisdom and pleasure. Please remind us that our kids are just goofy little humans—junior bozos on the bus—who will not, under any circumstances, always be happy, no matter how hard we try. Please watch over all of us sleeping and waking in this imperfect world."

After my prayer I thought I heard the furniture heave a sigh of gratitude, sensing that the days of slam ball and backpacks and wet shoes were over. I patted the couch and assured it that, although it would never enjoy the prim isolation of couches in childless homes, I was ready to set some limits. Then I went upstairs to bed and fell into a hopeful sleep, certain that in the morning something good would arise from the ashes.

The next day the same group of kids got off the school bus and headed toward our house. When they reached the front door, I steeled myself for an uprising, but instead Jonah explained to them, in a dramatic voice, that the evening before he and Rahm had witnessed the Great Movement of the Couch, and the tragic and untimely end of slam ball. They then convinced me to allow them to move the couch one more time, so that slam ball could live on, preserved forever on videotape. Impressed by their inventiveness, I conceded, and for one more deranged afternoon, the sounds of slam ball resounded through the house.

I sat in the viewing stands (the couch), watching the last game with glee as Jonah and Rahm took turns filming. My heart filled with a poignant sense of love toward my sons and their friends, and toward myself. I had taken a stand, and the kids had responded with creativity. Sure, there were a few grumbles, but they all seemed to understand the logic of my decision and accepted my authority with surprising goodwill. After the final match, they retired to my office to type up a slam ball instructional manual. Then they put their coats back on and went into the woods to shoot a movie about an FBI raid.

The Great Movement of the Couch was significant to the kids in that it essentially ended slam ball, since no other parents were interested in hosting the game. But along with their disappointment, I sensed relief in my sons—relief that I had resumed the role of boss. Children do not want to be in charge of family life. They may act like they do, but they don't. Not when they're toddlers, and not when they're kids, and not when they're teenagers. Children need their parents to lead the way, to show them how to navigate the waters of real life. I also was relieved by something revealed to me through the Great Movement of the Couch: I saw how resilient children are—how much better able they are than adults to accept and work with what is. They are interested in making the most of each moment, while we are trying to string the moments together into a preconceived picture of life. They're alive in the moment; we're stuck in normal.

After the Great Movement of the Couch, my quest for normalcy mellowed. I'd be dishonest to say it disappeared overnight, but I took new vows and began to put them into action. I vowed to honor the flawed authenticity of real life. Instead of expending wasted energy longing for the way it was supposed to be, I vowed to make what *was* as harmonious and vibrant as I could. I vowed to honor the family we already had, and to include and respect every member—me and my kids, their father, and later their stepfather and stepbrother, and their stepmother and her family, and their new brother who would come along a few years later. The full catastrophe! I renew my vows every day, and thank slam ball for bouncing such a big lesson into center court.

Gift

There's a card I keep above my writing desk, tacked to the wall with other icons of inspiration, that I would never have imagined receiving when I first became a stepmother. It's a pink cut-out card of Glinda, the good witch from *The Wizard of Oz*. Inside the card, in my stepson's unmistakable Neanderthal handwriting, is this message:

> *In a world of wicked stepmothers, you are my Glinda.*
> Love, Michael

Michael gave me that card when he graduated from high school, ten years after our families joined in that most awkward amalgamation called the "blended family." In those ten years, Michael and I climbed a steep learning curve, in which he learned how to calm down and trust, and I learned how to loosen up and love. Sounds pretty tidy on the printed page, but it was anything but tidy raising three sons, one of whom arrived as a seven-year-old toting some awfully heavy chimidunchik.

From the outside, it all looked pretty perfect: He was the son of the man I loved, equally spaced in years between my boys, and a sweet-hearted child with gobs of energy and enthusiasm. At first, Michael lived during the school year in Los Angeles with his mother and stepfather, and spent school vacations with us. By the time he made the difficult choice to move to our home he was eleven, and had crisscrossed the continent more times each year than a traveling salesman. It seemed he was continually suspended between time zones and his mother's and father's worlds. In L.A., he was raised by a nanny and exposed to things I didn't think were good for kids—lots of television, junk food, and late-night parties. When he was with us, we went hiking and river rafting, and ate health food. The contrast was striking, and it created tension between Michael and me when I tried to control what I considered unacceptable behavior. I was used to the antics of boys, but as I perceived it, Michael was from another species altogether. He was so full of nervous energy that he literally bounced off the walls.

A combination of events motivated Michael to move from his mother's home in L.A. to ours in upstate New York. The constant travel was hard on him; he was unhappy at home and in his school; his father wanted nothing more than to protect and nurture him; and from the beginning, Michael and my sons had decided they were brothers. So it seemed right for him to move in. My husband was ecstatic, my sons were excited, and Michael was ready. Only I was wary. It wasn't that I didn't love *Michael*; it was *me* I was concerned about. I was afraid I would turn into a hypercritical witch—a wicked stepmother—if I had to incorporate Michael's rambunctious energy into our daily life. I had already seen and not liked who I became on the vacations he spent with us. I did not want to know anything more about those parts of me—the parts that cared more about being in control than about a little boy's need for love.

A couple of months after he was with us, we began to wonder if Michael's perpetual motion was caused by something more than just his natural exuberance. Sometimes he was barely able to sit still; he twitched and fidgeted and seemed physically uncomfortable. We took him for tests and discovered that he was suffering from Tourette's syndrome (TS), a neurological disorder that manifests in tics and hyperactivity. Although it was mild, and many people never knew about it, Michael's condition was hard on him. His symptoms made him self-conscious. He tried to mask his tics with constant activity.

I began to feel as if there were two strangers living in my home: one was Michael—a little, wild stranger; the other was myself—a big, controlling stranger. I became a stranger to myself. At work, I was the one known for her sensitivity and kindness: I listened to coworkers' problems; I championed our scholarship fund; I labored to make our staff more diverse. Now someone who needed my kindness was living with me, and our family had become more diverse. But I didn't want diversity in my own home, and I didn't feel like being compassionate. I wanted Michael to calm down, to sit still, to fit into the mold.

I may have been the fairy godmother at work, but at home I was becoming the wicked stepmother.

I'd always wondered about wicked stepmothers. Fairy tales are rife with them: Cinderella and Snow White each had one. Hansel and Gretel's stepmother was so awful that she convinced their father to abandon the children in the dark woods. Now I could see the stories from both sides—from the innocent side of the child in need of love *and* from the painful side of the adult who can't give it. My heart would ache whenever I'd come home from work proud to have helped two colleagues get along better and then lock into a battle of wills with Michael. What did it matter if I had to cook different food for him, or if he let his pet rat run around the living room, or if he did back flips when we were trying to watch television? If this was what he needed in order to deal with TS and adjust to a new school, new friends, and a new family, then why couldn't I help him? I didn't want to be like Hansel and Gretel's stepmother. I didn't want to lose Michael in the woods of my own selfishness. But day after day, I failed in my attempts to rewrite the myth of the wicked stepmother.

The year before Michael had come to live with us full-time, I had wanted a Fresh Air kid—a child from a disadvantaged inner-city home—to spend the summer with our family. Why not share the bounty of our life with a kid who needed the kind of love we had to give? I argued to my husband. He argued back that there was already enough chaos in the house and we'd better wait until we were more stable. After Michael moved in, my resistance to his behavior became a prickly issue not only between Michael and me but also between my husband and me. One night, after the kids had gone to sleep, my husband said something that finally broke me open: "Remember that Fresh Air kid you wanted?" he asked me. "Well, here he is! He's Michael."

That was the push I needed into a new Phoenix Process. In the light of the flames I began to see how my need to control extended far beyond my relationship with Michael. I made a practice of stopping myself every time I made a subtle (or not so subtle) attempt to change Michael's behavior. I'd ask myself a few things: Who made me the authority on what was acceptable behavior? How did I know what was best for Michael? And even if I did, would forcing change really work? Wouldn't patience and support work better than pressure and intolerance? As I became more honestly self-aware, I began to see the impatient, intolerant side of myself reflected everywhere. It showed up at home with my husband and family, and at work with my colleagues. I even saw it in the way I regarded people with different political views or social backgrounds. As long as others believed what I believed and acted in familiar ways, I was magnanimous; take me out of the safety zone for more than just an exotic vacation, and my largesse shrank.

It's easy to remain blind about ourselves when we stay within the safety zone—among people who are just like us, in a place that looks like home. We can trick ourselves into thinking that we are far more open-minded and big-hearted than we really are. It's when we must walk our talk in the complex landscape of a messy life that self-righteous ideals are whittled down into the honest truth. Seeing myself fail and learn as a stepmother, and fail again, and learn some more, and take small steps in the direction of loving-kindness has humbled me. I'm less of a know-it-all now; I've discovered there's much more room in the heart of an I-don't-know-it-all.

When Michael was a sophomore in high school, parents were invited to offer a series of classes that the kids could choose to take on Wednesday afternoons, during their half-hour independent study time. I volunteered to teach a six-week meditation course. I wondered if any high school students would be interested in silence and stillness, and assumed that certainly none of my boys would be caught dead in a "hippie" class taught by their mother. *Hippie* was Michael's term for all the health food and nature walks and psychobabble that he politely tolerated in our home. Meditation would most likely fall into the hippie category.

When I entered the classroom on the first Wednesday afternoon, I was surprised by how many kids had chosen my class. But more than that, I was surprised to see Michael in the group. I talked a little about my qualifications to teach meditation and about its varied benefits and uses. Then, before I led them in a short session of silent sitting, I asked the kids to write a few paragraphs about why they wanted to learn to meditate. I couldn't wait to get home and read the responses. Mostly I wanted to see what Michael had to say.

In response to the question "Why do you want to meditate?" some kids filled both sides of the paper with information about the stress in their lives, or their belief in UFOs, or their ailments—headaches, asthma, inability to concentrate. This was all very encouraging. We were going to have a serious and lively class. When I got to Michael's paper, there was only one line, scrawled at the top of the page by my question, "Why do you want to meditate?" Michael had answered, "To chill with Ram Dass."

This pithy response was pure Michael. It was a joke—which was his preferred way of communicating—but it was also not a joke. It was an olive branch of sorts, a white flag that Michael was holding up, as if to say, "See? I don't really think you're so weird. I like salads and hiking and even that kooky friend of yours, Ram Dass." Ram Dass (the famed meditation master and spiritual teacher) was a code name in our family for all the exotic, un-L.A. people and things Michael had met and done through me. Now here he was declaring that he wanted to learn how to meditate.

As the weeks went on, a handful of kids dropped out of the class. Just as I thought, sitting still was not a terribly popular activity among teenagers. But Michael hung in to the end. He was my most devoted student (as well as the class clown). Sometimes I'd open my eyes during a group meditation and look at him sitting on the floor, so quiet and calm, like a veritable Buddha in the forest, and my heart would fill with respect for this young man who had navigated difficulty and change with good humor and a flair for life. When the meditation was over, he'd jump up and end the session with a gymnastic flip, and I would laugh, and feel proud of myself, too. Michael may have learned from me how to calm down, but he had taught me how to lighten up. I had been his devoted student as well.

By the time he graduated from high school, he was a gifted basketball player and actor. He was admitted to a prestigious university and graduated with a degree in theater. And then he moved back to Los Angeles to pursue acting. He and I started up a lively e-mail relationship, sharing news about our lives, sending jokes and articles, and kidding around with each other in a language all our own. One day he sent me the most remarkable note. He had gone to see a documentary movie about Ram Dass—the same Ram Dass I wrote about in Part Two. It was being shown in cities across the country, and it had reached Los Angeles. The film chronicled Ram Dass's childhood, his university years, his faculty position at Harvard, his journey to the East, his books and teachings, and finally his stroke and present condition. For Michael, it was a revelation to see Ram Dass portrayed as a cultural figure, and not just as one of his stepmother's friends. He wrote about that in his e-mail to me and ended it with these words:

That movie was amazing. It had me in tears for most of it. Ram Dass is an incredible person. But I guess you already knew that. I was really interested in hearing him talk about his stroke. He handles it so differently than most people seem to. It is one of those medical problems—like my Tourette's syndrome—that Western medicine can't really fix. All that is left is how you deal with it psychologically. He likened his symptoms to Sirens—the Sirens in the *Odyssey*. (See? I really did read it.) I can identify with that, and I've never heard it put so articulately. Ram Dass says that when his symptoms start to drag him down, he feels like Odysseus, who strapped himself to the mast to keep from swimming to the Sirens. He says he sometimes has to work that hard not to give in to the pain and fear. But from the looks of it, I bet he sails right by the Sirens and gives them a high five.

I'm not quite there yet, but he's given me some insight. Dealing with TS is my Sirens experience. It made me a stronger person than I would have been without it. I remember when I was little and Dad took me to the neurologist. He gave me that medicine—it kind of took the symptoms away. Unfortunately, it took something else with it. I only took that stuff a few times, and when I stopped I specifically remember feeling lucky that I had TS, because it gave me a reference to the world that most people didn't have.

I don't really look at TS as a disease anymore, or let myself get stuck in the symptoms as much. Of course, sometimes it happens. Then I turn into a twitching mess. Getting tangled up in the symptoms makes them worse because I'm fighting them. I think, after seeing the film, I'll have a whole new way of looking at it. Now I really do want to chill with Ram Dass.

Recently, at the funeral of my father-in-law—Michael's grandfather—Michael and I huddled together under an umbrella as an early spring rain fell on the prairie grass and gravestones. The cemetery was full of family and friends, people who had known each other their whole lives. Michael and I felt like outsiders—the only folks there who hadn't grown up in that small West Texas town. We stood off to the side, a little out of place yet safe in the warmth of our own familiar love. It was then that I realized families are defined not by blood but by love, and Michael and I were family. After all the years of adjustment and learning and failure and success that Michael and I experienced, as I became his Glinda and he became my son, we are left with the hard-earned gift of love—the greatest gift of all.

All you need is love. The Beatles said it, and the Bible said it, and every wise saint who has ever spoken has said it. But Michael taught it to me. Sure, there are other great things in life: knowledge, and power, and spiritual understanding. "But these shall pass away," Paul writes in the New Testament. "Where there are prophecies, they will cease; where there are tongues, they will be stilled; where there is knowledge, it will pass away. . . . And these shall remain: faith, hope, and love. But the greatest of these is love."

The Vroom, Vroom Gene

Babies are their own gender. There are males, females, and babies. I don't think I fully grasped that my babies were boys—and not just amazing little creatures—until they became walking and talking toddlers. When I was potty-training my first son, he loved to pee with abandon all over the toilet seat. I was horrified. My husband thought it was funny. Once again, I realized how being raised in a world of girls had taught me little about boys. I would have to learn.

When I had my second son, and as both boys grew, I felt like an anthropologist in my own house. What strange customs the tribe members had! They spent hours rolling around on the floor together. Their love of sports and their penchant for armed conflict bewildered me. They were physically strong yet emotionally fragile—the tiniest hint of anger in my voice reduced them to tears. Their honest affection and the way they wanted to protect me touched my heart. And they were so funny, so noisy, so genuine. I was thoroughly confused yet utterly charmed by their boyness.

For me, entry into the world of boys was like diversity training for those who have never been around people of a different race. Growing up in a house full of women, with a father who was usually forty miles away at work, I related to boys the way an extraterrestrial might regard earthlings. I was curious about them, but their behavior was unfamiliar and unnerving. My first education in men came from the unlikely area of feminism, and since I was practically a blank slate, I took as gospel what the feminists of the 1960s had to say about men and women: that we were born basically the same; that only nurture created behavioral differences; and that we would live one day in a gender-free world.

Then I had my babies. Had I not been blessed with boys, I may never have made one of the most important discoveries of my life. When my babies grew into boys, I came across the "vroom, vroom gene." And the vroom, vroom gene turned the nurture versus nature debate upside down. I first discovered the vroom, vroom gene when my first son was about two years old. In his play-group, the boy toddlers would get on their hands and knees and push dump trucks and backhoes around, making a *vroom, vroom* sound, while the girls played with dolls or scribbled pictures. The more I hung around little boys, the more I witnessed the innate primacy of the vroom, vroom gene. The boys made the sound all the time. To a feminist like myself, this observation was discon-certing. But as a spiritual seeker I was interested more in the unsettling nature of the truth than in the safe confines of doctrine.

As my boys grew, I could not deny what I was observing every day: Give them a truck and they made the *vroom, vroom* sound; give them a stick and they turned it into a spear. Certainly there were shades of masculinity and femi-ninity, and some boys received larger doses of the vroom, vroom gene than oth-ers. But no matter what I did to raise my boys in a "gender-free zone," they made the *vroom, vroom* sound, and most of their little girl friends did not. My boys had an undeniable, subterranean knowledge of who they were, and who they weren't, regardless of my concepts.

I did buy my sons dolls, and my second son actually took to one—a boy doll, dressed in a clown suit, that he named Baby Joko. Baby Joko went every-where with Daniel for about a year. He often allowed the girls in his preschool to borrow Joko for sleepovers, and I sometimes wondered if his thing with Baby Joko wasn't just a precocious attempt to impress the girls. When he tired of Joko, Daniel began to collect little plastic beings: farm and zoo animals, elfin creatures called Smurfs, army men, and action figures. He could spend whole afternoons arranging families and amassing armies. I would hear him in his room acting out secret dramas and archetypal wars.

I once asked Daniel why the little green army men fought with each other, and he answered, " 'Cause that's what they're supposed to do."

"Well," I suggested, "maybe they could play instead."

"No," Daniel said, matter-of-factly, "that's what the Smurfs do."

Daniel knew at age four what some of us forget as we age—that there are undeniable forces at work within us and in the world. Watching my boys play without trying to influence their choices, I began to understand that they were working out inner conflicts, aggressive urges, and the competitive, creative, and communal instincts that all children need to express. Better to allow my boys to act out their unformed urge for power before it morphed into an evil version of its original impulse. Whenever I heard them making explosive noises of one sort or another, I would stop myself from telling them to "play nice." Instead, I made sure I balanced things out as best I could by reading to them, drawing with them, teaching them how to cook, and nurturing genes other than the vroom, vroom sort.

When my second husband and I joined our families—my two boys and his one (and a house full of their friends)—I was seriously outnumbered. The tables had been turned; I now knew how my father must have felt. My anatomy and hormones made me "the other" in the family. My sons' behavior and interests made them different from me—but how different? I wanted to know. I would find out only if I got my own preferences and prejudices out of the way and took interest and pleasure in the course they charted for them-selves. So I threw myself into their world.

Often, on the sidelines of a soccer game, or in the Little League bleachers, screaming my head off when our team scored, I would have an out-of-body ex-perience: Was this really me? The me who had spent idle childhood time read-ing Laura Ingalls Wilder books or dressing up with my sisters? Not even in high school would I have been caught dead at a football game. I was a hippie girl who forged sick passes to get out of gym class. Now I was spending a good part of every week watching one kind of ball or another being kicked, thrown, or hit.

At home any attempt I made at quieting things down or tidying things up was met with blank stares. Every question like "Why do you beat each other up all the time?" or "Why do you have to be so loud?" was answered with a wrestling move or a joke that would leave me a reluctant partner in their an-tics. There were only two things I could do in my minority role in the house: (1) learn to respect and enjoy their energy, and (2) teach the men in my life how to value the ways of their female compatriots. I wanted to show them that men and women are the same in some ways, and different in others; that di-versity is good; and that until both male and female value systems are given equal respect, our world will suffer.

What I have learned living among boys for many years is that all of us can come much further in each other's direction than we think. Rumi says:

Out beyond ideas
of wrong doing and right doing
There is a field.
I'll meet you there.

I met my boys in a field of action and energy, and they have met me in my gardens, my kitchen, my books, and my heart. They have never stopped surprising me with their willingness to learn about and appreciate what I love and value. It gives me great hope to see how comfortable they are around women, and how they respect and care for their girlfriends.

Given that things seem to even out in life, whether we try for symmetry or not, I am not surprised that the first part of my life was spent in the company of women, and the second primarily in relationships with men. Women still nurture and sustain me, but it is men who call me to grow, to examine my presumptions, to widen the boundaries of my heart. Husbands, lovers, spiritual teachers, colleagues, but more than these, sons, have been my greatest teachers in the art of living and loving and letting go.

Letting Them Go

When my oldest son was little, he was a man of few words, and a faithful, kind, and funny friend. When his brother came along, Rahm was just three and a half, but from the start he was protective and eager to love. He was also clear about the pecking order in a benign yet steadfast way. By the time he was seven, I was a single mother, and I came to rely on his sharp mind and his navigational skills. In fact, once when I drove without him, I missed the exit on the thruway and sheepishly reported to him my mistake after I finally got home. He seemed relieved when I remarried, and genuinely loved the new family members. He was the child who made sure our stepfamily held together harmoniously, even as he called the shots.

Rahm paved the way for his brothers at school, on the soccer field and baseball diamond, and later on the basketball team. He pioneered other teenage territory as well—a tame way of describing what went on in our house when three teenage boys and their friends dominated the landscape. My teenagers tested me vigorously. In their quests to "individuate" (as Jung called the process of liberating one's essential self from the self conditioned by family and culture), they went through several classic initiations into adolescent behavior—a fancy way of summing up the frightening and potent mixture of teenage boys, cars, girls, and God knows what else.

I often think that God has a plan in making it so difficult for parents to live with teenagers: When the time comes for our beloved children to leave home, we're more than ready. Even so, it took me an awfully long time to awaken from the trance in which my children never grew up and I remained the mommy forever and ever. It wasn't until Rahm's senior year of high school that it dawned on me that children *do* leave home, and that I was going to have to live without him in a very short time. I went into a prolonged period of preemptive grieving—mourning Rahm's leave-taking even before he left. Poor first children! Always a few steps ahead of their parents, they must suffer through being learned on, while their younger siblings bear the fruit of the first child's involuntary martyrdom.

Shortly before Rahm graduated, I realized that while my grieving might be important for me, Rahm needed something entirely different. He needed some wisdom, some warnings, some direction. I looked around for the tribal elders—the fathers and grandfathers smeared with frightening face paint; the crones and wise women with knowing smiles—to come and take Rahm into the adult world. Whoops! Wrong culture, wrong century. How could I—a mother whose instincts were to shield her children from all that is harsh and hard—prepare him for that world?

I felt as confused as I had been when I was the mother of an infant. I knew that I had to let Rahm go, but I also wanted him to retain a strong sense of his connection to his family. I wanted to avoid what I had believed could cripple children as they left home: either a sense of being untethered to any home base or a feeling of guilt about leaving parents and family behind. I wanted to be able to tell Rahm (in a way he could hear me) that I believed in him, that I took joy in his freedom and self-responsibility, that the road ahead was not always going to be easy, and that he could come to us with both his successes and his failures. I wanted to be able to thank him for our life together thus far without lapsing into the kind of sentimental blather that would turn him off. Beyond writing a letter, which I would never be sure if he read, I wondered how to do this.

And so I risked several talks with Rahm—conversations that we both had been avoiding because we didn't know how to have them. We talked about his feelings concerning the divorce of his parents, his anticipation of the future, the transition I was going through, and our love for each other. These were not easy conversations. I had to make them happen. But I undertook them as one would a religious ritual, because even in their difficulty I could feel a river moving in both of our hearts.

One of the traditions at my children's school was to offer the chance to each member of the senior class to speak at graduation. Since graduating classes were small, usually only twenty kids, most class members did indeed speak for a few minutes to the friends and family gathered at the ceremony. I had been to previous years' graduations and been moved by the power of the day. I looked forward to hearing from Rahm, although I could not imagine what he would say. A couple of weeks before the ceremony, I asked him what he was planning, and he replied, in standard teenage dialect, "I don't know. I'll do it later." This was certainly one of the places for me to practice letting go. I was famous for giving my kids excessive help with their school projects, but this time the work was Rahm's to do or not to do.

The day came. The seniors gathered on the stage; teachers and school administrators spoke; the school choir sang. Parents and grandparents sat in the audience, proud, happy, sad. The headmaster spoke, as did a few teachers and alumni, and then it was the seniors' turn. One by one they came to the podium and addressed their community. Some were funny, sarcastic, and brief; others were political, symbolic, and long-winded. When Rahm rose to speak, I felt my heart pounding: What would he reveal about himself? What would we learn about the essence of this person who was poised between childhood and the rest of his life? He stood at the podium, a tall young man who looked vaguely like the little boy he had been only yesterday. Well, here you go, Rahm, I thought. Tell us about yourself.

When I started thinking about what I was going to do when I got up here today, I had a lot of good ideas. I thought that I would get up here and say something inspirational that would be indicative of my high school career. So I started to write about something that I thought was pertinent. But the further I got into my speech, the more I realized that it wasn't what I wanted to say at all. So I started again. I wrote about something completely different. When I started I thought that it was good, but again it wasn't what I wanted. I tried again. And again I got nowhere.

Each idea that I wrote just didn't seem to be the perfect closing to my high school career. And then I realized why. It wasn't because none of my ideas were good enough. It was because every one was very good. It was because every emotion that I have for today is so strong that when I was writing about one I felt myself wanting to write about the others.

I have so many emotions, and they're all so jumbled. For every emotion that I'm feeling I am also feeling the exact opposite equally strong for something completely different. I am feeling happiness and sadness. I am feeling nervous and confident. I feel strength and weakness. I am on top of the world, yet at the same time I am overwhelmed by the moment.

Very soon I will be receiving my diploma—a moment that literally ends my secondary education and in some way signifies the end of my childhood, my dependence on my parents, and life as I know it. It's a frightening thought. In fact this could be the scariest moment of my life. And even though at this moment I am scared to death of what the future will hold, I have complete confidence in my ability. Even though I am very sad to be leaving a world that I know so well, I am also extremely happy to be entering a new one. And although I am sorry to be leaving this school with all that it has done for me, I am very glad to be going somewhere new.

I look out on this audience, and I see so many people who mean so much to me. I am sad to be leaving all of you, and I hope that you are sad to see me go. But at the same time I am proud of myself and my class-mates, and I hope that you are too. It is rare to be in a place that is filled with so much sadness and at the same time so much joy. Everyone's emo-tions are split, including mine. I look forward to my future, yet I will miss every one of you dearly.

I was stunned by Rahm's speech. Many people were. One of the parents who knew his laconic style well, said, "Who would have thought that Rahm would speak for the heart of the class?" I felt tremendous gratitude to the school for creating a modern coming-of-age ritual. They had allowed a young man—one who usually kept his feelings to himself—a rare opportunity to share his soul with his world. Forever I would know, in moments of wonder or worry, that Rahm has what it takes to make it through the wilderness of life. He was open to his feelings; he was realistic about the contradictions in life; he was self-confident but also self-aware.

A month after Rahm graduated, he left home to work at a summer camp in Vermont. I knew that even though he would return for two weeks before heading off to college, this was the end of his living at home; this was the end of an era. For the first time in my adult life, I was alone with my husband in the summertime. All of the boys were gone for the months of July and August—our younger ones attending their summer camps—and the days stretched in front of me, full of a bewildering freedom.

One day in early July, I sat inside, stumped by a work project, feeling bogged down by a vague burden in the chest. From the corner of my eye, I sensed movement, and I turned to the window, looking up from my writing to the tops of the tall trees. A high wind was making each leaf flutter like a flag of youth. The light changed dramatically as the wind moved the clouds and branches across the afternoon sun. Bees swarmed in the front yard, adding their darting yellow bodies to the swirl of moving colors—wisps of wildflower pollen, blue sky, white clouds, the shockingly green leaves of the summer trees.

How could I be depressed on such a day, I asked myself. Things around the house that had looked beautiful yesterday seemed like projects I was too lazy to tackle today. Outside, the summer day was whirling around in the sky, free of my heavy spirit. I tried to work, but I kept looking outside, as if my heart might be won over by the same wind that was moving the leaves and the clouds. No such luck: I sat there, at war with myself, part of me longing to join the world of flight and the other part dragging me down into the underworld.

Finally I gave up. I surrendered to the underworld and let myself sink fully into its downward gravity. Once again I understood what one would think any simpleton could grasp: It is better to go in the direction the river flows than to swim like a drowning person against the current. It is wise to move with the motion of the heavy heart—to ask it to show us the cause of our grief, and to trust its messages and its deliverance.

"What's wrong?" I asked my heart. Am I worried about work? No answer. That disagreement my husband and I had last night? Nothing. Unsettled by the lack of routine in these childless summer months? "I just hate not having a routine," I heard myself say. "I hate not knowing what the next weeks will bring." My heart stirred a little. Go this way, it suggested. Maybe if I sat with the calendar and got a firmer grasp of my summer plans, I'd feel better.

Studying the little blocks of July and August, I realized I hadn't been able to plan anything without knowing when I could visit Rahm at his summer job. He had called the week before and asked if I would come up on his day off and take him and a friend out to dinner. But he didn't know yet when his day off would be and had told me to call him in a few days to find out.

As I thought about calling Rahm, my heart lifted, and I felt the life in my body moving. My eyes went back to the window, back to the treetops. Okay, I'll call him now, I decided, buoyed by the quickening. It was lunchtime at the camp, and as I waited for him to come to the phone I heard the din of boys' voices in the background. I closed my eyes and imagined their faces and bodies, the mess and the energy, the life force of 150 boys. And suddenly the wind filled my sails, the river flowed, and finally I knew my way: My depression was about missing my son and dealing with the changes of his growing up and leaving home. "Yes," I said to myself as I heard Rahm's voice on the phone. "Yes, this is it."

We shared a quick conversation and made a date to meet. Rahm had to get back to his kids, an idea that made me marvel at his newfound maturity. He ended by saying, "I love you, Mom. Can't wait to see you." I put down the phone and let the tears come. I missed him so much now, away for the summer. When he went off to college in the fall, I would miss him even more—his sense of humor, his intellect, his habits and ways of being that I had known intimately over eighteen years of shared living. He would leave a big hole in the family structure, and change the nature of our life at home. His brothers would miss him, too, and things would never be the same. I let all of this enter my heart.

To my great surprise, I was overcome with powerful sobs that I could almost see, building in size and strength, far off the shore of my rational mind. As if sitting on the beach, watching an enormous wave roll in, I let the crying come. Both fearful and curious, I let it come.

Accompanying the wave of tears were images of the years Rahm and I had spent together as mother and son. And as in those moments before death, when people see their lives played out before them, I relived vignettes of our history that needed to be felt and remembered. I saw the early years, when Rahm was a willful and needy baby and I was a willful and untrained young mother. I remembered the struggle we went through as I learned to sacrifice my own youth to the demands of motherhood, and he learned how to live in this world. I cried for my mistakes and asked his forgiveness for being a less than perfect mother. I watched us grow up together through his childhood— through my maturing into a more confident woman and mother and his unfolding into the fullness of his personality and gifts. I thanked him for the joy he brought me and forgave him for the trials he put me through, especially in his uncommunicative teen years. I let my heart know how wounded he had been when his father and I divorced, something I had never wanted to feel fully. I sat with both of our sorrows and grieved for the years of insecurity he had known because of a decision his parents had made.

And then I saw him emerging into his manhood and walking alone into his destiny. I felt the pride of a long job completed, and the sadness of losing the daily company of my beloved firstborn son. As my tears washed up onto the shore and then drew back, I sat alone, cleansed and opened to the truth. I knew that I was not really losing him, rather, I was stepping out of the way so that he could now find his own path. I felt his gratitude and love, and I knew he was taking a piece of my heart with him, for his good and for mine. Sitting there, alone on the shore, I watched him move away in his own sturdy boat, and I silently prayed that I had done the best I could to prepare him for his adulthood. I also knew that part of the pain I was feeling was the death of one way of being his mother and the birth contractions of another. I prayed for the strength to let the old way die and for the patience to let the new way emerge. "How should I be in this new way?" I asked. "What is too much mothering now, and what is too little?" A poem came to mind, by the fifteenth-century Japanese Zen master Bunan:

> *Die while you're alive*
> *and be absolutely dead.*
> *Then do whatever you want:*
> *it's all good.*

My self as the mother of young children was dying. That self would be asked to die again and again as Rahm continued to mature, and as my younger sons left home. I would strive to become *absolutely dead:* absolutely surrendered to the process of stepping aside and letting my children become adults. And then my prayers would be answered—I would know how to be this new kind of mother, and it all would begin to feel natural, genuine: *good.*

I am writing this after all my sons have left home and gone out into the world. I must be honest: I was a very slow learner and a reluctant letter-goer. But I got a lot of practice, and after many transitions I am, at last, a new kind of mother. Indeed, *it's all good.* Years ago my sister gave me a refrigerator magnet that reads, "Insanity is hereditary. You get it from your kids." Yes, and if we can let them go with grace and Godspeed, we also inherit the ability to love and to keep on loving as the object of our love grows, changes, and sets sail.

Iron John

When my children were little, and each day seemed to drag on interminably, more experienced parents would say things like "Enjoy it now, before they're teenagers," or "Don't miss a moment of it. It all goes by so fast." I hardly knew how to respond to such advice. At the end of a long day, when the kids were all finally fed, bathed, and asleep, I would count up the years left of juggling being a mother and wife, a career woman, and a sane human being, and wonder if I could make it through even one more week of such relentless exertion, much less an entire decade! Now I hear myself saying the same thing to young mothers. "It all goes by so fast," I warn them. "Try to enjoy every crazy moment when your children are little. You will miss your little ones when they become teenagers, and then you will even miss your teenagers when they leave home."

Around the time my sons were beginning to turn from little bunnies into the creatures called teens, I decided to do some research into the process of separation and individuation between teens and their parents. I wanted to see if there was some way for a parent to help a young person individuate. Or at least not get in the way too much. Or maybe it was the parents who needed the help. I certainly did. Suddenly I found myself holding on to my sons, full of fear about their readiness for the world and not wanting them to grow up at all.

But every now and then, as I felt myself resisting my sons' attempts at individuation, I would hear Daniel's three-year-old words ringing in my ears: "Why doesn't the mommy let the bunny do what he wants to do?" I wanted to see if there were any models out there for making the transition from bunny-parent into the parent of young adults. Being the mother of boys, I was especially interested in the ways in which mothers and sons might better navigate the waters of separation.

Part of my work at Omega has been to search out the culture's most original thinkers. When we organize a conference around any theme—be it new trends in medicine, the common ground between organized religions, or being a parent in the twenty-first century—I immerse myself in the subject until I have found some leading voices in the field. In this way, I have come across some true geniuses over the years.

One of these people is the marvelous poet and astute social critic Robert Bly. When I began to research the ways mothers and sons interact during the teenage years, Bly's name kept surfacing. He is best known for his controversial book about men, *Iron John.* This book is reviled by some, mocked by others, and deeply appreciated by thousands of men and women who find in its pages a road map for understanding the mind of the modern man. *Iron John* is Bly's retelling of a Grimm Brothers' fairy tale, and a series of essays that explore the ways men have repressed their zest for living (and the price society pays for that repression) under layers of shame, anger, and unfelt grief.

I had been hearing about Bly's "wild man" retreats for several years before the publication of *Iron John* and sensed that he was tapping into a vein of longing in contemporary men—a longing to feel more, to express more, to grieve and enjoy more, but to do so in a way that felt natural to their masculinity. The women's movement had provided support and inspiration for young women as they set out on their journeys away from home. What would provide that kind of direction for young men? Perhaps Robert Bly had some answers.

The press had portrayed the men who attended Bly's gatherings as a laughable bunch of maudlin guys going into the woods to drum and cry around campfires. But I knew Bly. He had taught poetry and writing workshops at Omega for years. I knew he was way too cynical himself to participate in anything that smacked of sentimentality. I invited him to lead a men's retreat at Omega.

During that retreat, and others he did in the following years, I had some excellent talks with Bly about raising sons. He showed me portions of *Iron John* before it was published, and we argued about some points and agreed on others. When the book was published, I bought copy after copy to give to young men and women, to mothers and fathers, and to friends and family. I believed in what Bly was saying—that to experience real masculinity, men must be vigorous and strong as well as tender and loving. This kind of male was not to be modeled after either the macho John Wayne figure or the sensitive-New-Age-guy. Somewhere between the two, another man was waiting. Bly set forth a plan for men to find him. It included retrieving and feeling repressed grief, learning from positive male mentors, and reviving the capacity to act with potency and heart. All of these steps would lead, he said, to a stronger, healthier male identity at work and in the world, and to more engaged and responsible fathering, better relationships with women, and wise ways of dealing with crises such as addiction and divorce.

But the most consistent message in *Iron John,* as told in the language of the fairy tale, was that a boy had to "steal the key from under his mother's pillow" before he could become a man. This was the part of the book that enraged some women. For a while it enraged me. I thought Bly was merely parroting Freud, whose theories on male neurosis all led back to the mother, and to her inability to release the son. I was sick of men pinning their penchant for anger and violence on overbearing mothers. To me, the Oedipus myth was old news. But the more I talked with Bly, and read his book, and discussed with my husband what went on in Bly's wild man retreats, the less defensive I became.

I took some of Bly's observations into the laboratory of my own home and became aware of my motherly compulsion to keep my sons tucked safely under the warmth of my wing. My reluctance to push them out of the nest and into the wild world wasn't a fault; it had served its purpose well for many years. But I began to understand that a child of twelve or fourteen or sixteen needs to leave the nest. Older boys and girls alike strain under the heavy wing of a mother. Their very self is trapped under that wing. To borrow the words of the Iron John story, one of the most crucial keys to a child's individuality is to be found "under the mother's pillow."

Often in indigenous societies, a boy is taken from his mother's house by his male elders for a few days and nights of initiation into adulthood. When the boy returns to the village, it is understood that the relationship between mother and son is changed. But since there are no such rituals in our culture, it is difficult for a modern mother to know exactly when to stop being one. Bly talks about this in *Iron John;* he also addresses the confused status of fathers in our society. He notes that boys and girls are held back in their individuation process as much from a lack of mature male direction as from overprotective mothers. Mothers are often placed in a lose-lose situation when their children reach the teen years. Single-parent families, fathers who skip out on the difficult role of parenting a teenager, and the busy pace of contemporary life all conspire against a mother knowing how and when to let a child go.

If all of this sounds academic, it's because my understanding of *Iron John* didn't drop down into the deep guts of my life until I began the arduous process of lifting my wing and letting my boys fly freely into their own lives. I tried to be a model Iron John citizen, but I found myself up against some pretty powerful urges within myself, and some dangerous territory out in the world. How does a mother let a child go when all of her instincts rise up in resistance? How much is too much protection in a world that includes drugs and AIDS and automobiles? When a father's work takes him away from the daily life of a son or daughter, and a mother is left to grapple with these questions on her own, where does she find the courage to let the bunny run away?

I don't really think there is any way around it: A significant change in the relationship between a parent and child usually requires some sort of painful Phoenix Process. Fortunately, if we can relax just a little, our children will lead us to the flames. They know the way. And that way usually involves a period of distancing themselves from us through experimentation with behaviors that are meant to frighten parents. There is no polite or gentle way for a child to "steal the key." When my own sons began to individuate and I began to panic, I dipped back into *Iron John*, where Robert Bly had this to say:

> The key has to be stolen. I recall talking to an audience of men and women once about this problem of stealing the key. A young man . . . said, "Robert, I'm disturbed by the idea of stealing the key. Stealing isn't right. Couldn't a group of us just go to the mother and say, 'Mom, could I have the key back?' " . . . No mother worth her salt would give the key anyway. If a son can't steal it, he doesn't deserve it.
>
> Mothers are intuitively aware of what would happen if he got the key: They would lose their boys. The possessiveness that mothers typically exercise on sons—not to mention the possessiveness that fathers typically exercise on daughters—can never be underestimated.

Different kids and parents traverse the teen years in different ways. I can speak only from my experiences. Each of my sons matured in ways that matched his personality, yet all of them put me through my paces. In order for them to step boldly into their own lives and to discover their purpose and their power, they had to steal the key. I couldn't do it for them. In fact, they needed my resistance in order to push through their own fears of independence and responsibility.

I have the luxury of writing this on the far side of the Iron John process. My sons are all in their twenties now. In the old primers on raising sons, the experts said that when boys got older they stopped talking to their mothers, they lost interest in the family, and they ventured far and wide and rarely called home. While my sons did travel the globe, they not only called but also invited me to join them. And yet these invitations came only after difficult periods of disconnection—when they pulled away from me so that they could get closer to themselves and to the new women in their lives.

I am as close now to my sons as many of my friends are to their daughters. Other friends with sons report the same thing. I tell you this so that parents of teenagers can keep hope alive through the demanding years when the bunnies leave the nest and enter the dangerous world. If you find yourself holding tight to your children long past appropriateness or helpfulness, perhaps it would help if you took down an old copy of *The Runaway Bunny*. Sit on the couch next to your stunned son or daughter, and read the book aloud. Only this time, change the words. Read it like this: *Once there was a little bunny who wanted to run away. So he said to his mother, "I am running away." "If you run away," said his mother, "I will let you go. For you are grown now. I trust you to find your way in the world. Run away, bunny!"*

Widening the Circle

The problem with the world
is that we draw the circle of our family too small.
—Mother Teresa

It is the end of a hot and humid August day, and I am in my vegetable garden with Eli, squatting over the fuzzy leaves of a vine, searching for the perfect-sized cucumbers to make what my mother calls "refrigerator pickles." These were my favorite garden treat when I was growing up, as they were for my sons and now are for the current youngest member of the family, Eli. Eli is my ex-husband's nine-year-old son from his second marriage, my sons' half brother, and a frequent visitor to our house, especially during August, when we make pickles together.

It has been a great summer for cucumbers, and the vines twist and climb all over the garden. Eli and I are amassing a huge harvest and enjoying the soft air and the buzzing sounds of late summer when he says, "What is your title to me?"

"What?" I ask, not understanding what he means.

"Are you my mother-in-law?"

"Oh." I laugh, suddenly grasping what he's getting at. "You know, I don't think there is a title for what we are to each other. There should be."

"You're not my stepmother," he says. "I know that. I think I'll call you my double-stepmother. Double-step for short."

I look at his beautiful face, which has always reminded of my first son's face, and I am struck by the ways in which love will grow like an unruly cucumber vine if you give it enough time and space. Years ago, when Eli was about to be born, my heart shriveled in anticipation of a baby who would be my boys' brother but not my own child. I felt about as spacious as a clam.

But my sons fell hard for Eli the moment he was born. They liked to babysit for him at our house, which after about a half hour meant me taking care of him. I figured they were responding to some sort of instinct from an ancient and tribal time, when a family's structure was less narrowly defined. So, instead of banishing Eli from my heart, I followed the lead of my kids, and I fell in love with him. Fortunately, my bighearted husband, who has never met a child he didn't like, was equally enamored of Eli.

Soon Eli was part of our family. I kept his favorite juice in the refrigerator and the sweets he wasn't allowed to have at his own house in the cupboard. Before he learned my name, he called me Cookie Lady. He seemed unconcerned with bloodline, and equally comfortable with all of us—his brothers, my husband, my stepson, and me. Even after the boys left for college, he visited us. I think it was mostly for the cookies and the pickles.

When Eli said, "What is your title to me?" he was really asking, "Where do I stand in the circle of your family?" Mother Teresa said: *The problem with the world is that we draw the circle of our family too small.* It is not that hard to understand what she meant. The nightly news is filled with stories of small circles. Some people are called to widen these circles through important work in the world. But you don't have to be a delegate to the United Nations or a volunteer in a soup kitchen to do the noble work of drawing bigger and bigger circles. Our friendships and families, our marriages and work relationships—all of them are circles begging for more spacious boundaries.

We need wider circles, and titles that relate us to each other, rather than those that divide us into smaller and smaller groups—family groups, political groups, religious groups, racial groups, tribal groups. I think this may be the only way to save the world from the meagerness of our own hearts. It took a child to show me this. I had to start somewhere. So I started with Eli. I figured that if I couldn't let a child into the circle of my family, I had no right to have an opinion about *the problem with the world.*

We all have closed loops in our lives and people whom we have exiled to the outside of the circle. A good question to ask is, Do I really need to keep that person on the outskirts anymore? What would it take to give him or her a new title? Haven't I stayed angry or shut down long enough? Vengeance or protection or coldheartedness may have served a purpose in the past, but could forgiveness be a better balm now? If so, take a few small steps toward expansion. Push gently on the edges of your circle, and see if there is room within it for the exiled ones. And like the proverbial pebble thrown in the pool, as your circle widens it will ripple out and set a widening pattern in motion for the world.

Despair and Dulcimers

Today, like every other day, we wake up empty
and frightened. Don't open the door to the study
and begin reading. Take down the dulcimer.
Let the beauty we love be what we do.
There are hundreds of ways to kiss the ground.
—RUMI

L ast night, at the end of a long week of late nights, I went to bed at 2:00 A.M., then tossed about like a small boat on a choppy sea. My sons and their girlfriends were visiting from their far-flung homes, and though my heart was full of love, my mind was awash with worry. Outside, the warm September weather changed as the night wore on. Rain blew in on a cold wind, and in the darkness, the first yellow leaves fell before their time. Middle-of-the-night despair pooled in my little boat, like water from a slow leak. I couldn't stop the forlorn flow: I marveled helplessly at how my children were growing older and taking their tenuous places on life's stage. They seemed so young and unprepared, and the world so fast and impersonal. I held each son in my mind's eye and allowed worst-case scenarios to run amok.

Despair is a nondiscriminating fellow. When he throws a late-night party, he invites in every hopeless situation that troubles the mind. When I was done despairing about my kids, I thought about how my body was changing—and not for the better. Then I moved on, and worried about the repetitive lunacy of war as our country entered into yet another one. And, adding one more drop of angst to the overflowing pool, I wondered how long my mother would live and if she was afraid, right now, in bed by herself, as she approached the end of her life. I loved her so much—what would it be like to live in this world without her? Nothing is stable, I thought, floating in my bed, listening to the rain. I brooded over my work, my teaching, and my writing. Do I know anything at all worth sharing? Anything with the power to fill the hole in my boat, and to keep it from sinking? Finally, despair grew bored and left the party. I drifted into a foggy sleep.

Today, like every other day, we wake up empty and frightened, Rumi says. This morning, I wake up empty and frightened. I get out of bed. Two of my kids have already left for early flights, one going back to school, the other to his job. I say good morning to my stepson, who is in his childhood room, smashing into his backpack the clothes I have washed and neatly folded. I stumble downstairs to the kind of mess I am no longer accustomed to. Knowing full well that coffee won't even make a dent in my fatigue, I brew a strong cup anyway, clear a space on the kitchen table, and sit, drinking the black potion, sorting through the images and feelings of my addled sleep.

I make a brief survey of my middle-of-the-night despair and give myself a stern talking-to: I can no longer make my children's boo-boos go away with a kiss, and my trying to do so just agitates me and annoys them. My long-distance dread is a burden that serves no one. Let them live their own lives. I make a mental check by the topic "Kids." Next? My body is in pretty darn good shape, but it is indeed a human body and therefore will continue to sag, droop, malfunction, and one day die. Stop fighting gravity. Check.

I continue my mental checklist: It seems that war might be around for a good while longer, at least until a critical mass of people decide there is another way to broker power and share resources. And who knows what the final outcome of this human saga will be? Einstein wrote that he wanted to know God's thoughts—that the rest was "just details." When it comes to the subject of war and peace, I'd like to know exactly what God is thinking. I'll keep praying for that perspective. Check. My mother—well, all I can do is love her and stand by her as she deals with the last and hardest task of being alive. Check. My work, my teaching, my writing: I am doing the best I can with each of them. Check, check, check. I pour the unfinished coffee down the drain and wash a few of the dishes piled in the sink. I look out the window. I wonder what to do next.

Rumi would tell me to go outside today—outside in the aftermath of the rain and wind. He would tell me to take a long and aimless walk into the woods amidst the rot and ruin of the downed yellow leaves. *Don't open the door to the study and begin reading,* he says. *Take down the dulcimer.* This is Rumi's prescription for dropping the complicated burdens we haul around, and the despair we so often feel.

Being as close as I can to the dirt is the way I take down the dulcimer. My way of plucking out a tune on a simple stringed instrument is to dig in the garden, or sit on the forest floor and scratch the matted leaves with a stick, uncovering the miraculous process of dying life turning into living earth. When the mood strikes, I pee outdoors, like an animal does, and watch the rivulets of my body's water run down the hillside until it sinks into the soil. My feet planted firmly on the ground, my eyes moving from earth to sky, my heart comes home to the blessed way things are. I am both animal and angel. Animals need the solid ground beneath them; angels long for flight; humans are caught in the middle. Just remembering that sets me free. I am a grounded angel! No wonder I get so confused.

The way *you* take down the dulcimer may be different—driving fast with the radio blaring, helping a friend, feeling skin on skin, whacking a tennis ball, stirring a soup pot. There are hundreds of ways for each of us to counter despair with an act that connects us to our most essential, simple self. Sometimes while doing laundry I take down the dulcimer. When the kids were young, pairing little sets of socks brought solace. When they got older, and struck the bathrooms with hurricane force, I rallied by washing and drying and folding towels. Sitting on the living room floor, smelling the cheerful clean cotton, I folded beauty back into our lives. *Let the beauty we love be what we do. There are hundreds of ways to kiss the ground,* Rumi says. There are hundreds of ways to put down our burdens, hundreds of ways to give and receive blessings, hundreds of ways to wake up grateful after a sleepless night.

The last kid drives away, my husband goes to work, and I am left alone in the house. I should write, I should call my office, I should finish the dishes, I should grip the reins again. But I think I will take Rumi's advice and go out into the bright autumn day, kneel down in the leaves, and kiss the ground. As I breathe in the dark smell of earth, I will worship animals and angels. I will stop trying to solve anything. I will revere the mystery. Then I will raise my face to the brilliant blue sky and receive the sun on my skin. I will wash myself with gratitude. I'll promise to trust the wisdom of the unseen hand in my children's lives. I'll grant them their God-given right (as if I have any say in the matter) to fall down and get up again. I'll notice, for the umpteenth time, that I am a small creature, looking at the smallest segment of a huge painting. Here, from our little corner of the canvas, how can we fathom the purpose in the design, the overarching message, or the end of the story? And so today I will just stretch out in the leaves and drift into space. I'll let myself be a child, safe in the arms of the Great Mother and the Great Father.

PART V

Birth and Death

I HAVE BEEN A STUDENT of death and dying since childhood, when I appointed myself undertaker of the birds, turtles, and chipmunks who died in my neighborhood. I was one of those morbid little kids who got off my bike to inspect roadkill as my friends pedaled past, holding their noses and screaming. My fascination with dead things did not come from any great courage; rather it was a response to fear. I was afraid of death. I lay in bed at night and wondered, Who will I be when I am no longer me? Where will I go? Does it all just end? I would work myself into a panic—my heart pounding in my chest, the word *forever* rolling around on my tongue like one of those sourball candies, hard and bitter, yet strangely sweet.

As I grew up, the fear of death was my closest companion. It led me around and made choices for me: It introduced me to insightful people; it encouraged me to find a spiritual teacher; it made me become a midwife, and had me sit with the ill and dying. Over the years my companion has mellowed, but it is with me still, as constant as my breath. Our friendship has given me an intense appreciation of life; I never forget the closeness of death.

"The secret cause of all suffering," Joseph Campbell said, "is mortality itself, which is the prime condition of life. It cannot be denied if life is to be affirmed. . . . The conquest of the fear of death is the recovery of life's joy." I cannot pretend to have fully conquered my fear of death. But I have recovered much of life's joy through an engagement with death. And by death I mean not only the final death of the body at the end of earthbound life but also the Phoenix Processes we undergo, and the smaller deaths we experience every day.

Carl Jung said that he never met a patient over forty whose unhappiness did not have its roots in the fear of death. I agree with Jung, but I would broaden his age range; I have never met anyone, of any age, whose unhappiness did not have its roots in the fear of endings, partings, and the dark unknown of death. Our uneasiness with mortality is always humming in the background of our consciousness. Some people are agitated most by the death of the body and the eternal mystery that follows. Some people do not fear the final death but are more afraid of arriving at the end of life not having fully lived it. Some are most unnerved by the "ego deaths" we encounter when we experience loss, when we must give up a sense of control, or when we don't get what we want. Whether we fear the big one at the end of life or the little ones in between, our awareness of death causes suffering in our daily existence.

I think it is a good idea to study death because, as Campbell says, it is "the prime condition of life." Life and death are two sides of one coin. Together—always together—life and death complement and complete each other. If we play dumb about death, life loses its vitality and meaning. We may never fully understand death while we are alive, but that does not mean that we should fear it, or deny it, or merely tolerate it with the weary attitude "life's a bitch, and then you die." Death has so much to teach us—it is our greatest teacher.

Turning a difficult transition into a Phoenix Process is good practice for dying. A Phoenix Process burns into us the same lessons that we learn from the study of death: All of what we crave in life—security, health, personal gain—is fleeting and out of our control; all of what we fear—conflict, aging, loss—will come to pass. It may not sound like a jolly curriculum, yet in a roundabout way it is, because the study of death holds the key to a life of wisdom and freedom and joy.

When we study death we see how everything is dying and being reborn as something else, over and over, every day, everywhere, in all kingdoms, species, elements, and forms. Nothing is wasted, everything has its purpose, all things are connected, and therefore eternal, in the vast cycle of birth and death. When we understand this, we can let go of our crippling compulsion to hang on tight to who we think we are and to what we think we need in order to survive. We can appreciate how new life is always born out of the dark fertility of death. We can enjoy what is given with gusto, grieve what is lost with passion, and dwell with humor and faith in the vast, infinite mystery.

Many people worry that by studying death, or by confronting fear and releasing grief, they will become dour and depressed. In fact, the opposite occurs. When the hard shell of our resistance to death cracks, we are surprised to find the very optimism that had previously eluded us. Through the study of death, our limited ability to see beyond this life expands. New vistas of understanding open up beyond the border of fear.

When I teach workshops on death and dying, I break the study of death down into three simple rules. The first is that death is not something that happens only once at the end of life; from the moment we are born we are dying every day in all sorts of physical, emotional, and spiritual ways. The next rule for all of us dying people is that grief is good—that it is a sign of how well we have loved. And the last thing to know about death is that the death of the body is the start of an adventure. We may not know where that adventure will lead, but we can approach it with the same kind of hopeful anticipation and nervous butterflies that we feel before the start of a trip to a foreign land. The stories in this part of the book are about these three aspects of death. Except the first story, which is about birth—a prerequisite and a sequel to death.

Trailing Clouds of Glory

*But trailing clouds of glory, do we come
From God, who is our home.*
—William Wordsworth

Longing for a sense of the sacred as I navigate my way through the realms of life and death, I have read hundreds of spiritual books, made pilgrimages to holy sites around the world, and sat in meditation until my legs fell asleep. Sometimes these techniques have helped, and sometimes they haven't. But in my quest for the divine I have discovered one foolproof way that allows me to peek for a moment beyond the veil of my own limited vision. That way is the role of midwife.

When I was younger, I was a birth midwife. More recently I have begun to sit with people as they die. It is during these experiences, as a midwife to arriving and departing souls, when I am most able to step out of the way and be bowled over by something a lot grander than my own opinions, fears, and misconceptions. Maybe every citizen should be required to watch at least one baby being born, and to sit with one person as he takes his last breath. In the same way that you can't drive a car without passing a road test, you wouldn't be able to become an adult without witnessing the miracles of birth and death.

Being at the birth of a baby has humbled me, awakened me, challenged me, and healed me. Tending to the needs of a dying person has done the same. Following the first and last breaths of a human soul has connected me to that which came before life on earth, and that which follows. Wordsworth wrote that babies come into the world *trailing clouds of glory,* and I concur. I have also witnessed the dying grab hold of the same cloud and ride it back to God, *who is our home.*

The first time I assisted at a birth, I had the feeling that I belonged exactly where I was, that there was nowhere else I would rather be. Everything about the process of delivery and birth seemed familiar to me, even though I was just twenty years old, and the closest I had come to a delivery room was a barn in Vermont, where I had watched a lamb being pulled feetfirst from its mother.

I knew little about my own birth—something about a Catholic hospital, where I was delivered by nuns who scolded my mother for making noise during labor and knocked her out with ether when it was time to push. My mother glued our birth certificates, each with a tiny footprint in the upper right corner, into the family picture albums. I used to stare at my page and wonder what it had been like, having my brand-new foot dipped in black ink and pressed onto a legal document. My thoughts stopped there. In the antiseptic 1950s, things like birth and death happened somewhere else, and were handled by the experts. No one talked about being born or dying. My mother would go off to the hospital and return home a few days later with a baby sister and a new birth certificate. A neighbor, or my grandmother, would leave in an ambulance and never come home.

Any discussion about the two bookends that surround our lives—had been excised from everyday living and relegated to the upper reaches of religion and science. The messiness and ecstasy of birth had been cleaned up; the nobility and power of death, anesthetized. This was not always so. The ancients knew that the rites of birth and death are valuable opportunities to part the veil that separates human life from eternal life. The midwife who sat with the babies being born and the old people dying was held in the same high esteem as the village shaman or priest.

When I first watched a baby making its way out of the birth canal, trailing not only clouds of glory but also blood and mucus and amniotic fluid, I felt no queasiness but only a sense of wonder. Perhaps my childhood attraction to the insides of plants and creatures had prepared me. From an early age I liked to dissect dead bugs and birds, to pull apart beehives and anthills, and to dig into my father's compost pile to watch the worms transforming mucky, old vegetables into fresh soil. I liked the smell of new life emerging from decay; I still associate that smell with the miracle of transformation.

Childbirth seemed a similar miracle of nature. It had the sounds and smells of a barn. It was earthy, yet elevated; common, yet mysterious. Only one thing frightened me at the first birth I attended. In the last stage of labor, a baby's soft head conforms to the bony length of the birth canal. Especially if the pushing stage of labor is long and hard, a baby can be born with a misshapen head. Even in an easy birth, when the head is only slightly molded, the first peek at the baby is unsettling. With its hair slicked and darkened by blood and mucus, and its crown ridged and puffy, a newborn can appear deformed. I was sure that there was something horribly wrong with the first baby I saw born. But within minutes an astonishing change occurred. As the midwife washed the baby's tiny face, the swelling subsided. When she laid the baby on the mother's belly, his skin was pink and his head was perfectly round. And the mother, who just minutes before had been screaming in pain, was radiant and peaceful. The baby's descent had ended in life; the mother's pain was transformed into love.

During my career as a midwife, I always warned the first-time fathers what to expect when their babies' heads crowned. Still, several fathers fainted at that very instant, and I understood why. Birth is shocking—it is graphic and gory, painful and intimate. For these reasons many people shy away from the delivery room. And yet, once again, it is through the very terror of the birth process that the miracle is revealed.

It is not easy to stay conscious during a painful and frightening process. We would rather turn away, drug ourselves, or feign indifference. It requires a delicate blend of curiosity, fortitude, and patience to trust in the wisdom and purpose of pain. Understanding what's happening on the inside is key. At the beginning of the prenatal class series I used to teach, I told the expecting mothers and fathers that they would get a passing grade only if they fell in love with the uterus. This always got a laugh, but I was serious, because I had discovered that, while breathing and relaxation exercises were helpful during labor, understanding the anatomy and physiology of the birth process helped even more.

Normally, we don't pay much attention to the hidden ways of our bodies. Most of us know more about the carburetor of a car than about the function and location of our own gallbladder or kidneys or uterus. But a little knowledge of the body goes a long way. Moving beyond habitual squeamishness and fear, and into an attitude of openness, increases our desire to care for and work with the body. If you know how your digestive system works, you're less likely to fill it with junk food. And if you can picture the color and fragility of the lungs' inner lining, you'll find it easier to quit smoking.

If a woman knows how her uterus works, she will be less reactive to the tsunami strength of a labor contraction. The uterus is really a collection of muscles, closed at its base with a feisty little muscle called the cervix. Grip your hand tightly in a fist, and you will have a good idea of what the prelabor cervix looks like. Now take both hands and form a wide circle with your thumbs touching at the bottom and your index fingers touching at the top. This is the size, give or take a few inches, that the cervix must stretch to in order to let the baby's head pass through. That's a lot of stretching in a short amount of time, and to a laboring woman, it feels like being torn inside out.

In the same way that you would flinch and draw back if someone threw a punch at you—or screw your face into a tight knot anticipating a shot at the doctor's—a laboring woman instinctively tightens when the pain of a contraction begins. But a woman who has fallen in love with her uterus knows that a contraction is really the uterus's brilliant way of stretching the birth canal and loosening the cervix so that the baby can move down and out. If she fights back as her uterus does its work, she will only slow the progress of labor. If she greets the pain with all the love and respect she can muster, her cervix will stretch, her heart will break open, and her baby will be delivered.

Although I am no longer a practicing midwife, I use the metaphor of falling in love with my uterus all the time. If I can approach change with an understanding of the process and an openness to the pain, then my daily labors will be swift and fruitful. As the surgeon Bernie Siegel says, "Life is a labor pain; we are here to give birth to ourself."

The Hundredth Name

While I have witnessed many babies being born, I have been with only a few people as they died. One cannot exactly invite oneself to deaths, and I do not plan to become a professional death midwife. But I do expect that in the years to come I will sit with a few more people as they leave the human form and travel beyond. I want to know how to be with the dying for two important reasons. First, dying people seem to want others around them as they struggle to let go of life. From my own experiences and from stories told to me by nurses and doctors, I have come to believe that no one wants to die alone. My second reason is that each time I have witnessed a death, I have been enriched beyond measure—deepened in my capacity to confront my own death and inspired to live with more immediacy and passion.

Given that those who are ill and dying need the presence of others, and that those who are well and living can gain so much at the bedside of a dying person, why do we banish death to intensive care wards and nursing homes? Why do we turn away from something so precious, so significant, so needed? Perhaps we think that by hiding the process of illness and death we will somehow forget the fact that people do die, that *we* will die. Bruce Talbot, a writer friend of mine who has Parkinson's disease writes:

Get this, sick and healthy people alike: The plot is the same for all of us. We were born; we're living; we're going to die. Those of us with a chronic disease have a certain advantage over you healthy people. I don't mean to make light of this rotten illness or the circumstances of anyone else, but for those of us with a chronic illness, the plot can be simpler and in some important respects (dare I say it?) easier. As we lose, in other ways we gain.

We have the advantage of lives ratcheted up a few significant notches. We have the enlivening clarity that our days are quickly passing through the hourglass.

This is what being around death and dying has done for me—it has ratcheted up my life; it has convinced me of its beauty and its brevity. I was in my early thirties when I first sat with someone dying. I did not plan to do this. In fact, I had banked on something altogether different. I wanted to grow old with my friend Ellen.

We met at the commune, when our children were babies, and we became close friends right away. We shared a few sensibilities—like common sense and a sense of humor—that we agreed were in short supply at the commune. But almost from the beginning of our friendship Ellen was sick. She was often tired and came down with all sorts of minor illnesses. Then, when our sons were just three years old, she was diagnosed with leukemia. I helped her through her many attempts at healing, from carrot juice to chemotherapy, and was overjoyed when the cancer went into remission. During the next couple of years, as our kids grew older, and we both moved with our families from the commune and set up homes near each other, we stayed hopeful that Ellen had beat the odds.

Five years after her remission, she received the news that the leukemia was back in full force. Now all she had were questions that no one could answer: Should she go for another round of painful chemotherapy even though the prognosis was poor? Should she tell her son that she was going to die? When would she die? She was tired of fighting but terrified of leaving her son motherless. What should she do? Would I stand by her and help her die? I had no idea how to do this. I knew about the birth process, but I knew nothing about dying.

The last time I had been around anyone sick enough to die was when I was four years old and my grandmother had cancer. I remember my grandmother's death the way I remember old movies—in scenes and snippets of conversations and songs. She had been living in our house, in the bedroom down the hall from the room I shared with my older sister. She enjoyed being around her little granddaughters, singing old tunes to us and brushing our hair. But we were afraid of her. Her skin was yellow, and her hands shook.

I remember the time my mother went grocery shopping and left me home to take a nap. I took my pillow and slept on the landing at the top of the stair-case. That way, I'd be as far from my grandmother as I could without going downstairs, something my mother had told me not to do. My grandmother heard me in the hallway and called me into her room. She offered me gum from a yellow and red box of Chiclets, and I felt obliged to take a piece. When my mother returned home, she found me asleep on the stairs, with gum in my hair.

One day an ambulance took my grandmother away. I never saw her again. Now, decades later, I was being asked to help someone die. Fortunately, Ellen was a good teacher. She softened into her death. Months before taking her last breath, she was already taking her leave. You could see it in her face and in the way she was with her husband and son. This woman who had been such a fighter, whose wit had often masked her emotions, began to say surprising things: "If only people realized what they had in life," she told me one day, "they would not be able to contain their joy!"

One scene, during the winter of Ellen's demise, stays with me, all these years later. A few friends had gathered at her house for dinner. I looked around the room. There was her husband, sitting alone in the corner, worn out from work and worried about everything else. Two friends were haggling over who should go to the grocery store to get an ingredient they had forgotten. I was being short-tempered with my children and Ellen's son, who were running around as I tried to prepare dinner. Then I looked at Ellen, paper-thin and wrapped in a blanket in a rocking chair. She was watching the snow fall out-side the window. She turned to us and in a small voice said, "Would you all please love each other?"

In the middle of a December night, Ellen slipped into a coma. I arrived with my children the next morning, as we had planned weeks before, to take her Christmas shopping. I found her lying on her bed, breathing very lightly, a thin trail of blood coming from her mouth. Her doctors had warned us that at any time her body could reject the blood transfusions that were keeping her alive. That time was now.

Ellen's husband took their son and my boys to a friend's house while I called the hospital to get directions for a journey I had never before taken. I was fortunate to speak to a doctor who knew what Ellen had wanted and was brave enough to honor it. He guessed that she had suffered a brain hemorrhage and that nothing more could be done for her. He reminded me that Ellen wanted to die at home, and that if we brought her to the hospital they would put her on life support machines and prolong her life for a while, but that she would suffer and never regain full consciousness.

"What should I do? Should we come to the hospital? What would you do if it was your wife?" I asked, panicking.

"I can't tell you what to do," the doctor said.

"When is she going to die?"

"I don't really know. Soon. You'll know what to do."

"How?"

"Just watch her breathing. Just be with her."

All through that day, and into the night, I sat with Ellen, her husband, and an old friend who had also chosen this of all days to visit. It was apparent that we were meant to take this voyage together, with Ellen as our ethereal guide. Tears slipped through her closed eyes and ran down her pale face. Her breath was weak and halting. Was she in pain? Did she know we were there?

Morning became afternoon as we held Ellen's hand, breathed with her, and read to her. We told her that her son would be loved, that she could leave him. This seemed to deepen her breathing and stop her tears. At one point, I curled up on the bed next to her and found myself chanting a song I barely knew— one that Ellen had learned from a beloved teacher when she and her husband had traveled to the East. I felt the presence of that teacher. He had died the year before; perhaps he was coming for Ellen now. I felt others with us too—strange forces come to escort her across the divide.

As the evening blew in and the room got colder, the spaces between Ellen's breaths became longer. We sat around her, three lost sailors in a rudderless ship, with Ellen's breath filling our sails. We gave ourselves over to the sea of space that was taking her away. And then the pauses between Ellen's breaths got so long that there was only space—huge, abiding space. We sat in the immensity of space with Ellen. We went a little way with her and then turned back when we noticed that she had not taken a new breath for a long time. She had gone on and we were still here, sitting on her bed, holding her cold hands.

In the Qur'an, Allah has ninety-nine names. Allah's last name, the Hundredth Name of God, is hidden. In the Sufi tradition, one bead is always missing from the rosary to signify the mystery of God's true name—which is our true name and the name we will discover, it is said, when we take our last breath. When Ellen took her last breath, a window opened in my mortal mind for a brief moment. There on the threshold of life and death, I thought I heard the heavens whispering the Hundredth Name, but before I could know for sure, the window closed, and I returned to the living. Every now and then, especially when I remember my last moments with Ellen, the window opens a crack again, and I hear the Name.

No Birth, No Death

Rien ne se crée,
rien ne se perd.
(*Nothing is born,
nothing can die.*)
—Antoine-Laurent Lavoisier

One of the world's most revered meditation teachers is the Vietnamese Zen monk Thich Nhat Hanh. I have attended several retreats led by Thich Nhat Hanh—or Thay, as students call him. Once I invited an old friend who had no experience with spiritual practice to join me at Omega for a retreat with Thay. For years I had hesitated to bring this friend to an Omega program. He was a high-strung, high-powered music producer from New York City; his cynicism and caustic wit were on the level of a stand-up comic. I just couldn't imagine him being able to handle the peaceful atmosphere or the people at Omega. But recently my friend had been diagnosed with a serious illness. For the first time in his life he was confronting his mortality, and he had absolutely no resources to draw upon. My overtures to him about making peace with illness and death made him cringe; he said they sounded like New Age pabulum.

I thought that if anyone could reach my friend, it would be Thich Nhat Hanh. There is something about this small, unassuming monk—his clarity, his modesty, his choice of words, his voice—that calms people down even as it wakes them up. Thay has a poignant voice. It is soft and wise, but it is also playful. It is tinged with sadness, and it is profoundly peaceful. Born in Vietnam in 1926, Thay became a Buddhist monk at the age of sixteen and lived through years of war that ravaged his country and his people. Throughout those years he devoted his life to helping victims of war cope with overwhelming suffering. He lost family members, witnessed torture, and risked his own life as he tried to exert political pressure through peaceful resistance. Exiled from Vietnam for his leadership of the Vietnamese Buddhist Peace Delegation, he moved to France, where he continued to work for peace. Martin Luther King, Jr., nominated him for a Nobel Peace Prize.

Thay's personal history—the suffering he witnessed and the loss of his friends, family, and homeland—makes his present demeanor even more remarkable, for he is the most peaceful person I have ever encountered. His infrequent visits to the United States attract thousands of people who want merely to sit in the presence of a quiet man who practices what he calls "being peace."

More than eight hundred people had gathered at Omega to be with Thich Nhat Hanh this time—a splendid Indian summer weekend in October, the kind that makes living in the Northeast worth our miserable, cold winters. My friend reluctantly agreed to take part in the retreat, commenting that sitting still with a Vietnamese monk was probably deserved punishment for choosing to go to a rock concert instead of an antiwar march back in 1968. I stood in the parking lot waiting for him, drinking in the deep blue sky and the brilliant sunshine, the orange and brown leaves of the maples and oaks, the yellow bees in the late flower gardens. Hovering with the autumnal beauty was a peacefulness that always gathers around people in a meditation retreat.

My friend arrived characteristically late, as the program was about to begin. Just as he got out of his sleek black car and rushed to greet me, Thay was walking with a Vietnamese nun in the opposite direction toward the lecture hall. Monk and nun walked slowly and silently in their simple brown robes, like two autumn leaves drifting through the blue sky.

My friend stopped in his tracks, watched the two approaching, and bowed his head as they passed, a very uncharacteristic move on his part. No words were shared. He turned and continued to observe Thay and the nun make their steady progress toward the hall. An American Zen teacher, Richard Baker Roshi, has described the way Thay moves as "a cross between a cloud, a snail, and a piece of heavy machinery—a true religious presence."

When I reached him, my friend was still standing in the same spot, head slightly bowed. His hand was over his heart. "What was that?" he asked.

"That was not a what," I said. "That was Thich Nhat Hanh."

"Wow," he said. "That was weird. I felt as if I couldn't move. That guy was so, so . . . slow!"

Perhaps it was the marked contrast to his own rushed drive from New York City; perhaps it was the visual impact of a Buddhist monk and nun walking through a glorious fall day; whatever it was, my friend was already changed by the encounter. He sat patiently in the lecture hall in silence, surrounded by people whom he usually would have torn to shreds with snide remarks. He listened intently to Thay's simple words.

That day Thay was talking about death. I was so glad that my friend was present. I was so glad I was present. Thay spoke for two hours in his gentle, singsong voice, as the crowd sat, listening with rapt attention. At one point I noticed that my friend was asleep. I pulled his coat over him and figured that Thay's words would find their way into my friend's dreams (and knew that he could purchase the audiotape and listen to the talk all over again on his drive back to the city). Here is a condensed version of what Thay told us that autumn day at Omega.

In our minds, when we think of death, we think of suddenly becoming no-one. We cease to be. We cease to exist. That is our understanding. In the same way, we think of birth as our beginning. What does it mean to be born? We think that to be born means that we arrive here from nothing. That from nothing you suddenly become something. From no-one, you suddenly become someone. That is our definition of birth and death. Because of these notions, there is always fear deep within us. But the Buddha discovered something different, something called no-birth and no-death. The Buddha invites us to bring our fear up and look deeply into the object of our fear: fear of dying, fear of non-being. That is the cream of the Buddha's teaching. You cannot afford not to learn it because it is the best thing to learn in all of the teachings.

There are many non-Buddhists who have discovered the reality of no-birth and no-death. Let us talk about, for instance, the French scientist Lavoisier. He was called the father of modern chemistry. He looked deeply into the nature of things and he declared that nothing is born and nothing can die: *"Rien ne se crée, rien ne se perd."* I don't think that he had studied Buddhism.

Suppose we try to practice this idea of no-birth and no-death with a

sheet of paper, because a sheet of paper is what we call a thing. Let us practice together now, by looking deeply into this sheet of paper. [Thay holds
up a blank piece of paper.] You may think that this sheet of paper had a
birthday—that one day it was produced from nothing, and it suddenly became something, a sheet of paper. Is it possible? Look closely at the sheet of
paper in this very moment. Look into the true nature of the paper. What
do you see? You see—in a very tangible, scientific way—that paper is made
of nonpaper elements: When I touch the paper, I touch the tree, the forest,
because I know that deep inside there is the existence of the tree, the forest. Right? I also touch the sunshine. Even at midnight touching the sheet
of paper, I touch sunshine. Because sunshine is another element that has
made up the paper. Another nonpaper element. Without sunshine, no tree
can grow. So touching the paper, I touch the sunshine. I touch the cloud.
There is a cloud floating in this sheet of paper. You don't have to be a poet
to see the cloud. Because without a cloud, there would be no rain and no
forest could grow. So the cloud is in there. The trees are in there. The sunshine, the minerals from the earth, the earth itself, time, space, people,
insects—everything in the cosmos seems to be existing in this sheet of
paper. It is very important to see that a sheet of paper is made of—only
of—nonpaper elements. Our body is like that also.

So is it possible to say that from nothing, something has come into existence? From nothing, can you have something? No. Because before we
perceived it as a sheet of paper, it had been sunshine. It had been trees. It
had been clouds. The paper hasn't come from nothing: *"Rien ne se crée."*
Nothing has been born. The day you believe to be this paper's birthday is
something you should really call a "continuation day." The next time you
celebrate your birthday, instead of singing happy birthday, you can sing
happy continuation day.

"Rien ne se crée, rien ne se perd." Nothing is born, nothing can die. Our
true nature is the nature of no-birth. Our birth certificate is misleading. It
was certified that we were born on that day from such and such hospital
or city. But you know very well that you had been there in the womb of
your mother long before that. Even before the day of your conception, you
had been there—in your mother, in your father, in your ancestors, and
everywhere else, also. So if you try to go back, you cannot find a beginning
of you.

Let us now try to eliminate this sheet of paper. Let us burn it to see whether we are capable of making it into nothing. [Thay strikes a match and sets the sheet of paper on fire, holding it up as it burns in his hand.] Observe to see if it is possible to reduce something to nothing. Ash is what you can see now. You also see that some smoke has risen. The smoke is a continuation of the sheet of paper. Now the sheet of paper has become part of a cloud in the sky. You may meet it again tomorrow in the form of a raindrop on your forehead. But maybe you will not be mindful and you will not know that this is a meeting. You may think that the raindrop is foreign to you, but maybe it is the sheet of paper into which you have practiced looking deeply. So, can you say that the paper is now nothing? No, I don't think you can. Part of it has become the cloud. You can say, "Goodbye, see you again one day in one form or another."

It is very difficult to follow the path of a sheet of paper. It is as difficult as it is to find God. Some heat of the burning paper has penetrated into my body. I almost burned my fingers. It has penetrated into your body, also. It has gone very far. If you had fine equipment you could measure the impact of the heat even from a distant star. Because the impact of a small thing on the whole cosmos can be measured. It has produced some change in my organism, in your organism, and in the cosmos, also. The sheet of paper continues to be there, present. It is difficult for our conceptual eyes to see and discern, but we know that it is always there and everywhere, also. And this little amount of ash may be returned to the earth later on. Maybe next year you will see it in the form of a new leaf on a tree. We don't know. But we do know that nothing died. So the true nature of the sheet of paper is no-death.

Looking deeply into our self—our body, our feelings, our perceptions—and looking into the mountains, the rivers, and another person, we can see the nature of no-birth and no-self. It is right there, but we are assailed by so many ideas about birth and death that we get scared. Because of that fear, true happiness is not possible. Deep looking helps us to remove the fear. In Buddhism, there is a word that upsets many people. That is *nirvana*. *Nirvana* means "extinction." Touching nirvana is the purpose of our practice. But a good question may be asked: Extinction of what? We have to learn what a word like *nirvana* really means. One of the best ways is to ask questions. "Dear Buddha, what do you mean? What do you mean by *extinction*? Extinction of what?"

Extinction first means extinction of ideas—like ideas of birth and death, being and nonbeing. The idea of a self is an idea to be removed in order for you to touch reality. The self is made of nonself elements. The moment you realize that, you lose all your fear.

This body is not me. These eyes are not me. It is a mistake to identify yourself with this life span, to imagine that you are separated from anything else in space or time. You are everything at the same time.

If you are locked into the idea of a separate self, you have great fear. But if you look and you are capable of seeing "you" everywhere, you lose that fear. I have practiced as a monk. I have practiced looking deeply every day. I see me in my students. I see me in my ancestors. I see my continuation everywhere in this moment. I have not been able to go back to my country in the past thirty years. I left Vietnam in order to call for peace, to stop the killing, and I was not allowed to go home by many succeeding governments. Yet I feel that I am there, very real. I don't have that kind of painful feeling of a person being in exile because friends of mine go to Vietnam, and new monks and nuns are there. I see myself in them. I don't think that I am not present in Vietnam right now, just as I do not think that I will cease to be someday.

This teaching of the Buddha about no-birth and no-death is the cream of the whole body of the teaching. You have come to this retreat in order to learn this, and therefore to transform some of your sufferings. Yes, that is good, but don't miss the real opportunity. I am inviting you to go deeper, to learn, and to practice so that you become someone who has a great capacity for being solid, calm, and without fear, because our society needs people like you who have these qualities. And your children, our children, need people like you in order to go on, in order to become solid, and calm, and without fear.

After Thich Nhat Hanh finished his talk, he bowed to us and rang a bowl-shaped meditation bell. The clear sound vibrated out from the belly of the bell, swirled around the room, and seeped out of the doors and windows. It merged with the autumn air and was carried on the breezes to the tops of the trees. From there it spanned out, mingling with clouds and weather patterns and the myriad vibrations that hover in the earth's atmosphere. Perhaps that one strike of the bell traveled across oceans and made its way to Vietnam, to the town where Thich Nhat Hahn was born. There, in a simple village temple, a young nun looked up from her meditation and felt a wave of courage enter her heart. *Rien ne se crée, rien ne se perd.* Nothing is born, nothing can die—not a piece of paper, not a person, not even a sound made by a monk striking a bell.

Since the retreat with Thay, my friend the music producer has taken some long strides toward healing, both in body and in soul. He has become more solid and calm. He has slowed down. He is less quick to judge, and more likely to smile. He gives credit to a small monk in brown robes.

Visitation Dreams

My father remained a constant throughout my life. As I grew and changed, he stayed the same. At eighty-five, he was as gruff and remote as always, and as curious and energetic as well. He still climbed mountains, skied, and mowed his own fields around the Vermont farmhouse where he and my mother had moved many years before. He still stood perched over the radio while listening to the news, as if ready to attack any commentator with whom he disagreed. He still sent me newspaper clippings that might apply to my work, with terse notes explaining how things should be done. He'd end all of his correspondences and phone calls and visits with parting words he must have learned in the army: "Keep up the good work!" he'd write, or bark into the phone, or say, thumping me on the back. I think this was his way of telling me that he approved of the way I lived, maybe even that he loved me.

One cold February morning, before I had awakened, the phone rang. I picked it up and said hello as I dug my way out of sleep.

"Elizabeth?" It was my sister. "Dad died last night," she said in a wondering tone, as if she was reading an unusual headline from the paper.

"What?" I gasped, struggling to make sense of such outlandish news. Her words felt like a blow to my gut. "But . . . but . . . what happened?" I stammered.

"He'd been skiing all day," my sister said, in the same kind of voice you use to tell a fairy tale to a child. "He came home and had dinner, went to bed, and never woke up." Although she was a nurse, she seemed stunned that an old man could die in his sleep, and although she lived in the same town as my parents, she sounded as if she was stranded alone on the moon. "You better get in the car now and come here," she begged.

I woke my husband and said these strange words: "My father died." I lay like a confused little girl crying in the cradle of his arms. How could it be that my father—the man who never changed—had suddenly died? Oddly enough, for someone who has spent a lot of time thinking about death, the whole notion of my father dying had rarely crossed my mind. As my oldest son said a few days later, "I thought Grandpa would never die. He's just not the type."

Driving north to my parents' town, and up the long dirt road to their house, I wondered if the call had been a dream. Would my father meet me on the road as he always did, wearing his old boots and battered winter coat? Would he be out there, fixing the long stone wall, waving to me in the frosty Vermont air? But it hadn't been a dream; he wasn't on the road. By the time I arrived, my mother—not one to tarry—had moved my father's body to a funeral home. I drove to the next town and found my newly configured family waiting for me.

And there we were—the girls. Just the girls now, helplessly giggling and weeping in the funeral home. My father would have said that we were acting "just like girls," but we were behaving as do many people who are surprised by death. Too shocked to feel grief, we were giddy with change. We laughed as we wrote his obituary and cried as we chose the urn for his ashes, and all the while we felt his presence—his pride in us, his modest affection, his disdain.

Before we left I asked to see his body. The pale, overweight funeral director unlocked the door to the large walk-in cooler where my father was stretched out on a gurney. "Don't stay in there too long," the man said. "It's cold." He shut the door behind me, and I stood next to the body, not touching, as always. My father was naked, covered with a sheet pulled up to his shoulders. He head looked huge and heavy—his whole body seemed dense, as if in the few hours since his last breath he had become antimatter. A cool, blue light vibrated all around him. He was being eaten by death, digested and used by a force I could feel in the room. All I could think was that I had been wrong: Death was not nothing; it was something different—something massive and shimmering. My father was leaving our house and going somewhere else. All these years of my trying to leave his house, now it was over; he had left.

But where had he gone? For several months after he died, my father came to me in my dreams. I recognized in the atmosphere of those dreams the same blue light that had hovered around his body in the funeral home. In every dream he was radiantly happy, and his face was young and beautiful. His pleasure at seeing me was palpable, even in my sleep and in his death. I began to call these dreams "visitations," because they were so vivid, so authentic. Perhaps I would be in the middle of another dream, and quite suddenly, out of context, he would just show up—like a festive character from the wrong play. And always, the unspoken message flowing between us would be that we loved each other. Nothing fancy or sentimental—just a clear, sweet exchange of a profound depth of feeling.

In one of the visitation dreams, my father and I spoke to each other. I was with my mother and sisters in my parents' old bedroom. Suddenly the door opened, and my father was there. We were all so glad to see him. I was shining inside, with a silvery happiness. My father looked so handsome.

"How are you?" I asked him.

"Wonderful!"

"What is it like there in the afterlife?" I asked.

"It's much different than you think. You have to make your keep," he said.

"Really? You have things like money there?"

"No, not really, but you have to make your keep," he repeated. "Like this weekend I have to go do some work in Alaska."

I got the feeling that it was some kind of Good Samaritan angel work he was speaking about, like cleaning up an oil spill. Then he turned to leave, but before he did, he went over to my mother and asked her to marry him again.

My sisters reported similar "visitations." Only my mother never had one, until one night, a year after he died, he came to her while she slept. The next morning she left a message on my answering machine: "Elizabeth! At last it happened! Your father was there in my dream last night, and in my dream I knew I was dreaming him and I said to myself, 'I can't wait to tell the girls that I saw him.' There he was, clearer than anyone has ever appeared in my dreams. He looked so beautiful! I got just a brief look at him before he was lost in a crowd of people, and I didn't see him again. But that first view seemed to last for several minutes. It was in living color and so real. I thought you'd like to know."

I've had visitations not only from my father. Peter, my friend who died of AIDS, visited me several times shortly after his death. For many years after Ellen's death, she would appear in my dreams—healthy and young, and talking only about her son. I've made an unscientific study of visitation dreams by talking with friends and strangers. I had a conversation with a young man on an

airplane about a remarkable visit he had with his twin brother after his brother
had died in a car accident. I met a woman in one of my workshops whose
mother regularly appears to her when she is most in need of direction. Most
recently, I met a man at a Bruce Springsteen concert whose visitation dream
brought me to tears.

Before the concert began, I was hanging around backstage with a crowd of
other die-hard fans, trying to act cool but not pulling it off, since I was thrilled
out of my mind just to be there. A large man from New Jersey struck up a conversation with me. His name was Ray, he owned a chain of restaurants, and this
was his forty-fifth Springsteen show, he said. He asked me how I came to be
backstage, and I told him that a friend who was aware of my shameless Springsteen worship knew someone in the band. I asked him the same question, and
Ray told me that his father had died recently and a roadie had given him a
backstage pass as a healing gift. I asked him how he was doing with the loss of
his father. He said fine, now that he had had a dream about him.

"A visitation dream?" I asked.

Ray looked at me with astonishment. "Exactly!" he said. "How did you
know? He visited me. It was him, plain and simple. It wasn't really a dream,
but that's what I say, otherwise people would think I'm nuts. But you nailed
it—it was a visitation. Most people don't really want to talk about it."

"Well, you've found someone who does!" I laughed. "I don't think you're
nuts at all. I'm actually making a study of visitation dreams."

"Well what do you know," Ray said. "They even have a name for it." And
as the crowd waited for the show to begin, we pulled two chairs off to the side,
and Ray told me his story. His father had struggled with alcoholism and had
been absent during most of his childhood. But in the past couple of years Ray
and his father had been establishing a friendship—something that meant the
world to both of them. They talked on the phone every week, and spoke of
spending time together in the future. Ray was in the middle of building his
dream house and couldn't wait to finish it so that he could show his father. He
wanted his dad to see how successful he had become. He wanted to feel his father's pride in him. He just knew that when they stood in that house everything would come together for them at last.

But before that could happen, Ray's father was killed in a car accident. Ray
was devastated. He had lost his dad again. Soon afterward Ray and his wife
moved into their new home. One night, as they slept in their beautiful bed-

room, Ray woke up to find his father standing by the bed. He looked young and beautiful. He told Ray that he had come to see the house. Ray asked him about the accident, but his father acted as if he knew nothing about it. He only wanted to take a tour of the house and to tell Ray how proud he was of what he had done with his life. Ray showed him each room, and his father asked detailed questions about the building and planning, and about Ray's wife and children. As they walked through the house, his father apologized for not being a better parent when Ray was a boy. He told Ray that he had always loved him, and that he'd make up for lost time by being with him now, whenever Ray needed him. And then he was gone.

"That dream changed my life," Ray said.

"How so?" I asked.

"Now I know that my father loved me and was proud of me. I don't know if he could have told me those things while he was still alive. I know it was him. It was his voice, his face—it was him. I feel I can go on now. I'll have my father with me forever."

Like Ray, I have been comforted and reassured by nocturnal visits from people who have passed on. I have tried on occasion to initiate visitations, but it never works. Apparently visitation dreams cannot be ordered up, like room service or a pay-per-view movie. One can prepare the ground, though, and the best way I know of doing that is to grieve—to grieve the loss of beloved friends or family members well and long; to keep a space in the heart for them, even at the risk of keeping alive unfinished feelings and painful memories.

Good Grief

Let the young rain of tears come,
Let the calm hands of grief come.
It's not all as evil as you think.
—ROLF JACOBSEN

Thich Nhat Hanh says that studying death can help each of us become "someone who has a great capacity for being solid, calm, and without fear." Even so, we often feel anything but solid and calm when someone we love dies. Death stirs up conflicted feelings in the hearts of those left behind—some of us feel shaky and tender; others are shocked and angry; almost everyone is confused and unsettled. All of these feelings are included in what we call grief.

There is an art to grieving. To grieve well the loss of anyone or anything—a parent, a love, a child, an era, a home, a job—is a creative act. It takes attention and patience and courage. But many of us do not know how to grieve. We were never taught, and we don't see examples of full-bodied grieving around us. Our culture favors the fast-food model of mourning—get over it quick and get back to work; affix the bandage of "closure" and move on.

I am not a big fan of "closure." It sounds so abrupt, so tidy, so final. I prefer old-fashioned words like *mourning, lamentation,* and *grief.* They suggest a slow and sloppy process—one that involves emotional upheaval, interrupted activity, and dark nights of the soul. They describe the true nature of family gatherings and memorial services, which are never easy or neat. Grief is messy and painful. No wonder we may want to steer clear of it.

But grief is also a tonic. It is a healing elixir, made of tears that lubricate the heart. This is *the young rain of tears* that the poet Rolf Jacobsen speaks of. When a friend or family member dies—or when the world loses one of its beloved citizens—we should not hold back our tears. Our tears, and *the calm hands of grief* that follow, are not signs of some tragic and evil reality. *It's not all as evil as you think,* the poet says. Grief is the proof of our love, a demonstration of how deeply we have allowed another to touch us.

Grief is often confused with depression or self-pity. While one can certainly go into a woeful tailspin during the grieving process, in the long term, grief is not the same as depression. If we gloss over our grief, we might become depressed. Unfelt feelings and unexpressed grief have a way of dulling life. It is as if with every grief we do not feel, we stuff another handful of our vitality underground, until we are numb or sick or embittered.

I have counseled many people whose lives took destructive detours because of unfelt grief. A couple came to one of my workshops after a crisis in their marriage. The husband—whom I'll call George—had lost both his mother and his father to cancer shortly after he and his wife married. Then his brother drowned in a boating accident. With each loss, George threw himself more fervently into his work as an environmental lawyer, traveling extensively and taking on more and more responsibility. His wife complained that he was never home; his children rarely saw him. His family's requests for attention and intimacy confused and angered him. He thought he was doing all he could for them by working hard, caring for their financial needs, and creating a stable home. Now they were asking him for something more, something he couldn't access, something he was dead to within himself. His wife and children became living reminders of his numbed heart.

He began to spend even more time away from home. When he traveled, he drank heavily, "just so I could feel something," he said. One night, on a two-week business trip in Brazil, George brought a woman back to his hotel room. He knew he was playing with fire; he knew this could be the beginning of the end of his marriage, but he did it, he said, "because I couldn't feel anything anymore. Because I was numb. Because I was afraid if I didn't do it, I would freeze to death." All during that business trip, he worked long hours with an international conservation organization, then came back to the hotel to drink and spend the night with the woman. He stopped calling home.

On the last day of the trip, he came back to his room, and there on the hotel's voice mail was a message from his wife. She was filing for divorce. The

shock of the message, combined with the events of the week, exploded a dam in
George's heart—a dam holding back years of unfelt grief. He huddled in his
bed, terrified by the waves of anguish that swept over his normally laced-up
emotions. His business partners left Brazil without him. He stayed on for several days, swimming in an ocean of sorrow. There, alone in a room thousands
of miles from home, he traveled back in time. Images of his mother and father
and brother haunted him; he mourned their deaths as if they had just occurred.
He spent hours on the phone with his wife, weeping, apologizing, listening,
telling the truth. Wrung out, yet finally alive, George flew home and joined his
marriage and family as if for the first time.

When I met them, George and his wife were celebrating two anniversaries:
one year of sobriety for George and one year of a new marriage for both of
them. Things were still shaky, they said, and they knew they were not out of
the woods yet, but George had come back from the dead. He had done it by
descending into darkness, falling apart, and grieving. He had finally opened
the space in his heart that had scarred over when his parents and brother died.
In it, he found his life.

When my father died, I was stunned by the size of the space that his sudden departure had left. I wanted to fill it with something that would take away
the emptiness and the pain. I wanted to go back to work right away, or take a
trip, or do something, anything to get back to "normal." But I sensed that I
should sit tight with my grief, that I should allow the pain to have its way with
me. I took time off from work and gave myself over to what Dietrich Bonhoeffer calls "the gap." Bonhoeffer was a Lutheran theologian who lost many
friends and family members in World War II, and was eventually executed by
the Nazis. He wrote:

> Nothing can make up for the absence of someone whom we love, and it
> would be wrong to try to find a substitute; we must simply hold out and see
> it through. That sounds very hard at first, but at the same time, it is a great
> consolation, for the gap, as long as it remains unfilled, preserves the bonds
> between us. It is nonsense to say that God fills the gap; God doesn't fill it, but
> on the contrary, keeps it empty and so helps us to keep alive our former com-
> munion with each other, even at the cost of pain.

I lived for a couple of weeks in that gap after my father died. It was not an
easy experience. I felt restless, despondent, and naked. I cut myself off from

others because I felt like an alien in the living world. Sometimes I worried I would never leave the gap; at other times I felt I was bathing in a spiritual sea and didn't want to leave. During those times, I would talk to my father. I would tell him things I never did while he was alive—loving things and not so loving things. He would explain himself to me, and I to him. Often I was confused. I didn't understand my feelings. Did I really miss my father so much? That did not seem possible, because while I did love him and respect him, I also had a complex relationship with him, replete with poor communication, frustration, and resentment. Fortunately, understanding is not required for entrée into the gap. All one needs to do is to stay in it, to keep it empty of diversions and expectations, and to communicate with the person who has died.

When my best friend was dealing with the death of her mother, she was horrified to find that, six months after the loss, she was still feeling overcome by grief. Her despair kept her in the dark unknown, day after day, week after week, and month after month. Her grief made some people uncomfortable. Some said that she was depressed, and that she should take medication. Others told her to get busy, to go on a vacation, to read this or that book. All of this sounded right to her; she felt guilty and abnormal for being so weak. Yet the more she tried to cure her sorrow, the worse she felt.

I gave her the Bonhoeffer quotation and suggested instead of fighting the grief, or trying to fill the gap with books or medication or distractions, that she allow it to stay empty. That she wait. That she remain as deeply connected to her mother as she needed to. This helped her. Every time she felt ashamed of how long it was taking her to recover, or afraid that she would *never* recover, she'd go back to the gap. She would clean it out, and make a wide-open space for her mother. This process energized my friend in a lonely sort of way. She was alone with her mother, there in the gap, estranged from this world, yet connected to another. Eventually, after a few more months, a few visitation dreams, and some plain old-fashioned patience, the dark cloud lifted, the hole in her heart became less gaping, and my friend could say that she was ready to enter life again.

What happens when we keep the gap empty? "Nothing happens," writes the Jungian author Robert Johnson, "which is enough to frighten any modern person. But that kind of nothingness is the accumulation or storing of healing energy. It is genius to store energy. Though one has no idea what that energy will be used for, to have a store of energy accumulated is to have power in back of one. We live with our psychic energy in modern times as much as we do with our money—mortgaged into the next decade. Most modern people are exhausted nearly all the time and never catch up to an equilibrium of energy, let alone have a store of energy behind them. With no energy in store, one cannot meet any new opportunity."

Keeping the gap open after a loved one has died is a way of storing valuable energy. Without knowing it, I had stored a lot of energy during the months of grieving for my father. One day, after months of sadness and lethargy, I noticed that I was no longer living in the gap. The clouds had lifted. I felt a new sort of energy moving in me—some of it seemed to be my father's. I was ready to return to my life and put the gifts of grief to good use. I decided to mark the passage with a ritual of sorts. I took down a few objects given to me by a teacher who had frequently worked at Omega. Ed Benedict is a Native American leader from the Mohawk Nation. He once led an Iroquois condolence ritual at Omega and afterward gave me the doeskin pouch, dove feather, and clay bowl used in the ceremony. Now I had a use for them. I filled the bowl with water, placed it by a picture of my father, and read aloud the Iroquois prayer:

> *Some of you may have suffered the loss of a loved one. Perhaps it is*
> *something else that has caused you pain. It may be that your eyes have been*
> *clouded over by tears and that you can no longer see the beauty of the*
> *Creator. Perhaps the soreness of the grief that you have suffered through your*
> *eyes now blocks your vision. If this is the case, I offer you in symbolism a*
> *white doeskin that I take from the sky of the Creator. The skin of the doe is*
> *soft and comforting and with it I wipe the tears of soreness of old wounds*
> *from your eyes, so that you may see clearly once again.*

I took the doeskin pouch and touched it to my eyes.

> *I fear that you have suffered the loss of a loved one. Perhaps you may have*
> *suffered many losses. It may be that the cries of grief now echo in your ears so*
> *that you no longer hear properly. If this is the case, I offer you a white*
> *feather—a gift from the Creator—that I take from the sky. I take this*
> *feather and in symbolism I will clear the cries of grief from your ears, that*
> *the silence may rest and comfort you and that you may hear properly once*
> *again.*

I took the dove feather and brushed it over my ears.

It may be that you have suffered the loss of a loved one, perhaps something else caused you pain. If this is the case, perhaps you have uttered many cries of grief and done much weeping and a great sob has become lodged in your throat. This may be keeping you from speaking the truth of the Creator. If this is the case, I will reach into the sky and take for you a bowl of pure water. This water is sweet and pure and comes from the Creator. It will wash the lump of grief from your throat so that once again you may speak clearly and properly.

I held the bowl to my mouth and drank the water.

All of these things are offered you in symbolism so that you may be relieved of the pain of whatever losses you have suffered, that once again we may join hands and with open hearts and minds offer gratitude for this day to the Creator.

Karaoke

Doesn't everything die at last, and too soon?
Tell me, what is it you plan to do
with your one wild and precious life?
—MARY OLIVER
"THE SUMMER DAY"

When I met Peter, he was HIV positive. This was in 1985, long before anyone had a chance of surviving AIDS. But Peter was different. There was no way he was ever going to die, of anything. At least that's what I thought. Or wanted to think. Peter was a larger than life figure, and a perfect friend. He was able to meld within his personality disparate qualities not normally found in one person. He was social and silly, but also monkish and sensible. He was a party animal with a steady and meaningful job; a compassionate therapist with a wicked sense of humor; a political junkie on a spiritual path. He was up for anything and interested in everything. Who else would have called me late one night from his apartment in New York City to see if I had been watching a political fund-raising speech on television, and to ask my opinion: Should he put his coat over his pajamas and take the subway downtown to where the gala was being held in hopes he could meet the presidential candidate as he left the Plaza Hotel?

"Why would you want to do that?" I asked him.

"So I can tell him that he needs to articulate his foreign policy more clearly," Peter said, with an exasperated tone of the obvious.

"Well, sure, if you want to go out at this time of night," I said, knowing that I probably should, but never would do such a thing myself. But Peter did it. And sure enough, the next day the candidate *did* articulate his foreign policy more clearly.

Peter often called me late at night to discuss politics, fashion, food, TV, theater, the Mets, music, his love life. So when he called me one cold winter night at ten o'clock and asked if I wanted to go out with him right then to sing karaoke tunes at a bar in a town nearby us, how could I say no? I had always wanted to perform pop songs in a karaoke bar—I knew it was as close as I would ever get to fulfilling my secret desire of singing backup for Aretha. And who else but Peter would ever do this with me? So began our three years of meeting once a week in the barroom of a local Holiday Inn to sing duets like "I Got You Babe" and "Endless Love" under the tutelage of a woman whom Peter dubbed our "Karaoke master."

Each Thursday evening after work, Peter would make the two-hour bus ride from New York City up to his country home in my town. I would meet him at the bus station, and we would drive together to join a most unlikely group of wannabe pop stars, waitresses, car mechanics, video clerks, and other assorted oddballs, to be coached by Vivian, the Karaoke master, in the fine art of singing to the strains of a machine while reading lyrics on a video screen. But that was not all! We also received bits of life-coaching and healing advice from Vivian, who was a cross between Dolly Parton in looks and Mother Teresa in character. And free voice lessons from Jimmy, Vivian's husband—a lounge singer and Elvis impersonator.

At first, our friends were amused. Some even joined us at the Holiday Inn and suffered through two hours of cigarette smoke and awful renditions of Bee Gees songs. But when they realized that we were dead serious about our new group of friends and mentors, they left us alone on Thursday nights. One Christmas we hired Vivian and Jimmy to shepherd our flock of friends through a holiday karaoke party at my house. Although resistant at first, everyone— even my husband and Peter's longtime companion—sang his or her own solo with talentless abandon. It was thrilling to witness our friends succumb to the power of karaoke to remove inhibitions and rejuvenate the life force.

Peter and I kept up our once-weekly karaoke therapy longer than I wanted to and he should have. He continued because it helped him stay alive; I went along because it gave me the excuse to be with him. I was beginning to accept that Peter was dying. Anyone would know from just one glance that he was not long for this world. His face had the look—the sunken eyes, the yellow skin, and the tired gaze. But my ability to judge how long Peter would be alive was seriously compromised by my desire for him to live.

One fine Sunday morning in October, Peter called to see if I would go with him to the county fairgrounds, where an antique car and motorcycle show was being held.

"*Now* you're interested in old cars?" I asked.

"No," he said. "Vivian and Jimmy have a booth there. I thought it would be great to do my new song in the open air."

Peter had been butchering Frank Sinatra's "That's Life" for a few weeks at the Holiday Inn. Did I really want to hear him do it again? Did I want to spend a precious autumn day at the dusty fairgrounds, hanging around with karaoke-singing car fanatics? No. But I went, because I did want to spend a precious day with a friend who would not grow old with me.

Peter was quiet on the drive. When we crossed the bridge, he didn't even look up to see the trees on the other side of the Hudson River, spread like a red and yellow blanket over the hills. The year was dying, and so was he. In the winter the trees would stand bare, waiting for spring. Peter would step outside his body and journey on into the mystery.

But today he wanted to sing "That's Life" at an antique car show at the fairgrounds. Hundreds of people were there—vintage car fans, motorcycle gangs, and whole families eating hot dogs and having a good time. As we spiraled our way into the innermost ring of exhibit booths, past shiny Model Ts and beefed-up Corvettes, we realized that Vivian and Jimmy and their karaoke machine were featured aspects of the show. Someone was singing an off-key karaoke version of "King of the Road" over the entire fairgrounds's sound system. A thrilled look came into Peter's eyes: He was going to sing to hundreds of unsuspecting strangers.

At the karaoke booth, Vivian greeted Peter as if Frank Sinatra himself had arrived. She rushed us past a long line of people waiting their turn to sing, gave Peter a glass of water, and flipped through her CDs, looking for "That's Life." I sat down in a chair next to Jimmy, who was dressed in full Elvis regalia. When the microphone was free, Peter—who just the year before had been a handsome six-foot hunk of a guy—stepped to the platform, balding, skinny, and pale. The opening bars of "That's Life" began, and then Peter's wavering voice was heard over the sound system, crooning the words,

That's life—that's what all the people say.
You're ridin' high in April, shot down in May . . .
That's life, and I can't deny it:
Many times I thought of cuttin' out but my heart won't buy it.
But if there's nothing shakin' come this here July,
I'm gonna roll myself up in a big ball . . .
And die.

It was a classic Peter moment, when the most improbable extremes of life came together in one spectacular and comic flash. I would remember it at his hospital bedside months later, keeping a vigil with his friends and family as Peter left this world. The memory of him standing at the fairgrounds singing about life would help me find my way to that place of magic where our existence can be both tragic and funny, grievous and full of joy.

At the end of Mary Oliver's poem "The Summer Day," she writes these lines:

Doesn't everything die at last, and too soon?
Tell me, what is it you plan to do
with your one wild and precious life?

Peter died at forty-four. Gorgeous, bright, full of love and life: *too soon.* His death broke my heart. In the beginning, I missed him terribly. Five years later, I still think about him almost every day. Whenever he visits me in my dreams, he tells me the same thing—to live my life fully. I have tattooed that message on the diaphanous skin of my *one wild and precious life.* But still, I forget; I worry, complain, resist the ways in which life moves and changes. Today, as I write this, my neighbor is dying from cancer. He is sixty-two, an age that now seems quite young to me. Too young to die. His wife and he have recently retired, so excited to start the next phase of their life together. They bought and renovated the house next door when our previous neighbor died at 101. She was a painter and a celebrated figure in town. Even she died too soon!

So, tell me, what is it we should do with our one wild and precious life? This, indeed, is the question. The answer can only be discovered by living life to its fullest. One day the sun and the earth will tilt out of balance, and the thin-skinned salamander and the furry bear—all of us—will dry up and turn to dust. On another planet, far away from here, on the same day, something mysterious will tip the scales of emptiness in the direction of life, and the story—with all of its magnificent diversity and colorful confusion—will begin anew. Will we meet there again, in some other form?

Practicing Death

We do not know where death awaits us:
so let us wait for it everywhere.
To practice death is to practice freedom.
A man who has learned how to die
has unlearned how to be a slave.
—MICHEL DE MONTAIGNE

My mother, who taught high school English, used to read us all kinds of poetry, from traditional children's verses to the ecstatic ramblings of Walt Whitman and the strange riddles of Emily Dickinson. She especially liked the work of the American poet Theodore Roethke, who spoke in images of black snakes, white lilies, still waters, and sunken trees. His poems scared but also thrilled me. They were like ghost stories.

My mother started teaching when I was in grade school. She loved her work and was an excellent teacher, but she was often full of anxiety about her students, the administration, and her performance. Once, in describing her apprehension, she told me a story about Roethke, who taught for many years at colleges and universities. When he was at Bennington College in Vermont, his fear of failure was so great that he would vomit behind a specific tree before every class. Soon afterward he suffered a mental breakdown.

My mother never vomited before class, and never had a breakdown. But she did endure many restless nights anticipating a new school year or a faculty review. Despite her occasional cold feet, she had a long teaching career and continues, in her eighties, to tutor children.

I had forgotten all about these stories of teaching anxiety until I started lecturing and leading workshops and was racked with worry for weeks before each event. One of the first workshops I taught was at a conference on alternative medicine for doctors and nurses at Harvard University. The organizer of the conference had read an article I wrote about the spiritual dimensions of the dying process, and she asked me to teach a workshop. I tried to tell her that I had never taught a workshop on death before, especially not one for medical professionals, but she was undaunted. "There's a first time for everything," she replied in a sunny voice. I reluctantly agreed. The minute I hung up the phone I was terribly sorry I had said yes. And from deep in the recesses of my anxious brain, I flashed on an image of Roethke, brought to his knees outside of a classroom, turned inside out by his gut-wrenching dread. I now could imagine doing that behind some old chestnut tree on the Harvard campus.

As the date approached, I regretted the decision more and more. No matter how much I prepared and rehearsed, I couldn't shake the feeling that I was an impostor, and that the bigwigs at Harvard would find me out. As I drove to the conference, I wondered if I would end up not only vomiting behind a tree but also dragged away to a mental hospital, like Roethke. By the time I reached Boston, my sense of self had unscrewed itself. I was a mess.

Once at Harvard, I found my way to the building where the conference was being held, listened to the keynote speaker, met a few people, screwed my head back on, and marched with shaky confidence to my assigned classroom. My workshop, called "Death, Grief, and Healing," was being held at the same time as a few others and was in a room right next to a workshop called "Humor, Laughter, and Healing." The walls separating the classes were thin; in fact, they weren't really walls at all but room dividers in a large auditorium. As soon as I began to speak, so did my next-door neighbor.

I launched into my discussion about the importance of staying open to the feelings that arise when we confront death—be they fear or anger, regret or grief, numbness or wonder. When I began to lead the thirty or so doctors and nurses in my group into a grief meditation, the folks in the workshop next door were apparently playing a game. Shrieks of laughter could be heard as I played soft music and asked people to touch on the part of the heart where feelings may have pooled. Every time I would say something about fear or grief, the other workshop leader would call out instructions for a game. I felt as if I was directing a funeral at an amusement park.

Finally things got too much for one doctor in my workshop. She stood up, grabbed her coat and bag, and announced, "I didn't come here to get depressed! I'm going next door, where they're having a good time."

After she left, I stood tall and tried to salvage the workshop. "Does anyone else want to go next door?" I asked. A few people nodded their heads. "Please, go ahead." I waited for them to leave, then hunkered down with the brave souls who had stayed.

"Listen," I said, suddenly not nervous, and miraculously in command of my subject. "If you really want to have fun in life, if you really want to play— like they are doing next door—then it helps to come to terms with death. The death at the end of this life, and the deaths you go through all the time when things fall apart, or when you fail, or you suffer a loss. Joseph Campbell said that the conquest of the fear of death is the recovery of life's joy. My workshop is really a prerequisite to Humor, Laughter, and Healing. They forgot to say that in the brochure." My students laughed. I hoped the guy next door heard them.

It was at that workshop that I started thinking about leading a guided meditation on one's actual death. I remembered how a friend of mine, the painter Alex Grey, brought students in his New York University drawing classes to a city morgue. He told me, "In the context of an anatomy lesson, I take my art students to a morgue, where we study cadavers. This immediately becomes a lesson in confronting mortality. To see a dead body is shocking, not only because death is usually hidden or cosmetically 'enhanced' in our society but also because we project our own finality onto the cadaver. I talk to my students about the Buddha, and how he recommended using a dead body as an object upon which to meditate. Death heightens our appreciation of every moment we are alive and calls out to us: 'Soon you will die; what will you do with your life? What have you not done yet that you want to do?' Death is the best kick in the ass I know. It is profoundly confrontational and profitable for students to contemplate."

Since I would not have the opportunity to bring students to a morgue, I decided to create a way for people to role-play their own death. I have now led this meditation many times, with groups as intimate as ten cancer patients in a local hospital and as large as four hundred people in a conference room. Before I lead the meditation, we talk about death and dying, our resistances and fears, and our expectations and preconceptions. I explain that death is always with us. It shows up in daily life when things change, end, and then begin again in a different way. It greets us when our life in human form is over and we move on, into another form of consciousness. I talk about death anxiety, and how there are two kinds of people—those who fear the final death and those who are more concerned about not living fully while in human form. I ask people from each club to raise their hands—I never cease to be amazed by how the room divides evenly. It is helpful for all of us to understand that one's point of view about death is only that—a point of view—and that the truth is much larger than anything we can conceive.

Then I lead a twenty-minute guided meditation into what I imagine is the realm beyond human life, beginning with the experience of saying good-bye to the people and places we love, and to our attachments and disappointments and regrets. The death meditation is a powerful experience. People have told me that it changes the way they approach life and death.

At every death workshop I lead, there is at least one person who has had a near-death experience. Many studies have been done and books written on the near-death experience, which occurs when a person experiences clinical death and then is medically revived. After I lead the death meditation, I encourage anyone in the class who has had a near-death experience to share her or his story with the group. Many people are stunned to find similarities between the stories of near-death experiences and the experiences they just had in the guided meditation.

I was particularly moved by the near-death experience story of a person in one of my workshops. John was twenty-five years old when he was in a serious car accident. After being on life support for several days, he lapsed into a coma. His parents sensed that he was about to die and asked the family priest to administer last rites. Then they left John in the hospital for the night, sure they would never see their son alive again. But later that night when John's heart stopped beating, a team of doctors and nurses worked to revive him and brought John back from death. The next morning his parents found him alive and conscious.

In the months that followed, fragmented memories of his near-death experience came back to John, accompanied by the same sounds and lights and sense of love and beauty that other people who have clinically died also report. He writes:

When I was in the coma, I could see the doctors and nurses and my parents in the room, as if I was floating above all of them and my own body. It was very strange. I could see them, but I had no real feeling of connection. It was just like I was watching television. Then I felt something pulling me emotionally, although that is not really the right word, toward a tunnel that led into a huge field of light. There were people in that light—they were made of the light. They had no faces, but they didn't frighten me. I wasn't afraid of anything. I felt I knew these people; they were waiting for me. I wanted to join them, but they told me that it wasn't my time and I should go back, that I wasn't finished with my work. "What work?" I asked, because at that time I really didn't have any work to speak of. And they said that I would find this work and that it was important to do it.

And then the next thing I knew was that a doctor was pounding on my chest and I was feeling a lot of pain and confusion, and there I was, back in my body, back on earth.

For a long time I never told anyone about the experience. I had never heard of anything like it, and I didn't want people to think I had lost my mind. Now I can talk about it because more and more people have heard about near-death experiences. There are books about them and clinical studies. But I don't need the science to back up my experience, and I don't even care if people believe me. I'm not a near-death experience missionary. I'm not even particularly spiritual. I'm just an ordinary person. For me, the near-death experience was not mystical—it actually made me appreciate life here on earth more. It changed the way I was with my friends and family, and it gave me a strong desire to do good work in the world. It turned out that everything in my life is the work that those beings of light were talking about—my job, my marriage, my family. Life is full of possibilities to me because I am not afraid of death. I've been to the threshold of death and I know what it is. There is no reason to fear death. Life continues. You continue. I know this.

The French Renaissance philosopher Michel de Montaigne advised people to "practice death." "To begin depriving death of its greatest advantage over us," he wrote, "let us deprive death of its strangeness, let us frequent it, let us get used to it; let us have nothing more often in mind than death. . . . We do not know where death awaits us: so let us wait for it everywhere. To practice death is to practice freedom. A man who has learned how to die has unlearned how to be a slave."

By practicing death, Montaigne does not mean that we should set up shop on a city sidewalk with a sign announcing the end of the world. Nor does he mean we have to have a clinical near-death experience. He means that we can practice death by becoming conscious of the ways in which we resist life; we can practice death by approaching endings and partings and changes with more ease and faith. For a person like myself—one whose fear of death has been a lifelong struggle and quest—practicing dying is indeed the practice of freedom. I find ways to practice every day, every week, every year.

The Turtles and the Trees

Come, come, whoever you are,
Wanderer, worshiper, lover of leaving.
It doesn't matter.
Ours is not a caravan of despair.
Come, even if you have broken your vows
a thousand times.
Come, yet again, come, come.
—INSCRIPTION ON RUMI'S TOMBSTONE

It is a rainy June evening, around five o'clock. I am coming home from work, driving down Slate Quarry Road, the country route that winds through forests and fields, and leads to the bridge across the Hudson River, and eventually to the Catskill Mountains, where I live. It is a road I have taken hundreds of times, through all kinds of weather. Each bend holds significance for me: the turn where my car skidded into a tree on an icy winter night; driveways I have pulled into as I absorbed news on the radio; the old barn that folds into itself more and more with each passing year.

Today, as the spring rain slicks the road and makes the world around me green and vibrant, I am worrying about my most recent life-and-death obsession: the demise of several tree species in the Northeast. Stands of ash and hemlock are being killed by blights. Other species—like maples and the mighty sycamores, my favorites—are being weakened by acid rain. As I drive the bends of Slate Quarry Road, I search the top of the tree canopy for signs of die-off.

The death of trees offends me; it stirs up rage, and then grief. How could humans be so stupidly shortsighted as to allow the ravishment of the planet to reach such obvious proportions? Our lives are being diminished by the loss of nature.

Twisting along the curves with my eyes shifting to the tops of the trees, I sense a large shape in the road ahead of me. Before I can slam on the brakes, I come upon a huge snapping turtle, at least a foot across and just as long, making its slow way across the road. The marshy fields that flank Slate Quarry Road are home to snapping turtles that mate and lay eggs in the spring. It is common to see them crossing the road this time of year, and to see drivers stop their cars, get out, and help the turtles to safety. But I am not paying attention. I am preoccupied by the death of trees in particular and the loss of nature in general. I run over the turtle.

I pull to the side to survey the damage. The turtle is dead, its shell cracked, its soft body smashed all over the road. I stare at the carcass in disbelief. I love turtles as much as I love trees. I can hardly believe the sophisticated irony of the event. "Okay, Goddess Gaia," I pray to the Greek goddess of the earth. "What are you telling me?"

The next day I rise early. It is a glorious spring morning, the first clear day in a week of rain. As I look out the window into the front yard, I notice a strange shape in the garden. Putting on my glasses, I see to my amazement that the shape is a snapping turtle, just like the one I killed the day before, many miles from my home, across the Hudson River, on Slate Quarry Road. A turtle is parked in my garden, looking solemnly up at me. I stare back at her from the bedroom window. I have never seen a turtle, and certainly not such a large turtle, near my house. I call my husband to the window, and then we both go downstairs and out into the warm morning. We watch the turtle digging a hole in the soft dirt, noting that she had started other holes all over the lawn and garden. She uses her powerful feet and tail to bury herself in the dirt until all that is left is a tiny patch of shell and the tips of her nostrils. And there she stays for a day and a night.

I call a local wildlife organization, and the naturalist there tells me that the turtle is laying eggs. After she has deposited the eggs, says the expert, the turtle will leave. The eggs will rest and mature for six to eight weeks, and finally, we hope, they will hatch in the garden under our bedroom. We build a little chicken-wire cage to protect the eggs from raccoons and other animals, and we wait.

"So," asks my husband, "what is Gaia's message?"

"What do *you* think it is?" I ask him, too humbled by my crazy behavior to trust my own intuition.

"I would say that you worry so much about the environment," my husband says, "that you miss the point of how ingenious nature is. How creative it is. Look—you killed a turtle because you were worrying about things like turtles dying! And now, right here in your own backyard, the Easter turtle has left you a gift."

My husband's wise words remind me of the words of someone else. For years my hero of the natural world has been the poet and environmentalist Gary Snyder. In his poetry and essays, Snyder calls the earth Turtle Island, based on an old Native American tale. After the incident with the turtle and the trees, I e-mail him:

Dear Gary,

Perhaps you remember me from your visit to Omega a few years ago. I certainly remember you! And not only remember you, but continue to gain inspiration and forbearance through your words. If it is not too presumptuous, I am writing to ask you for a few more of those words.

For all of the spiritual work I have done on myself, and the environmental work I have done in my town, recently I have been struggling with an almost crippling sense of despair about earth changes. My heart aches when I confront things like overdevelopment, tree blight, loss of species populations, and the stupid choices we humans continue to make. When outside with others, my eyes go immediately to the top of the tree canopy and I rant about the ash blight, or the disease killing off the Eastern hemlocks, or the diminishing frog species, or the decline in the Eastern bluebird. I'm beginning to be a drag to be around!

I know that you too feel what the earth feels, and I wonder how you make peace with so much loss. If you have a spare moment, your thoughts on the matter might be of great help to this lover of Turtle Island.

Love, Elizabeth

Gary Snyder responds right away:

Dear Elizabeth,

I remember my visit to Omega quite fondly—and the trail that went up to a small green broad-leaf deciduous tree-covered knoll. Such a wonderful Eastern woodland feeling. About the threats to the world and nature: I comfort myself with remembering that Gaia has multi-millions of years to work things out in, and we can neither really destroy nor save her. So, we get energized to work for the earth for ourselves. For character, and for style. And when things are this bad, anger won't help, so you better have a sense of humor. Coyote is one of my teachers!

Best, Gary

Later that day, I go up to the cottage on our property where I write. I work for a few hours, then open the sliding glass door to take a break. There in the grass is a tiny deer. Is he a newborn? Was he born right there while I was working? Have I once again missed the rebirth of nature while writing about its death? This is becoming a joke! Perhaps Coyote, the Native American trickster Gary Snyder invoked in his letter, is playing with me. I carefully approach the baby deer, who lies motionless in the grass. Maybe he is a stillborn; maybe his mother abandoned him here. When I am a few inches away from the deer, he opens his eyes, startles, and wobbles to his feet. Then he smacks straight into the side of the cottage and falls back down again.

Oh no, I think, I've done it again!

Backing away from the little deer, I see the mother in the woods, gazing at me warily. After I have retreated far enough down the path, she comes over to her baby and licks him until he stands. And slowly they move into the woods, resuming their wild life without me.

On Rumi's tombstone, in Konya, Turkey, are these words:

> *Ours is not a caravan of despair.*
> *Come, even if you have broken your vows*
> *a thousand times.*
> *Come, yet again, come, come.*

And so, once again, I have broken my vows not to despair at the mysterious ways in which God shows up—as beauty and loss, as Coyote and baby deer, as life and death. I have broken my vows a thousand times, but I can renew them a thousand times, and rejoin the caravan of the faithful. Like the alchemists who changed metal into gold, I can transform my worry into trust, and my despair over dying trees and dead turtles into a bright vision of eternal rebirth.

A Meditation for Practicing Dying

When we practice dying,
we are learning to identify less with Ego
and more with Soul.
—RAM DASS

Take a few minutes right now to look closely at your life, and at the way things are always beginning and ending, moving and changing. Make note of the way things really work: The car breaks down, you fix it or get a new one, and a few weeks, or months, or years later, you're back at the garage. You plant seeds on a peaceful April day, watch the flowers bud and bloom, and then in August, a freak hailstorm flattens the garden. You get a cold, you get better, you get sick again. You find the perfect house or the perfect job, you lose your job, you're downsized, you have to move. You find the perfect mate, you move in together, you discover she's a cleanliness freak, or he chews with his mouth open, or something worse—something that unravels a marriage and a family. You make peace with your parents, your parents die. You have children and everything changes; you fall madly in love with them, they drive you crazy, they get bigger, and then, just as you're getting the hang of things, they leave home.

Given the nature of existence, you don't have to wait until something big happens to practice dying. You can begin right now. You can carve out some alone-time in your day, sit down, close your eyes, and meditate on the fluid nature of your body, of time, and of life itself. Here is a meditation I use to practice dying.

> Bring your awareness to focus on something in your life that is changing
> or ending or dying right now. Breathe gently as you consider whatever
> transition is most significant right now in your life. Note any feelings that
> arise—trepidation, excitement, resistance, anger, annoyance, or grief. Every
> time your feelings get the better of you, become aware of your breathing.
> Meet your troubled and contracted feelings with your calm and expansive
> breath. Breathe, sigh, and stretch out on the river of change. Remember
> times when you have resisted change in the past. Regard how things turned
> out in the end—maybe not how you thought they would, or you wanted
> them to, but in the end, there you were. Wiser, stronger, still alive. Tip your
> hat to the poignancy of death and the promise of rebirth. Smile. Relax.
> Allow yourself to break open. Sit tall, with dignity and patience, watching
> your breath rise and fall, rise and fall. Pray for the courage to welcome this
> new change with openness and wisdom.
>
> Then open your eyes, go back into your life, and do what you have to
> do, but do it with grace, with hope, and with a lighter touch.

I have trained myself now—when something is not going my way, and I feel rising up within me a big, hard *No!*—to take a breath or two, and to counter that *no* with different counsel. I tell myself to "die to it." Sometimes just saying that little phrase—"die to it"—is all I need to do to clear my head of the emotional storm clouds. What must die? Any resistance to the bigger truth. Any holding on by that part of me—my little ego part—that cannot see beyond its own nose. If the situation involves another person who appears to be getting in the way of what I want—even if that person is being led around by the nose of his or her own little ego—it is still only necessary for me to "die to it." When I can clearly see the whole picture, then I'm free to choose wisely my own next steps.

Practicing dying means living as close to reality as we can in each moment. It is the ultimate bravery. The spiritual warrior stands undefended before the truth—not some concept about the truth but the stripped-down reality of the most mundane, day-to-day situations: when you are arguing with your mate; when you get sick; when you are in a meeting at work; when you confront again, for the hundredth time, the same issue with your parent, or child, or friend. Every day you are given an embarrassingly rich array of opportunities to die to your resistance to what is so about yourself, your life, and those you share it with. Try it. Next time you are at work and you feel anger rising up to meet a situation that you think is outrageous or unfair or inept, tell yourself to "die to it." Take a few meditative breaths and get your little ego out of the way. Size up the whole story, and not just your small piece of it. Take a clean, objective look at what *is*, and not what you think should be. If you must, walk away from the scene, sit quietly, and practice dying.

Ram Dass says that *when we practice dying, we are learning to identify less with Ego and more with Soul.* Who would want to be an ego, when we can be a soul?

PART VI

The
River of Change

L IFE IS ALWAYS CHANGING; we are always changing. We live in a river of change, and a river of change lives within us. Every day we're given a choice: We can relax and float in the direction that the water flows, or we can swim hard against it. If we go with the river, the energy of a thousand mountain streams will be with us, filling our hearts with courage and enthusiasm. If we resist the river, we will feel rankled and tired as we tread water, stuck in the same place.

If we had the patience and a high-powered microscope, we could sit and stare at our hands and watch the river of change flowing through our own bodies right now. We could watch our cells changing and dying and being replaced, over and over and over. From year to year, every one of our cells is replaced. Literally, who we were yesterday is not who we are today. Our skin is new every month, our liver every six weeks. When we inhale, we breathe in elements from other organisms to create new cells, and when we exhale, we send parts of ourselves out into the atmosphere—into the living, breathing universe. "All of us," writes the medical doctor Deepak Chopra, "are much more like a river than anything frozen in time and space."

"I've known rivers," writes Langston Hughes. "I've known rivers ancient as the world and older than the flow of human blood in human veins. My soul has grown deep like the rivers."

Am I going to flow with my river nature today, or am I going to swim against it? This is what I ask myself when I get out of bed each morning. And when I go to sleep, I apologize to the river gods for any hard strokes I made against the current, and for splashing about like a drowning person. I pray that tomorrow I may once again know the pleasure of following my soul downstream, because I've known rivers—and once we've known rivers—once we have stretched out on the dark waters, trusting the river gods, going in the direction of life even if it is headfirst toward the rapids—we want to taste that water again; we want our souls to grow deep like the rivers again.

Enjoying the
Passage of Time

The secret in life
is enjoying the passage of time.
—Richie Havens

I have a visceral memory of what the passage of time felt like when I was a child. Sometimes a color or smell will spark a childhood memory and I'll enter the realm of magic, where a year seemed to take forever and the seasons existed mainly as backdrops for holidays. Halloween was the color of candy corn, pumpkins, and school buses. Christmas was a sparkling ornament, all shiny gold and green. It was pine trees, mittens, snow days, and the thrill of giving and getting presents. And then, there was Valentine's Day, with those exciting heart-shaped cards and red-hot candies. Spring meant Easter, and eggs painted in pastel colors, longer days and lighter evenings, and the birds making noise in the morning. Summer vacation stretched out like a lazy, green carpet leading to my birthday in August.

I longed for my birthday—for the party and for the changes one more year would bring. There was something about the month of August that just begged for time to move faster. After my birthday would come the new school year. I would be a year older, and in the next grade. I liked the way time kept moving, pulling me along, showing me new things, expanding my world. I was curious about what would come next. Third grade would be better than second, fifth so much more important than fourth. Junior high would be a huge improvement over elementary school. And there was high school to look forward to, and college. In one of my favorite songs from the sixties, Richie Havens sings, *The secret in life is enjoying the passage of time.* Children know that secret.

Sometime during college, instead of enjoying the passage of time, I began to drag my feet. I didn't want to leave my twenties. Thirty sounded *old.* Instead of joyfully anticipating the seasonal round, I began to set ultimatums for myself: By Christmas I must lose ten pounds; in the new year I'll be a more patient mother; when the kids go the school I'll concentrate more on work. When I entered my thirties I set the bar higher: By thirty-two if my marriage still feels like this, I'll do something about it; before I'm forty I *must* have written a book. The passage of time was now punctuated by approaching deadlines, and a nagging fear that the future wouldn't measure up to my fantasies of what life was supposed to be. I dreaded the passage of time. I stopped looking forward to my birthday in August. As the years rolled on, parties and presents lost their luster—in fact they were vaguely disappointing. I never seemed to get the perfect gift, the one that stopped time in its tracks.

At my fortieth birthday, I gathered with my closest women friends and held a ritual for myself. I decided that this would be the last time I celebrated my birthday with a party. I wanted out of the whole system! I was going to revise my relationship to time. I no longer wanted to live year to year, from birthday to birthday, or even from one season to the next. I wanted to live each day, moment to moment, enjoying the fact that nothing ever stays the same and nothing ever turns out the way we expect. I decided to experiment with a major attitude shift. Instead of freaking out about how my face was beginning to sag, I'd look in the mirror and say, "Wow, life is interesting when everything changes." Instead of worrying about my parents aging, or my kids growing older, or the world warming up (or blowing up), I would try to lighten up. What would it be like to regard change—whether it be a change of body or a change of heart—as merely proof of being alive?

My last birthday party took place on a warm summer night. I had invited my sisters, my mother, some of the women I worked with, and my friends to help me celebrate. After dinner and the usual party patter, we went down to the field where I had laid a big fire. I gave each woman a pinecone. I threw a match in the fire, and as it burst into flames, I told everyone to think of something she wanted to get rid of. "Something you want to burn to ashes, so that new life can emerge," I said.

We sat quietly under the stars, our faces lit by the fire's glow, each woman thinking about something she wanted to invest in the pinecone and toss into the flames. I had led this ritual before—at workshops and New Year's Eve parties. But there was something about being with a group of women that heightened the experience, and made it at once more serious and more comical. One friend pitched in her boyfriend. Most tossed something about themselves that they longed to burn and transform. My sister stood at the fire's edge and announced she was tossing in her fear; a friend from work threw her need for control into the flames.

I was the last to toss my pinecone. I had cheated and written down what I wanted to say beforehand. Well, I *was* the birthday girl, even if it was for the last time. Standing before the fire, I read, "I am throwing into the flames my resistance to time passing, my fear of aging, and my big *No!* to change. And out of the ashes I pray that a new way of being in life will emerge. I want to say *Yes!* to all of it—the good, the bad, and the ugly. I want to live by the secret law of the universe: I want to enjoy the passing of time."

Indeed, that was my last birthday party, although it certainly was not the last time I resisted change. In the ten years that have passed since I gathered with my friends around the bonfire, I have had many opportunities to practice the passage of time. My children grew up and left home, my father died, and my body began to age in more obvious ways. While I still found myself saying *No!* to transitions, I must say that the birthday ritual did burn a bright new pathway in my consciousness. It reminded me to say *Yes!* more often. It reignited what I knew as a child, and gave me a more innocent and hopeful way of measuring time.

Now when August and my birthday roll around again, I throw myself an un-birthday party. I sit quietly and recommit to the secret of life. I reverse the wheels of worry, and tip my hat to the never-a-dull-moment nature of time. Who knows what dimensions the soul will travel through after this one? We may look back on our sojourn through time with great nostalgia. I can imagine one angel saying wistfully to another, "Remember how we were never bored when we believed in time?"

The Workshop Angel

Each time I lead a workshop, I get the feeling that the universe has a central casting agent who sends the full array of human personalities to the dramatic stage of the workshop. It never fails: Wherever I teach, whatever the size of the group, or the subject matter, central casting supplies a rich blend of people, including shy souls, eager beavers, shut-down resisters, true believers, complainers, mystics, pretenders, wise guys, and what I call mental cases—people who live primarily in their rational minds. There's also a know-it-all, a class clown, and a sad sack. There's always someone whose heart has recently been broken. Central casting makes sure a couple of people who don't want to be there are in attendance; these people keep their arms folded and their eyes fixed on the ground. And then there's the person whom I call the workshop angel—the one whose presence and story gives all of us the courage we need to return to our lives renewed. The workshop angel is always sent.

Each player is critical to the success of the workshop. We all contribute to one another's growth. The class clown shows the shy soul how to come out of her shell, even if she must risk appearing foolish. The sad sack helps the class clown touch his deeper feelings, even if he has to descend into grief. The mental case encourages the sad sack to take a break from her feelings, while the mystic gives the mental case permission to seek out the magic hiding in the heart. No one's presence is arbitrary, and everyone is essential.

I recently taught a three-day workshop. It was around Christmastime, at a beautiful mountain lodge by the edge of a lake. Fifty people joined me to contemplate the direction they wanted to take in the coming new year. Sure enough, within minutes of starting our retreat, I noticed that central casting had once again made sure that each human archetype was represented. As the weekend progressed, we all took our places on the stage, fulfilling the destiny of our roles.

On the second evening, we met for an hour before going to sleep. A gentle snow was beginning to fall. We had been together for two long days, during which we had shared some painful revelations and some freeing realizations. One woman had spoken often about the miseries in her life. She seemed caught in an endless cycle of anger and regret. Central casting had sent her to the workshop for her own healing, and to teach others compassion, and the ability to sit patiently with someone else's pain without trying to fix it.

At the end of the evening session, I sensed that we had done all the work we could do for one day. I turned off the lights in the room and we sat in silence, watching snowflakes drift out of the dark sky, swirl by the windows, and land lightly on the frozen lake. Something about the soft darkness, the silent settling of the snow, and the warmth of our little community allowed us to drop our defenses. A sense of deep peace gathered in the room. It was as if we had become one breathing organism, and together we were releasing a deep sigh. The angry woman began to cry. I knew this was good. I knew she needed to spin her anger into grief before any healing could begin. I said nothing, enjoying the grace of human beings allowing themselves to put down their burdens and just be.

When I turned the lights back on, an elderly woman who had said little during the workshop's first two days rose and raised her hand, as if she were in grade school. She had a refined and almost translucent face and was dressed in a tailored blue wool suit, in contrast to the sweatpants and T-shirts most people were wearing. Her hair was tied in a soft silver bun at the back of her neck, and she was wearing a string of pearls. I sensed that the workshop angel had arrived.

"May I say something, dear?" she asked me.

"Of course," I said.

"I am ninety-two years old." she chuckled. Everyone gasped. She was such an elegant and energetic woman—that no one would have correctly guessed her age.

"I am speaking to all of you, but especially to you," she said with great warmth, acknowledging the angry woman, who was seated across the circle. "I've had a life of adventures and a life of losses. I've lost two husbands and a son. But at ninety-two, as hard as I try, I can't find anything to be unhappy about! I know now that all of my difficulties made me who I am supposed to be."

Now she leaned forward and looked straight at the angry woman. "Do you know the poet Rainer Maria Rilke, dear? He wrote a poem that ends like this: 'In the difficult are the friendly forces, the hands that work on us.' Isn't that wonderful? Our problems are friendly! They are like hands that want to work on us. They want to make us strong. They certainly worked on me! Now, even though I am an old woman, I am stronger than ever. Every day I wake up grateful just to be alive. I can do whatever I want. I can watch birds at the feeder, or be with friends, or read, or do nothing at all. I have nothing to complain about. Nowhere to go, nothing to get. Nothing bothers me. I want to tell you, my dear, that if you get to my age, all of your problems will seem like old friends. I promise you."

No one said a word as the woman sat back down in her chair. We were touched by her sudden gift. Some people smiled, and some had tears in their eyes, but the angry woman was unmoved. After a period of silence, she turned on the elegant old lady and demanded, "So, you mean I have to wait fifty years before I'm happy?"

"Ah, my dear," said the workshop angel. "Don't worry. They will be the fastest fifty years of your life."

When Grapes Turn to Wine

*When grapes turn
to wine, they long for our ability to change.
When stars wheel
around the North Pole,
they are longing for our growing consciousness.*
—RUMI

My son Daniel goes to college in Santa Fe, New Mexico. When I visit him, I stay with a friend—an American Zen teacher who lives in an impeccably beautiful monastery in the hills above town. Santa Fe is a notoriously enchanting place. It sits at 7,000 feet, surrounded by the higher peaks of the Sangre de Cristo and Jemez ranges in the Southern Rockies. When D. H. Lawrence saw Santa Fe for the first time, he said, "Something stood still in my soul."

I live a double life when I visit my son in Santa Fe. At my friend's Zen center I stay in a little monk's cell, in an old adobe building off to the side of the spotless meditation hall. I arise early and join the monks and residents for an hour or two of *zazen,* the Japanese word for sitting meditation. I watch my breath, empty my mind, and wait for those moments in meditation when something stands still in the soul. Then I eat a silent breakfast with the monks, wash my wooden bowl, bow to the Buddha, and leave for the day.

I pick up my son at his funky house in town, with its decidedly non-Zen college decor, and go with him to the campus. There, I sit in on a class or two and relax on the quad amidst the noise and squalor of college students. While the purpose of Zen meditation is stillness and emptiness, the purpose of going to college is to fill each day and night with as much activity as possible. When in Rome, do as the Romans do, they say. At the Zen center I slow down and empty out; at my son's school I speed up and fill my cup to the brim. The two seem to cancel each other out. I always leave Santa Fe with a roguish feeling—as if I have eaten rich chocolate every night but never gained weight.

During my most recent visit, it was springtime, and the high desert was suddenly green and alive. The lilacs were blooming all along Canyon Road, and the normally dry creek beds were running swiftly with the melting snow from the mountains. During the morning, in the meditation hall, sunlight streamed through the thin, clear air, and warm breezes carried in wafts of lilac to mingle with the Japanese incense. After Zen practice, before going to see my son, I stood outside in the strong sun and watched little desert flowers—pink and white and yellow—blooming in the cracks of the adobe buildings. The place was perfectly peaceful and quiet, except for the swishing sounds of a couple of monks, sweeping the paths in their crisp, black robes.

Up at the college, it was graduation week. Finals were over, and the kids were gearing up for major partying. There was an air of wildness and general disorder that contrasted sharply with the Zen center. As the week went on, I began to skip the early morning meditations, because each night I came back later and later. I felt like a kid, sneaking home when the rest of the family was sleeping. One evening I went with my son and his friends to the movies, then out to dinner, and later to a bar, where I had two beers. Combined with the air and altitude of the high desert, the alcohol went straight to my head. I was already in an altered state of mind, brought on by a diet of meditation, spiked with the enchantment of Santa Fe and the love I felt for my son and his friends. When I left the bar I couldn't figure out if I was drunk or sober, in a trance or as clear as the crystalline New Mexico night.

Driving home at about fifteen miles an hour, I kept the windows wide open and breathed deeply of the night sky. The sky in New Mexico is something that Easterners never get used to: It is huge, clear, and close; at night the stars seem near enough to be plucked and pocketed. Poking my way up the mountain to the monastery, and then down the long dirt driveway, I thanked God for the fullness of my life—for its order and disorder, its heights and craters, its plodding difficulties and its flashes of magic. I felt suspended between the poles—free suddenly of distinctions and differences. There was no good or bad, happy or sad, loud or silent, empty or full. Was I drunk or enlightened? It didn't even matter.

When I pulled into the parking lot, it was way past midnight. The Zen center was dark and silent. I opened the car door, made it to a stone wall, and simply sat there. The little dog who lived at the center barked once and trotted over. He looked puzzled, as if he had never seen a human up this late. Monks go to sleep early, and drunken women who stay out past dark are not standard guests at the monastery. I patted the dog's head. He sighed and leaned quietly against my legs. A warm wind swished through the piñon trees high in the surrounding mountains, then fluttered in the willows that flanked the riverbed near the guest quarters. Coyotes cried in the distance.

I sat as if in meditation. With each out-breath I dissolved into the space between the glittering stars, and with each in-breath I opened my heart fully to the life force coursing through me—the same force that was driving the wind and warming the coat of the little dog. How funny to stumble upon this kind of peaceful awareness outside a meditation hall, where just hours earlier I had soldiered on in my lifelong pursuit of an open heart and a quiet mind. Now I was sitting with a dog on a stone wall, drunk in the middle of the night, blasted open to the sky, and held in the embrace of a vast silence. So this is what those crazy God-intoxicated mystics were talking about!

Rumi says:

> When grapes turn
> to wine, they long for our ability to change.
> When stars wheel
> around the North Pole,
> they are longing for our growing consciousness.
> Wine got drunk with us,
> not the other way.

Here I was, almost fifty years old, outside a Zen center at 2:00 A.M., as drunk as a coyote and as sober as a mountain. And in that moment, I realized that I had indeed made some progress on this thing we call the spiritual path. I had given in to the grapes and the stars. My deepest desire was the ability to change. If I'd learned anything from my descents and rebirths, it had been to trust the Phoenix Process. Having died a few times, and been reborn as many, I had faith now that whatever came my way was fuel for my growing consciousness.

In the distance, I heard the sound of wheels on the gravelly road, then saw car lights winding toward me. Out of the dark night, a yellow taxicab pulled up beside my car, and a Pakistani man with a white turban opened the driver's door and stepped out. In my drunkenness I wondered if this was a Woody Allen film. Had a New York cabbie followed me to Santa Fe?

"Excuse me, madame," the cabdriver said with a strong Pakistani accent, "but is this a Zen center?"

"Uh, yes it is," I answered, holding on to the barking little dog and pretending that it was perfectly normal for a cab to deliver a customer to a remote mountain monastery in the middle of the night.

"I have come from the Albuquerque airport to bring this young woman to your center. She has traveled all the way from Thailand today," said the cabdriver in a formal tone, as if he was announcing the arrival of royalty. "She says she has come here to study, but I told her that I would not leave her alone way up on the mountain so late at night. Therefore, I am glad you have stayed up to greet her. Now I will not fear to deliver her." And with that he went around to the passenger side of the cab, opened the front door, and helped out a tiny young woman. I stood up to greet her.

Speaking in faltering English, the young woman introduced herself and explained that she was spending the summer at the monastery before beginning her studies at the University of Virginia. A devotee of a Buddhist order in Thailand, she had met my friend the Zen teacher in Bangkok. Now she was here, in the southern Rocky Mountains. She had been traveling for thirty hours, across twelve time zones. It was the first time she had left her country, the first time she was away from her parents' house.

"I'll help her get settled," I told the cabbie, who still seemed worried about his passenger. He took the young woman's bags out of the trunk and shook her hand.

"Thank you," she said to him, holding on to his hand with both of hers. "My mother said not to worry because people have Buddha nature in every country. She said I find many people to take care of me in my travels. You are first person. Thank you."

"God bless you," the cabbie said solemnly, bowing his head. "And welcome to America."

The cab pulled out of the parking lot, and I helped the young woman lug her bags to the visitors' dormitory. On the dirt path, she stopped for a minute and looked up at the stars. "So big, American stars," she said. I figured I would wait until the morning to try to explain to her about the New Mexico sky, about the size of the United States, about the diversity of its land and people. I would wait till later, when she was rested, and I was sober, to tell her that she was a long way from Virginia, that New Mexico was not the same as New York, and that while her cabdriver did indeed demonstrate his Buddha nature, others would not. Or maybe I wouldn't tell her any of this. Maybe I would just let her figure it out for herself.

I helped the tired young woman find a bed, showed her the bathroom, and gave her a hug.

"You are second person," she said to me.

"Good night," I whispered. And then, thinking of the cabdriver and the poignant absurdity of it all, I added, "Welcome to America."

On the way back to my monk's cell, I quietly opened the tall wooden doors of the meditation hall and slipped inside. In the dimly lit room, I made the ritual bow to the Buddha statue and noticed his half smile, his round belly, his relaxed shoulders. His expression was so kind, as if he was saying, "There, there. Come. Sit and rest. You don't have to try so hard. You don't have to rush anything. Take a seat and see what happens."

And so I sat lightly on a cushion, mellow and happy, ripened and ready, like a grape turning into wine.

Ch-ch-Changes

Ch-ch-ch-ch-Changes
Turn and face the strain
Ch-ch-Changes
Oh, look out you rock 'n rollers . . .
Pretty soon you're gonna get a little older.
—DAVID BOWIE

Aging is not easy for anyone, but I think it is particularly unappealing to rock 'n' rollers. This is a story about a rock 'n' roller—me—who finally got it through her thick head that it was time to *turn and face the strain*. Only, up until I wrote this story, I thought David Bowie was singing, "turn and face the *strange*." For thirty years I would sing that line from the popular seventies song "Changes" whenever I confronted the strangeness of getting older. Now that I have checked the lyrics on the back of an old album, I see that what I had been up against all of those years—according to Bowie—was the *strain* of aging.

It's a good thing it took me this long to learn the real words, because it's only recently that aging has felt like a strain. Once my body started going through the big ch-ch-change, the word *strain* took on sudden relevance. *Strange* is discovering a gray hair when you're in your thirties and the rest of your body is still running on all cylinders. *Strain* is beginning to sound like your parents when you bend to pick something up.

Back when aging was more strange than strain, I met a family who would become part of my family, and who would move alongside me through all of our changes. Steven and Lila showed up one summer at the commune with their baby, Lorrie. They stayed for a year. Steven was a songwriter who looked like Jesus. He had big eyes, a long beard, and a striking face. Lila had long blond hair and a Southern accent that made everything she said sound as slow and sweet as honey dripping from a jar. She was one of the most beautiful women I had ever seen. Lorrie was as blond and beautiful as her mother. The sight of this family—a rock 'n' roll prophet, a blond goddess, and a little angel—turned people's heads.

Steven and Lila renovated a chicken coop near the big Shaker barn and lived there during the long winter I was pregnant with my first son. Sometimes when the baby's kicking woke me in the middle of the night, I would stand at the window of our room in the main Shaker building and gaze across the road to see smoke rising from the woodstove in Lila and Steven's little house. Just knowing they were there made me happy, as if they were long-lost relatives, as if the gypsy side of the family had moved home for a while. In the mornings, I would see them trudging up the hill through the snow to breakfast, looking like summer flowers that had bloomed in January.

And then, as suddenly as they had appeared, they left. It suited them, I thought, to travel around the world, to Europe and Afghanistan and India. I heard from them from time to time; we kept in touch through all of their moves and all of our changes. Years later they settled back down in my area, and we resumed our friendship as if no time had passed at all. By then, Lorrie was a teenager, and I had three sons. Steven and Lila had always wanted more kids but had never been able to conceive again. Then, within days of Lorrie leaving home for college, they discovered they were pregnant. By the time the new baby arrived, Lorrie would be twenty.

I was no longer a practicing midwife, but occasionally I coached people through the birth process. I agreed to do this for Steven and Lila, who—in true gypsy style—had decided to have their child at home. A few weeks before their due date, on an early spring evening, I came to their house and gave them a refresher class in labor and breathing. Lorrie was there, visiting from college.

Maybe it was the heavy breathing we did, or maybe just the suggestion of labor, but in the middle of that night I got a call from Steven telling me to come back; Lila was in labor. All births are miracles. I've never been blasé about witnessing a baby being born. But that night was especially infused with the spirit of the miraculous, as if we all had stepped off the earth and out of time, into a meteor shower of pure energy. Our ages suddenly meant very little—each one of us was just a different body, a different container, holding the same abundant life force. As the labor progressed, I could almost taste the freshness of that force; the house nearly quivered with it. I sensed how something sends new life at every chance it gets; how something wants us to know that life is eternal and good. I could feel this in the way Lorrie stroked her mother's hair as Lila bore down and pushed out her new baby girl; in the way little Kenna gulped for air and gazed with astonishment at the world; and in the way Steven cried and laughed at the same time as he took the baby from me and held her close.

A few years later, after she had finished college and gotten married, Lorrie called and asked if I would help her during the birth of *her* baby. Now this qualified as a ch-ch-change. Someone I had known as a baby was asking me to help her have one! How strange. I happily offered my services. Three weeks before the due date, I called Lorrie to set up a time to visit and practice labor breathing. Lorrie and I laughed, remembering what had happened to her mother after my visit.

"Are you ready to deliver this baby?" I asked. "My labor lessons have been known to have a certain effect on your family."

"Well," Lorrie said, in a tentative voice, "we still haven't painted the baby's room, but I guess I'm ready."

Now, I have been accused of ornamentation for the sake of a story's flow. But this is the airtight truth: A few hours after hanging up the phone, Lorrie went into labor. When I got to the hospital, the whole family was there: Lorrie, her husband, Steven, Lila, and little Kenna—as blond and beautiful as I remembered Lorrie to have been at that age. By then Lorrie had lost her sense of humor—a common side effect of labor—and didn't appreciate the laughter that welcomed me into the birthing room. "Here she is," Lila said to the doctor, "the troublemaker."

Hours later, after a long and hard labor, we brought Garrett into the world, and the first member of the family to hold him was his aunt Kenna.

They say that significant events come in threes, so when Lorrie became pregnant again, two years later, and asked me to coach her through labor, I reminded her of my track record with her family. I half-jokingly suggested that we stay away from each other during the pregnancy and that she call me only when she was good and ready to have her baby—the day before, or even the day after her due date! In fact, I was scheduled to be 2,500 miles away at a conference in Los Angeles two weeks before she was due. I wouldn't even be around to stir up trouble.

As Lorrie's baby grew slowly inside of her, through the summer and the fall, and into the winter, I went into a different type of gestation. To my surprise, I began to experience the early signs of menopause. It seemed shocking to me that I had arrived at this milestone. Wasn't it early? Although I knew statistically that some women begin the process in their forties, I thought it would be later for me, when I was older, when I was *old.* And certainly I thought (perhaps as all younger women think) I would sail through "the change." I was wrong on both counts. Menopause did begin in my forties, and it arrived with a vengeance. It derailed me; it took over my body and my mind. Every symptom I had heard about I got, until I was barely sleeping at night, waking up five or six times to change my sweaty shirt. During the day I was exhausted and depressed. I knew that my dark moods were caused by sleep deprivation and hormonal imbalance, but that didn't help. I sank deeper and deeper into a hopelessness that I hadn't felt since the years of B.D.—before the divorce; before the descent. Before the Phoenix Process.

You would think I would have recognized the signs of another Phoenix Process. You would think I would have known not to strain against the changes but to surrender to the flow of the river. You would think I would have realized that an old part of me was dying so that a new part could live. But I didn't want to admit that it was time for this rock 'n' roller to *turn and face the strain.* I had never associated David Bowie's "ch-ch-Changes" with this kind of change, yet the words to his song had never rung more true: *Pretty soon you're gonna get a little older,* he sang when I was a teenager. Well, pretty soon seemed to be now.

Each morning I woke up confused and afraid. What was going on with me, I wondered with alarm. Where was the zest that I had become accustomed to? Where was my faith in the meaningfulness of life? Why was I so depressed and anxious? Was it the terrorist attacks? Global warming? Was it that my children were spread out across the country? Had my marriage, or my work, or my writing sprung a leak?

All through that autumn and winter, through the terror and grief of September 11, and through the ongoing exhaustion of sleepless nights, I swam harder and harder against the changes happening within me, putting in long hours at work, finding temporary relief through herbal remedies, or exercise, or a couple of glasses of wine, and hoping that things would go back to normal soon enough.

Then, in the middle of the winter, I discovered a lump in my breast. For days I fingered it gingerly, telling myself it was nothing, pretending it wasn't there. Finally I went to the doctor, who didn't like what she felt and sent me to have a biopsy. Waiting for the results to come back, I felt strangely indifferent, as if I was already diagnosed and dead. And when the results did come back, and it wasn't cancer, and I was in the clear, I still felt dark and depressed.

Lorrie's due date approached. The day before I was to leave for Los Angeles, she called to ask me when I'd be returning and, in case I missed the birth, to remind her of a few important things: *How* do you recognize the signs of labor? *How* do you breathe during a contraction? What should she tell her two-year-old? We chatted for a while, and I told Lorrie to wait until I got back; I really wanted to help her through the birth. "Or"—I laughed—"you could have the baby tonight. I don't leave until noon tomorrow."

As if destiny had a sense of humor, at midnight Lila called to say that Lorrie's waters had broken and she was in labor. They were heading to the hospital. "This is unbelievable!" Lila said. "I guess three's a charm."

I dragged myself from bed, tired as usual, and headed out into the night. Driving through my empty town, I felt the mysterious power of the old road again: the midwife road, the birth road. I rushed straight through a red light, not a soul awake to care. I glided down the mountain highway and crossed the bridge over the Hudson. On the back route to the hospital, which twists through a state forest preserve, the moon was so bright that it illuminated stands of gnarly old oak and maple trees. Quite suddenly, as if falling from a tree, Dante's lines landed on my tongue, and I recited them aloud: *"In the middle of the journey of our life, I found myself within a dark woods, where the straight way was lost."* And then I understood what had been happening to me. Of course! I was in the middle again, in the darkness, in the woods. The straight way was lost; there was no going back; the new way would reveal itself when it was good and ready, when I had learned some new lessons, when I had surrendered to change and transformation.

I pulled the car over to the side of the road and shook my head. "Where have I been all these months?" I said aloud. "Why have I been fighting against change?" And just by asking the questions, I felt a veil lifting. I felt a thin shaft of hope break through the woods of my weariness. In all of those months, through September 11, and the scare with breast cancer, through long hours at work, and sleepless nights at home—I had been fighting the inevitability of change, what some would call the will of God.

Like an animal drinking fresh water after a drought, I dropped my head and began to pray. "Thy will be done, not mine," I whispered into the night. "Thy will, Lord, not mine." As I sat at the side of the road, I felt the tension of willfulness and worry melt away. I stepped to the side and gave way to something wiser than myself—to the mystery that knows the truth about the past, the freedom of the present, the route of the future. For a blessed moment, in the middle of the woods, I dropped the burden of my fearful will. I admitted that I had lost the straight way. I sat still, allowing God to take over. And once again I sensed, in the ash-strewn path, a way through, and a hand guiding me toward the light. Then I started up the car and headed to the hospital. From the woods to the path, from despair to hope, from death to birth.

Hours later I handed Kylie—pink and new—to her mother. As I watched her latch on to Lorrie's nipple and taste the first sweet milk, I realized that it's not always about survival, this life we are given; it's usually so much easier than that. It's about trusting the eternal life force that is flowing within us—letting that force lead the way through all of the inevitable changes we will face across the span of our time here on Earth. Before I left the hospital, I took Kylie in my arms and whispered into her tiny ear, "Thank you, little one, for bringing me out of the woods. And remember always, to trust in the changes, to trust God's will."

Now when I drive in the car and David Bowie's song comes on the radio, I sing along with confidence, and not only because I may be one of the few people in the world who knows the correct lyrics. I sing, *Ch-ch-Changes, turn and face the strain,* because I am trying to do just that. It works a lot better than fighting against the tide of life. So *look out you rock 'n rollers,* and everyone else, 'cause *pretty soon you're gonna get a little older.*

Comfortable with Uncertainty

After all of these years of being broken open by loss and love and life itself, I still resist the river of change. Whether it is something going on in my personal life, or at work, or in the world, I still instinctually tighten my grip when things feel out of my control. But that's okay. I'm used to the drill: Something I didn't want to happen, happens. I feel the resistance build within. I feel the pressure to control what is obviously out of my control. I become aware of what I'm doing—I become aware of the choice either to break down or to break open. I take a deep breath, uncoil my body, and stretch out on the river of change. Once again, I accept that life is uncertain—that the goal is not to become more certain about anything but to relax more into the mystery of not knowing what will come next. And then, miracle of miracles, out there in the deep and uncertain water, I come into a peaceful knowing—a faithful wisdom that surpasses control and certainty.

One of my favorite spiritual authors is the Tibetan Buddhist Pema Chödrön, whose book titles are so good that I don't even have to read the pages to remember to break open into the mystery. *Comfortable with Uncertainty* is one of Pema Chödrön's book titles that always helps me shed my anxiety and resistance. I glance at the cover and feel my jaw unlock and my shoulders move a few notches down from my ears. I remember that I not only have survived life's surprises before but I am better because of them.

Pema Chödrön learned about becoming comfortable with uncertainty from her teacher, the Tibetan master Chögyam Trungpa. His own life experience—the loss of his family, teachers, and country when the Chinese Communists conquered Tibet—broke him open so radically that being around him was an unsettling experience. During the years in which I studied with him, he provided little security or predictability for his students. He wasn't amiable or gentle or comforting. He was barely friendly. There was only his daring personality and his dignified bearing, which inspired me. I was humbled by his humor and his enormous faith. His ability to flow with the river—with style and grace—was extraordinary.

Trungpa did not teach people to pray for life to turn out a certain way. Instead, he encouraged his students to learn from the way life already was. He regarded everyday events as messages about reality. "Trust in those messages," he said. They are an accurate description of what came before and of what to do next. Don't fight with reality. Don't defend against it. Rather, read it like you would a newspaper. Read everything that happens to you and to others as pertinent news about the reality of being human, of being you.

Life in the world is full of pertinent news—not only news about Washington or Hollywood or the Middle East but also news about us. Everywhere we look we can find accurate information and useful statistics about our most personal behavior. In fact, there exists a brilliant feedback system that is working at all times, offering free information about how to—and how not to— function in our world. For every action we take, reality leaves little messages about its wisdom or folly.

Chögyam Trungpa describes the message system like this: If you take steps to accomplish something, that action will have a result—either failure or success. . . . Trust is knowing that there will be a message. When you trust in those messages, the reflections of the phenomenal world, the world begins to seem like a bank, or reservoir, of richness. You feel that you are living in a rich world, one that never runs out of messages. . . . Those messages are regarded neither as punishment nor as congratulations. You trust, not in success, but in reality.

I try to apply Trungpa's wisdom especially when I am at work and nothing seems to be flowing easily. The meeting that is turning acrimonious, the project that is failing, or the assistant who is moving on: Each of these situations is a reservoir of meaning, a bank of rich information. The answer to every problem is already wrapped in the problem itself. I need only stop resisting, open wide to reality, and decode the message.

For Hugo

I live in a small town. Friends who live in cities are horrified by the way everyone seems to know everyone else's business here. Granted, occasionally things can seem a little inbred: So-and-so used to be married to so-and-so; the guy who works at the gas station also sits on the town board; my doctor is the father of my son's friend. But I like the closeness of it all. Some of the values of earlier days are still intact. I still know my neighbors. I bump into friends whenever I go to town. We are a close-knit community that celebrates holidays together, and we try to help each other when things get tough.

One night the phone rang just as my husband and I were leaving the house to go out to dinner. It was my best friend calling to tell us that Hugo—the young son of a family we know and love—had been diagnosed earlier in the day with leukemia. The more serious kind of leukemia—AML—the most difficult kind to treat. The doctors could say only that Hugo would enter the hospital the next day and begin months of chemotherapy. He would have a bone marrow transplant if a match could be found and, they hoped, a long and healthy life when he went into remission and it held.

Hugo is only ten years old. His family has already faced an unusual amount of loss and difficulty. His stepmother is one of my oldest friends. His father is the kind of man who lives and breathes for his children. While I don't know his mother well, I do know what it is like to be the mother of a ten-year-old boy. I know how little distinction there is between the life of a child and the life of a mother, a father, a sibling, a family.

After receiving the news about Hugo, my husband and I went to dinner at a local restaurant where we often know so many people that, depending on one's mood, the social scene can seem like an imposition or a party. That night we bumped into some new friends, a couple who had just moved to town. It was a fortuitous encounter. Although they did not know the family, Maria and Roger knew the emotions all too well. Maria had lost her four-year-old daughter, Hannah, to cancer a few years earlier. She wrote a book about the ordeal—*Hannah's Gift*—that became a bible of sorts for other parents going through the illness or loss of a child. We sat down at a table together. Maria talked about what it was like when she first found out about Hannah's illness, and we listened with a new sense of urgency.

Sometime between the wine and the salad, I looked up from our conversation. My eyes wandered across the floor of the restaurant. And there they were—the family, the whole family: Hugo and his brother, his father and mother, and his stepmother and her two little girls.

"Oh, my God," I said to my husband. "Look who's over there."

We turned. They saw us and waved halfheartedly, almost apologetically.

"You have to go over to them," said Maria, practically pulling the chair out from under me.

"What should we say?" I asked, knowing full well that there was no answer to that question.

"Just show up," said Maria.

We went to the long table by the restaurant's fireplace, where I had sat so many times at birthday parties and other gatherings. The adults at the table looked like children—teary and scared. The children looked like adults—somber and serious. We hugged our friends and they cried. We hugged the children and they were suddenly shy. Hugo stoically showed me the intravenous port on his arm where they had taken blood that morning. Later that port would be replaced by a chest port, through which chemotherapy and blood transfusions would be pumped. Later a horrible mistake would be made and the port would leak chemotherapy into his lungs. Later Hugo would undergo emergency surgery to save his life from that mistake. Later he would be rushed in an ambulance from one hospital to another, where he would remain for months and months, hanging on to life, healing, having more surgeries, and finally going into remission. But at that moment Hugo knew nothing of the trials ahead of him.

"What are you thinking about, Hugo?" I asked.

"I don't want to think about anything," he said.

Children don't project far into the future, nor do they dwell in the distant past. Tonight he didn't want to think about being sick, or the fact that his family was scared, or that his life was suddenly different. I tried to chat with him about his dance recital, which he would now miss, and about school and friends. Hugo, who is a talented dancer, with a passion for any form of movement, from ballet to hip-hop, normally would have wanted to talk about his dance class, a performance he had seen, or an upcoming recital. But tonight he said little. So I stopped talking and just sat there with my arm around him. I did what Maria told me to do: I just showed up.

In the absence of small talk, as we sat in the fresh wound of Hugo's diagnosis, something I can only call a sacred presence wrapped its atmospheric arms around the table. I could almost see the presence sitting in the corner, quietly tapping its foot to a majestic rhythm. It was as if, because we were showing up, God could show up too—not the severe and judgmental God of tired religions but the God that children know about, the God that the Sufi poet Hafiz writes about:

> Not the God of names,
> Nor the God of don'ts,
> Nor the God who ever does
> Anything weird,
> But the God who only knows four words
> And keeps repeating them, saying:
> "Come dance with Me."

Hugo had a new dance partner. His illness would demand he learn challenging steps. But I knew that Hugo was up to it. He was an experienced dancer. He knew when to lead and when to follow, how to listen to his body's inner rhythms, and how to train for the long haul. He would have to practice diligently over the next months, and so would his family. His mother and father had some difficult dance steps of their own to learn—as individuals and as partners in a new dance. Could they bear the pain of seeing their child suffer? Could their hearts stay soft and open? Could they have faith in God's choreography, even when it seemed so clumsy and cruel? Could they leave behind their contentious roles of ex-wife and ex-husband and join forces as Hugo's parents—the two people who loved him most?

I felt then, at the table, that if everyone in Hugo's family could remember in the months to come the dancing God who'd joined them in the restaurant that night, then all would be well. No matter what the outcome, all would be well if they took their direction from *the God who only knows four words, and keeps repeating them, saying: "Come dance with Me."*

The dancing God is always with us, but often it takes a calamity to make room for him at the table. And when he shows up, we suddenly understand what the prophets and saints have been talking about for thousands of years. Suddenly we are part of what we have only heard tell of before—a love that lives on when all else has died; a love that links us together across boundaries of time and space. I saw that right after September 11 in New York City. I felt that when my father died. I was sensing that now, as my friends experienced the suffering of their child. I saw them standing naked and humble before the altar of the most unaffected kind of human love. I could practically see the "cracks in their Egos," as Ram Dass would say, allowing them to regard each other with the eyes of the dancing God.

There was no telling how long this bigger perspective would last, but for the moment they all seemed to know something that God knows: that we are sent here to love each other and to help each other—that our lives are about each other. All of our other plans fly out the window in such moments of awakening. Plans for great things are replaced by the greatest thing of all, which turns out to be love, in its simplest, most tender, most personal form.

Why is it that the cracks in the ego fill back in? Why do awakened hearts go back to sleep? Why is it so hard to sustain the wisdom and joy that visit us in times of heightened loss and love? For a while after September 11, it seemed that New Yorkers would never lose their generosity and kindness. After my father died, I felt nothing but gratitude for the people closest to me. That night in the restaurant, the sweetness of the connection among all those in Hugo's family was so palpable that we could have scooped it up and served it as a cosmic aphrodisiac to the whole room. After one bite, there would be no doubt as to the purpose of life. We'd stop messing around and get down to the business of loving each other.

So much of what we do each day is a diversion from what our lives are really about. A traumatic event is like a knife slicing through our diversionary tactics and exposing the vein of truth—the truth of what we really want, of how we really feel, of the wrongs we have visited upon each other, of the love we crave from each other. In our habitual lives, we exercise the foolish luxuries of complaining, avoiding, and blaming. We gossip about the annoying behavior of friends or colleagues, shutting them out of our hearts, turning our backs on their complicated beauty in favor of their obvious flaws. It seems easier to do this than to move toward each other, to take responsibility when it is ours to take, or to speak directly to others when it is theirs. All the while, the truth waits patiently, until it shows up in the eyes of a frightened little boy.

Hugo's illness would slice through the diversions of everyone in his life—his family, his friends, his teachers. Some would allow themselves to feel the wound; some would examine what was being brought to the surface; some would be broken open and indelibly changed. Others would turn away, close down, and choose new diversions. My prayer that night at the restaurant table was not only for Hugo's healing. It was also for his family's healing, his community's healing. I prayed to the dancing God for Hugo's illness not to be wasted, but for all of us to break open into greater capacities for loving and learning.

A couple of months after Hugo's diagnosis, I spent a morning with his father. Home for a few days from his vigil at the hospital, Ron was like a long-distance runner, taking a brief break in the middle of a marathon. Hugo's treatment to date had been grueling. He had almost died on several occasions, experienced wrenching pain from his burned lungs and nausea from the chemotherapy treatments. He had lost his hair and his physical strength. Now he was in New York City, in one of the country's best cancer hospitals, and was slowly healing. Throughout his struggles Hugo had dipped in and out of terror and depression—at one point asking his father if "they put people to sleep like they do when pets are in too much pain." But his dancer's joie de vivre had pulled him through the roughest times. When he finally allowed himself to believe that he would survive, he turned his attention to helping other children in the pediatric cancer ward, talking to them when they were down, helping them get through painful procedures.

What was his father learning? I wondered. What was changing in this man who had used his formidable will to overcome a difficult childhood? This man who had carved a highly successful path through an obstacle course of problems in his adult life?

"I think maybe I am softening a bit," Ron said to me. This was no small admission for a man who worked on Wall Street and had the stamina of a prize-fighter. "Many things, like my work and the kids' school, have taken on less importance as a result of living with Hugo's life-and-death struggle. I have become much more aware of the pain and suffering all around me. I am feeling the pain of others more acutely—I guess it's called compassion. My awareness has broadened from what I have been exposed to at the hospital—so many children and parents, so much suffering, more than I ever could have imagined. I don't know where this experience will lead me. I know I am inalterably changed."

He took a long pause, and I watched his face crumble as he reached back into the early memories of his son's illness. "I'll never forget that night when Hugo almost died," he said. "I was in bed with him, holding him, and he looked at me and said, 'I'm dying. Good-bye, Daddy.' At that moment his blood pressure dropped, he went into shock, and I felt him slipping away. And suddenly, it was as if the clouds parted in my dense brain. I knew then that none of my plans for anything mattered. I didn't care anymore if Hugo became a great dancer, or if I prevailed at work, or anything. I just wanted to really be there for the people in my life. I wanted to drive Hugo to school, to ride bikes with Jacob, to play with my girls, to be a family. All of my *ideas* about life meant nothing; the experience of being alive with those that I loved—that meant everything. I know I will never forget that moment. I hope it will be what motivates me in life from now on."

Thomas Merton, the Trappist monk and social activist, once said that as he grew older he came to understand that it was not ideas that change the world but simple gestures of love given to the people around you, and often to those you feel most at odds with. He said that in order to save the world you must serve the people in your life. "You gradually struggle less and less for an idea," Merton wrote, "and more and more for specific people. In the end, it is the reality of personal relationship that saves everything."

I have heard there is a difference between cure and healing—that a cure cannot always be found, whereas healing is always possible. I don't know if a child of Hugo's age can really fathom what he is up against, or what his family is going through. But I do know how much he is healed by their devotion, and how he is uplifted by the kindness they show him and each other, even when they are stressed and distraught. I know that if they can continue to say *Yes!* as the dancing God leads them in and out of difficult territory, they and Hugo will discover what healing is really about and what makes a life worth living.

Peaceful Abiding

I have met a fair share of famous people through my work. Some have become my friends. Having famous friends has taught me a solid lesson: I know that fame and fortune cannot alter the inner landscape of a human heart. Despite what our cultural illusions about celebrity lead us to believe, the roots of suffering and joy remain untouched by one's public image and bank account. Famous people are no different from you and me, except that they can't go anywhere on a bad hair day, especially in Los Angeles, where one of my most famous friends lives in a beautiful house on the ocean.

One morning when my husband and I were visiting, I sat at my friend's computer, checking my e-mail. I noticed a passage from a Buddhist sutra tacked to his bulletin board:

> *Unceasing change turns the wheel of life,*
> *and so reality is shown in all its many forms.*
> *Dwell peacefully as change itself*
> *liberates all suffering sentient beings*
> *and brings them great joy.*

Looking out of the floor-to-ceiling windows at the Pacific Ocean stretching to the west, I regarded the unceasing churning of the water—the wheel of life turning the waves over and over. Swiveling around in my friend's desk chair and gazing to the east, toward downtown Los Angeles, I noticed unceasing change in the form of human "progress"—the slow and steady gobbling up of the land and spitting out of condominiums and highways. Inside my head, reactions to the waves to the west and the development to the east joined the unceasing movement of the wheel of life. I turned back to the sutra. *Unceasing change turns the wheel of life, and so reality is shown in all its many forms.* My opinions, the ocean, the action of human beings: reality in all its many forms. The sutra says to dwell peacefully with all of these patterns of change, and to have faith that the unceasing turning of the wheel is spinning us all toward greater wisdom and joy.

Once, years previously, I had helped my friend through a difficult divorce. His type A personality had temporarily melted into a puddle of helplessness. Suffering—the great equalizer—had left him naked, stripped of his worldly identity. He was just a man, a man who was suffering. That experience broke my friend open. He found through his suffering a deeper connection to his friends, his children, and his own feeling heart. His story reminds me of the story of another man—a man who also had been isolated by his fame and fortune, and whose confrontation with suffering forged a path that millions have followed for more than two thousand years. That man was Siddhartha Gautama, a prince of India's ruling class who became the Buddha—the awakened one.

The author Aaron Shepard retells the legend of the Buddha in this story, "The Prince Who Had Everything":

In the royal city of Kapilavatthu, a son had come to the great King Suddhodana and his lovely Queen Maya. They named the boy Siddhartha, which means "He Who Reaches His Goal." Soon after the birth, the king was visited by a great seer named Asita. The baby was brought for him to see. To the king's alarm, the holy man burst into tears.

"Sir, what is wrong?" asked the king. "Do you foresee some disaster for my son?"

"Not at all," said the seer. "His future is supreme. Your son shall become a Buddha, an Enlightened One, and free the world from its bonds of illusion. I weep only for myself, for I will not live to hear his teachings."

Now, the king was distressed that his only heir might turn to a life of religion. He called upon eight Brahmin priests, all skilled in interpreting signs, and asked them to prophesy for the prince.

When the priests had conferred, their spokesman addressed the king. "Your Majesty, if your son follows in your footsteps, he will become a Universal King and rule the known world. But if he renounces home and family for the life of a seeker, he will become a Buddha and save the world from its ignorance and folly."

The king asked, "What would cause my son to renounce home and family?"

The priest answered, "Seeing the four signs."

"And what are the four?"

"An old man, a sick man, a dead man, and a holy man."

"Then none of these shall he see," the king declared. And he placed guards around the palace to keep all such persons away.

As Siddhartha grew to manhood, the king sought ways to strengthen the prince's ties to home. He married him to the lovely Princess Yasodhara, who in time bore a son. And he surrounded him with dancing girls to while away his hours.

The prince became a creature of pleasure and seldom left his luxurious apartments in the palace's upper stories.

But one day Siddhartha thought he would visit a park outside the city. The king arranged the outing, with strict orders to his guards to keep the road clear of the old, the sick, the dead, and the holy.

As the prince passed through the city in his royal carriage, people lined the road to admire him. The guards followed the king's orders as best they could. But even so, the prince spied in the crowd a man with gray hair, weak limbs, and bent back.

"Driver," said Siddhartha, "what is wrong with that man?"

"He is old, my lord."

"And what is 'old'?" asked the prince.

" 'Old' is when you have lived many years."

"And will I too become 'old'?"

"Yes, my lord. To grow old is our common fate."

"If all must face old age," said the prince, "then how can we take joy in youth?"

Not long after, the prince spied a man yellow-faced and shaking, leaning on a companion for support. "Driver, what is wrong with that man?"

"He is sick, my lord."

"And what is 'sick'?"

" 'Sick' is when your health has left you."

"And will I too become 'sick'?"

"It is likely, my lord. To be sick is our common fate."

"If all must face sickness," said the prince, "then how can we take pride in health?"

Before long, the prince spied a stiff, motionless man being carried along by four others.

"Driver, what is wrong with that man?"

"He has died, my lord."

"And what is 'die'?"

" 'Die' is when your life is finished."

"And will I too 'die'?"

"You will, my lord, without a doubt. Of all our fates, death is the most certain."

"If all must face death," said the prince, "then how can we delight in life?"

At last the prince spied a man with shaved head and saffron robe.

"Driver, what is that man?"

"He is a seeker, my lord."

"And what is a 'seeker'?"

"A 'seeker' is one who renounces home and family to wander about, living on what he begs. Avoiding pleasure, he subdues the passions; meditating, he controls the mind. And so he strives for freedom from this world of tears and the endless round of rebirths."

"Driver, return to the palace. No more do I care for parks or pleasure or anything that may pass away. Soon I too will be a seeker, renouncing this life that binds me."

That very night, Siddhartha slipped into the women's quarters for one last look at his sleeping wife and son. Then quietly he descended to the courtyard, mounted a white steed, and set out.

The city gate, too heavy for a single man, swung open by itself at his approach. And as the prince passed through, he made this vow:

"Never shall I enter this city again, till I've seen the farther shore of life and death."

Siddhartha then went into the wilderness, where he spent six years as a monk, fasting and praying, meditating and searching, until he saw "the farther shore of life and death." What he found there was the ability to dwell peacefully in this life, even with its promise of aging, sickness, and death. He discovered his eternal self—a self that was neither a famous prince nor a humble monk. He became the awakened one, the Buddha.

His teachings have been passed down through the ages. The one that found its way to the bulletin board above my friend's desk is now tacked on the wall in my office. I look at it every now and then. Sometimes I nod my head in agreement, and realize that I have indeed been dwelling peacefully with change in all of its many forms. On those days, I pat myself on the back and feel grateful for the rare and fleeting experience of liberation.

On other days, the sutra startles me, as if I am reading it for the first time. Then I realize that I have been running against the wheel of life—like when I was a kid in a department store and my sisters and I would run down an up escalator for that disorienting feeling of moving fast but getting nowhere. When that happens, I do a mini-version of what the Buddha did. For a few minutes, I close my eyes and slow my pace. Whatever is happening, whatever is changing, whatever is going or not going according to my plans—I release my hold on all of it. I leave behind who I think I am, who I want to be, what I want the world to be. I come home to the great peace of the present moment, to the wide-open wonder of my Buddha nature.

The Truth

MAN: *Doc, my brother's crazy. He thinks he's a chicken.*
PSYCHIATRIST: *Well, why don't you turn him in?*
MAN: *I would, but I need the eggs.*
—WOODY ALLEN

It is often easier to remain stuck in old behaviors and mind-sets even when they no longer serve us, even when they make us miserable. Like animals that won't leave their cages when the doors have been opened, we're more comfortable with what we know. We get attached to the way things are, no matter how ridiculous or destructive they've become. We may know that a change is long overdue, but as Woody Allen says, we need the eggs. We're trapped by our own version of reality; we're afraid of confronting the truth. We want to keep the illusions in place.

All of us could rewrite Woody Allen's joke to be about ourselves. We don't want to look too closely at the way we interpret our lives and the other people in them. We don't want to consider that perhaps we're wrong about a couple of things: perhaps our victim stance is a cover-up; maybe our ex or our boss or our parent is not the monster we've made them out to be. Maybe we need to ask ourselves, What's in it for us to keep seeing the world in a certain light? What eggs do we think we need?

In order to change habits and attitudes garnered over a lifetime, we must want something more than the eggs. We must long for the truth. We must pay attention to the voice that calls us out of the safety zone; we must be willing to lose what stands in the way of the true self. We must give up the eggs.

Life sends all sorts of foxes to raid the henhouse and steal the eggs. I try to look at the problems that come my way as opportunities to give up my illusions about myself and about life here on planet Earth. I try to welcome the fox into the henhouse; I try to surrender the eggs willingly. Usually I hold on to them and fight off the fox for a while. Sometimes my problems have to clonk me on the head until I see the stars of truth.

I am not suggesting that everything bad that happens to us is sent directly by a knowing hand—cooked up specially for our personal development. Nor do I mean that by using the stuff of life as grist for the mill you will learn what you need to learn and move on into a problem-free world. And I also don't recommend courting drama and disaster so that you can be broken open to the truth. A catastrophe is not a sign that God has singled you out for greatness.

What I do mean is that you can use anything—everything—as a wake-up call; you can find a treasure trove of information about yourself and the world in the big trials and the little annoyances of daily life. If you turn around and face *yourself* in times of loss and pain, you will be given the key to a more truthful—and therefore a more joyful—life.

Adversity is a natural part of being human. It is the height of arrogance to prescribe a moral code or health regime or spiritual practice as an amulet to keep things from falling apart. Things *do* fall apart. It is in their nature to do so. When we try to protect ourselves from the inevitability of change, we are not listening to the soul. We are listening to our fear of life and death, our lack of faith, our smaller ego's will to prevail. To listen to the soul is to stop fighting with life—to stop fighting when things fall apart; when they don't go our way, when we get sick, when we are betrayed or mistreated or misunderstood. To listen to the soul is to slow down, to feel deeply, to see ourselves clearly, to surrender to discomfort and uncertainty, and to wait.

It is in times of brokenness that the soul sings its most wise and eternal song. I cannot hum you a tune or tell you the lyrics; each person's soul has its own cadence. You will recognize its music, though, by the way you feel when you are listening: awake, calm, and suddenly relieved of the burden of control. You will take a big breath, you'll sigh and say to yourself, "It's okay. Everything's okay." You'll unfold your arms and lean back, and say to the soul, "Just sing me your song. Teach me the words. Tell me what you know."

And sometimes, in those moments of surrender, you will get to see how much you are like the man in Woody Allen's joke—how much you get from staying stuck in the way you see yourself and other people; how much you have invested in making someone else wrong so that you don't have to accept your own culpability; how you idolize others so that you don't have to claim your own power, take a stand, be your most noble and radiant self. Woody Allen's character knew his brother wasn't a chicken, but he still needed the eggs. You may know something true about yourself, but you protect the henhouse nonetheless. It's when you let the fox steal the eggs that you're left with the truth of who you really are. And who you really are is worth so much more than those imaginary eggs.

Epilogue

Drum sounds rise on the air,

and with them, my heart.

A voice inside the beat says,

I know you are tired,

but come.

This is the way.

—RUMI

Yesterday was my fiftieth birthday. Today a present arrives from my sisters. My sisters love me with undying devotion and a biting sense of humor. They have been my best friends my whole life, and the first to take potshots at every phase I have gone through. Their respect for who I am is boundless, even though they've been making fun of my spiritual nature since we were kids. When we were in elementary school and I naïvely read them my early stabs at poetry, they laughed hysterically. They overacted piety at funeral ceremonies I created for dead pets in the neighborhood and rolled their eyes when I asked my mother if I could convert to Catholicism. And when I joined the commune, and started Omega, and wrote a book, there they were, cheering me on as they snickered in the background. This is sister love.

The UPS man hauls a big box from his truck to my front door. I read the card before I open the box: "Happy Birthday. We found this little 'spirit house' for our little fifty-year-old spirit sister. We hope you love it as much as we love you."

A spirit house! I had seen these when traveling in Thailand—tiny temples perched high up on poles in every family's yard or garden. Thai Buddhists believe that spirit houses provide appealing shelter for heavenly deities who protect and bless the family. Protection and blessings: Who wouldn't want them safely tucked into a little house, keeping watch in the garden? I open the box carefully. There, surrounded by plastic packing bubbles, is an exquisite ceramic spirit house, shattered into pieces.

A broken spirit house. I have to laugh. I have spent the year finishing this book—a book about finding protection and blessings in the broken moments of our lives. I have told stories of blessings that come disguised as mess and di-

saster, not as cute houses secured in sunny gardens. I know that there is no tal-
isman to keep the evil spirits away, and that we wouldn't want to banish the
bad times even if we could. I trust that the darkness teaches us and leads us
toward the light. I know that we are protected most by our own fearlessness as
we make our way through the shadowy forests and the beautiful gardens. Still,
it would have been nice to have that spirit house.

Instead, I have the shards. I keep them in a basket in my writing room.
They give me wise council; they remind me that, while I am never safe from
breaking, I am always protected by spirit.

Over and over, we are broken on the shore of life. Our stubborn egos are
knocked around, and our frightened hearts are broken open—not once, and
not in predictable patterns, but in surprising ways and for as long as we live.
The promise of being broken and the possibility of being opened are written
into the contract of human life. Certainly this tumultuous journey on the
waves can be tiresome. When the sea is rough, and when we are suffering, we
may want to give up hope and give in to despair. But brave pilgrims have gone
before us. They tell us to venture forth with faith and vision. Rumi speaks for
them all when he says:

> Drum sounds rise on the air,
> and with them, my heart.
> A voice inside the beat says,
> I know you are tired,
> but come.
> This is the way.

May you listen to the voice within the beat even when you are tired. When
you feel yourself breaking down, may you break open instead. May every experience in life be a door that opens your heart, expands your understanding,
and leads you to freedom. If you are weary, may you be aroused by passion and
purpose. If you are blameful and bitter, may you be sweetened by hope and
humor. If you are frightened, may you be emboldened by a big consciousness
far wiser than your fear. If you are lonely, may you find love, may you find
friendship. If you are lost, may you understand that we are all lost, and still we
are guided—by Strange Angels and Sleeping Giants, by our better and kinder
natures, by the vibrant voice within the beat. May you follow that voice, for
This is the way—the hero's journey, the life worth living, the reason we are here.

Toolbox

EVERYTHING CAN CHANGE IN A MOMENT; we have little control over the outer weather patterns as we make our way through the landscape of a life. But we can become masters of the inner landscape. We can use what happens on the outside to change the way we function on the inside. This is the moral of the great teaching myths. The hero conquers a monster; the heroine completes a quest; the reward at the end was there all along—the true self, the awakened consciousness. Joseph Campbell said, "What all myths have to deal with is transformations of consciousness. You have been thinking one way, you now have to think a different way. Consciousness is transformed either by the trials themselves or by illuminating revelations. Trials and revelations are what it's all about."

When we have been through a trial and survived it—or better still, transformed its terrors into revelations—then we begin to approach other adversities with a different attitude. Change and loss may still knock us off the horse, but soon we are back in the saddle, stronger and wiser than ever. As life progresses, and we continue to transform and refine our consciousness, we gain more insight and humility, greater strength of character, and deeper faith in the meaningfulness of life.

But how do we do this? How do we transform terror into revelations? How do we stay sane and courageous in the midst of a trial? Throughout this book I have described the process of transformation as a journey of brokenness leading to openness, descent to rebirth, fire to Phoenix. Difficult journeys are best taken in a sturdy vehicle, or at least with a trusty guide and a helpful toolbox. In this appendix, I offer a toolbox of practices that have helped me on my journeys of descent and rebirth.

The practices I use most often to stay on track during a Phoenix Process are meditation, psychotherapy, and prayer. These tools continually encourage me to keep my heart open and my mind awake when I would prefer to shut down or go back to sleep. The practice of meditation has helped me develop a steady heart and a less reactive and agitated mind. Psychotherapy has opened me to an inner world of cause and effect. At a critical time in my life, it pushed me to take responsibility for my own happiness—to stop waiting for that elusive someone or something to mend and define my life. Prayer gives me solace and strength; it is a reassuring companion on the road. Together, these tools have helped me become an alchemist. They have shown me how to transmute pain into growth.

Other tools have helped me as well. Storytelling in group settings is one of my favorites. Telling our story helps us feel connected to others as we go through difficult times. When we sit with fellow wayfarers, sharing our trials and revelations and listening to theirs, our struggles seem less like personal vendettas and more like myths in the making. Writing in a journal is another tool that I use. It is often easier for me to be honest with myself in the privacy of the written word. All sorts of artistic pursuits, like writing or painting or singing, are alchemical. Physical exercise and movement—including sports and yoga and martial arts—are also basic to transformation. They keep us strong and lively; they bring our revelations all the way down into the body.

But the tools that I come back to most consistently, and the ones that I am best able to describe here, are meditation, psychotherapy, and prayer. I may have come through many of my dark nights without them, but I do not think I would have done so as quickly, or as fully, or with as much good humor.

Sometimes these tools—especially meditation and therapy—seem tedious and boring; at other times they can be intimidating and challenging. We may want to give up. But the hard work demanded by a Phoenix Process, and the courage required to break open and stay open, are worth every moment of struggle. The payoff is enormous: We come into the liberating presence of our authentic self.

The meditative, psychological, and sacred practices I offer here cannot be learned just from reading a book. They are best done with a teacher or therapist, and they may take several years of practice to bear fruit. Please use the brief instructions here to introduce you to a method that you can develop more fully in your everyday life, or to inspire you to revive an ongoing practice.

MEDITATION

I have been a student and practitioner of meditation for thirty years. I still find it difficult—at times boring and at other times confrontational. And I still find it valuable—nourishing, expansive, and illuminating. Sometimes I meditate every day; sometimes I go months without ever sitting on my meditation cushion. I have taken short meditation courses and spent most of my time waiting for the evening or weekend to be over. And I have gone on long, solitary retreats and surrendered to the practice, emptying myself of worry, falseness, restlessness, and complaints. Without hesitation, I can say that meditation practice has made a remarkable difference in my life.

People are attracted to meditation for a variety reasons, including these:

- to relax, physically and mentally;

- to keep the heart open and soft;

- to accept life on its own terms;

- to feel more alive, connected, and content;

- to find inner peace; and

- to make contact with other realms of consciousness, what some call the divine or God.

Meditation can help us achieve any of these—but only over time, and with dedication and work. We come to meditation feeling that parts of our life are difficult and that perhaps a meditation practice will make them less so. We want relief now. But that is not how meditation works. The desire for peace and happiness is noble; the expectation of instant results is unreasonable.

Meditation is a matter of slow and steady experience. It is not a cure. It is not a set of moral values. It is not a religion. It is a *way*—a way to be fully present, a way to be genuinely who we are, a way to look deeply at the nature of things, a way to rediscover the peace we already possess. It does not aim to get

rid of anything bad, or to create anything good. It is an attitude of openness.
The term for this attitude is *mindfulness*.

Buddhists call mindfulness meditation *maitri* practice. *Maitri* is often
translated as "unconditional friendliness." Meditation is the practice of unconditional friendliness toward whatever is happening in the moment—the
moment during which we sit in meditation, and all the other moments of life,
whether things are going well or falling apart. Meditation helps us find an internal witness with which to view external events. This might sound like a
small, easy matter, but it is not. In fact, discovering and developing an inner
witness may be the most important act of our life. Being able to observe ourselves honestly, with acceptance and friendliness, trains us to do the same with
others at home, at work, and in the world.

Mindfulness meditation trains us to be less reactive to whatever it is in life
that causes us suffering. It gives us an ability to experience our own pain without identifying fully with it, and therefore to be more free from it. Because of
that experience during meditation, we begin to fear life's pain less, to contract
around it less. We become more easygoing with ourselves. We still suffer, but
with much less of the dramatic flair that only adds to our suffering and makes
it overwhelming.

We may be drawn to practice out of suffering, but meditation is not just
for pain relief. It is also about joy. It is like a magnifying glass in the hands of a
child on a sunny day. He holds the glass steady; the light concentrates on a spot
on the ground; a dry leaf goes up in flame. Meditation can be a magnifying
glass that lights the fire of happiness in our hearts. All of the conditions for
happiness are available to us at any moment. Our job is to hold steady, to concentrate, and to allow our natural warmth to be released. Over time, mindfulness practice sensitizes our capacity for joy so much that even tiny physical and
emotional pleasures can bring great happiness. When our minds are quiet and
our hearts are strong, we see that the whole world is full of grace.

But how is this possible? How can sitting still teach us to relinquish suffering and embrace grace? The Buddha was reluctant to use words to answer
this question. Instead, he just said, "Come and see." Or, as my friend who is a
Jesuit priest says, "Everything gets sorted out in the Great Silence." Describing meditation is difficult, and it can make one sound like a moron, or a phony,
or a shyster. "There's a two-thousand-year tradition of finding it impossible to
describe," says Mark Epstein, a psychiatrist who uses meditation and psycho-

therapy in tandem. The difficulty of talking about meditation lies not only in its experiential nature but also in the fact that the meditative experience takes us deeper and deeper into realms where language and even thought lose their potency.

There are some teachers and authors whose words come close to describing meditation. In this beautiful passage, the Catholic priest Henri Nouwen counsels meditators to cultivate patience in their practice:

> Patience is a hard discipline. It is not just waiting until something happens over which we have no control: the arrival of the bus, the end of the rain, the return of a friend, the resolution of a conflict. Patience is not waiting passively until someone else does something. Patience asks us to live the moment to the fullest, to be completely present to the moment, to taste the here and now, to be where we are. When we are impatient, we try to get away from where we are. We behave as if the real thing will happen tomorrow, later, and somewhere else. Let's be patient and trust that the treasure we look for is hidden in the ground on which we stand.

This is meditation.

A woman in one of my workshops asked me if when she meditated she could concentrate on an image that brought her peace.

"What image?" I asked her.

"I like to imagine flowers by a pool of water," she said. "I like to picture myself sitting there, hearing the lapping of the water on the shore, seeing the flowers in the sunshine."

I hated to rain on her sunny glade, but I had to. "If you like to do that, you can," I said, "but that is not mindfulness meditation. When you are in a flower garden by a pool, be there. But when you are sitting in meditation, be exactly where you are, doing exactly what you are doing. Be in this room, sitting in meditation. Close your eyes, feel your body, observe your thoughts, experience your breathing. If your body aches, be with it. If you are tired and cranky, be with that. Don't layer flowers on top of a bad mood. Don't use a peaceful pool as a Band-Aid over your anxiety. Be right where you are and who you are. Why? Because if you can do that, then when you are really by a pool, gazing at a beautiful flower, you will be fully present. You won't be worrying about what is going on at home or wondering if there is a nicer pool somewhere else. And when you are with a person you love, you will really be with him—you will be less distracted, less judgmental. When you are at work, you will show up for those around you; you will bring the gifts of attention and equanimity. And when you are confused or unhappy or sick, you will stop fighting your feelings and just rest with them for a while. You will then know what you feel when you are feeling it, what you think when you are thinking it. You will know the peace of being present to whatever is happening.

"Don't visualize yourself anywhere but where you are," I told the woman. "Be exactly who you are, wherever you are. That is the practice of meditation."

You can see why meditation would be so useful during a Phoenix Process. It helps us sit in the flames long enough for transformation to occur. It encourages us not to bail out before the lessons have been learned. It helps us ride out the common experiences of fear, anxiety, and depression. Can meditation cure us? No, but it can give us a platform to climb up to whenever we want to survey the scene. From that perspective, we get to see how we are not our depression—or our fear or anger or sadness—but that these are merely states of mind, conditions of the heart. Meditation shows us that we are something much stronger and vaster than our passing thoughts and feelings.

As an acquired habit, meditation fosters an exquisite attitude toward the whole of life. It helps us to get through the rough times with more grace. It teaches us to resist attachment to the wonderful times but to enjoy them fully and with gratitude, in the moment. While these are the unique fruits of meditation, the practice part of meditation is like the practice part of anything we want to learn. Meditation practice is like piano scales or basketball drill. Practice requires discipline; it can be tedious; it is necessary. After you have practiced enough, you become more skilled at the art form itself. You do not practice to become a great scale player or drill champion. You practice to become a musician or an athlete. Likewise, one does not practice meditation to become a great meditator. We meditate to wake up and live, to become skilled at the art of living.

Meditation practice is truly a refuge during times of crisis and change, but we can find this out only for ourselves. Past the restlessness, agitation, and confusion of our daily consciousness, there is a state of clarity and fearlessness deep within. It is always waiting for us. Each time we sit in mindfulness meditation, we can touch on that deeper state. And then we practice again the next day. And we continue to do it until one day it begins to do us.

MEDITATION INSTRUCTIONS

Since I have studied a variety of meditation practices, from teachers and cultures all over the world, one might think I have a highly ritualized and complicated meditation practice. But actually my practice is simple. While it is surely informed by all of my study and experiences, I would be mocking the real meaning of meditation if I represented it as an exotic journey. Immersion into many forms of meditation has led me deeper and deeper into the most essential core of all of them: *mindfulness*—a nondenominational form of practice that teaches moment-to-moment awareness, a kind of falling in love with naked reality.

While books and tapes are good introductions to mindfulness meditation, I believe that they are not as powerful as working with a teacher or a group—what is called in the East a *sangha,* or a community of seekers. A teacher or a sangha keeps us on track, inspires us, and answers questions along the way. If meditation is something that appeals to you, I suggest participating in a weekend retreat or workshop in your area or at a retreat center. Many community churches or yoga centers have weekly meditation groups. The following instructions are meant to help you begin meditating, or to revive a stalled routine.

Chögyam Trungpa was one of my first meditation teachers. He taught meditation as a twofold process: first, as a way to access stability and dignity in the midst of any situation; and second, as a way to wake up, as if from a dream, into vibrant and genuine aliveness. Trungpa believed that at the core of life was what he called "basic goodness," and that each one of us is basically good, and more than that, wonderfully noble. "You can transcend your embarrassment," he said, "and take pride in being a human being." Trungpa stressed good posture in sitting meditation practice as a way of demonstrating our basic goodness. He said that keeping a straight back is a way to overcome our embarrassment at being a human being. He often used the image of riding a horse when he taught meditation posture. Sitting tall in the saddle tells the horse that you are the master. Sitting tall on the meditation cushion or in a chair tells your mind and body that you are the master. Sitting upright in the saddle tells the world that you believe in yourself.

Posture in meditation does not refer only to a straight back. Posture includes the whole body. The body and mind are inseparable in meditation, and a relaxed and energetic body creates a beneficial base for meditation practice.

Trungpa said that by working with posture in meditation, "you begin to feel that by simply being on the spot, your life can become workable and even wonderful. You realize that you are capable of sitting like a king or a queen on your horse. The regalness of that situation shows you the dignity that comes from being still and simple."

I use Trungpa's checklist of six body parts—seat, legs, torso, hands, eyes, mouth—as I sit down and assume a meditative posture. I elaborate here on each point:

1. **Seat:** It is best to sit on a firm pillow on the floor or on a firm-seated chair. If you use a chair, sit forward so that your back does not touch the back of the chair.

2. **Legs:** If you sit on a pillow, cross your legs comfortably in front of you, with your knees resting on the floor if they can. If you sit in a chair, put your feet flat on the floor, knees and feet hip width apart.

3. **Torso:** Keep your back comfortably straight, your chest open, and your shoulders relaxed. Philip Kapleau Roshi, the first Zen teacher I studied with, writes, "If you are accustomed to letting the chest sink, it does require a conscious effort to keep it up in the beginning. When it becomes natural to walk and sit with the chest open, you begin to realize the many benefits of this ideal posture. The lungs are given additional space in which to expand, thus filling and stretching the air sacs. This in turn permits a greater intake of oxygen and washes the bloodstream, which carries away fatigue accumulated in the body."

   A straight back and soft shoulders is a natural position. It does not have to feel forced or painful. In fact, after time, meditation breeds a sense of overall comfort. But often when we start to meditate, assuming a straight back makes us suddenly aware of discomfort in the body. This is why many people who meditate also practice yoga, or another form of physical exercise that strengthens and stretches the body.

   One of the best ways to maintain a straight back and open chest in meditation is to repeat silently a phrase whenever you feel physical pain. For example, if you feel yourself tensing your shoulders as you hold your back straight during meditation, you can inwardly whisper to yourself, "soften, soften," or "open, open."

A straight back, open heart, and relaxed body will help your meditation practice immeasurably. A straight back will lead to dignity and courage. An open chest will nurture acceptance of life. A relaxed body will remind you to go easy on yourself, to treat your meditation practice as a gift instead of a chore.

4. **Hands:** Sometimes, when meditation gets very quiet, our concentration coagulates in the hands. It sounds strange, but you may experience this yourself. It's not uncommon, as your exhalation dissolves outward, to feel as if all that is left of your body is your hands. Therefore, it is good to position your hands in a way that is both grounding and meaningful. You will notice in statues from a variety of religious traditions that the deities or saints hold their hands in intentional ways. These hand positions are called *mudras* in the Tantric Buddhist tradition—physical gestures that help evoke certain states of mind.

One frequently seen position is the forefinger lightly touching the thumb and the other three fingers flexed outward. Another common mudra is one hand resting in the palm of the other, thumbs touching. Many people like to meditate with their hands in the Christian prayer position of palms together, fingers pointing up. Some people meditate with their hands simply resting, palms down or upward, on their knees.

Each mudra evokes a specific quality that you can experience yourself merely by experimenting with them. For example, resting the palms upward on the knees indicates receptivity—openness to whatever comes your way. Hands placed downward on the knees produce a grounded feeling in the body, a sense of balance and strength. My personal favorite hand position is where the thumb and index finger touch and create a circle. There is something about the thumb touching the finger that reminds me to be *on the spot* in my concentration, yet delicately so. I gently extend the other three fingers and rest my hands on my knees. This position keeps me steady and balanced. I attach the words *on the spot* to the mudra and use both the position of my hands and the intention of the mudra to bring my mind back to meditation when it wanders.

It is a good idea to stick with one position for your hands per meditation session, so as not to get distracted by the switching-mudra game. It's very easy to turn anything into yet another way not to do the simple work of meditation. At the end of a meditation session, many traditions suggest raising the hands palm to palm and bowing. This is a way to indicate respect and gratitude for having meditated. It is also a way to experience a sense of humility as we bow to the universal forces of wisdom and compassion.

5. **Eyes:** Some meditation traditions recommend closing the eyes during meditation; others suggest keeping them open and directing the gaze downward, four to six feet in front of you, focusing on a point on the floor. Some suggest keeping a soft, unfocused gaze. I meditate with my eyes closed. You can experiment and see which way affords you the best relaxation and concentration. If you find that closing your eyes makes you sleepy, keep them open. If you find that keeping your eyes open is distracting, close them.

6. **Mouth:** We hold a lot of tension in the jaw. Let your jaw drop right now. Open your mouth wide, stick your tongue out, then close your mouth. Massage your jaw area from your ears to your chin. Now notice the difference. You can do this often during the day as a way to release tension. During meditation, it is not unusual for tension to gather in the jaw. The Vietnamese Zen master Thich Nhat Hanh recommends smiling slightly, while you meditate, a great way to keep the jaw soft. Or you can drop your jaw and open your mouth several times during meditation.

Understand that the pain or tension you may feel in your body as you meditate is both physical and psychological. If you experience pain, constriction, restlessness, or all of the above, do not be alarmed, and do not take the attitude "no pain, no gain." Adjust your position slowly and mindfully as many times as you want during a meditation session. The point of meditation is to be relaxed and awake. Therefore make sure you are comfortable, and at the same time sit in a way that keeps you alert.

At a meditation retreat I heard Thich Nhat Hanh answer a man who said he experienced pain in his shoulders and neck the minute he sat down to meditate. Thay asked the man if he felt that same pain the minute he sat down to watch television. He said that he did not.

"How do you sit when you watch television?" Thay asked.

"I usually sit on the couch, with my feet folded under me," said the man. "But after a while I may switch my position and stretch out my legs."

"How long do you watch television?"

"Oh, about an hour."

"Do you stay awake for the whole hour?"

"Yes," said the man.

"Well, then," Thay suggested, "take that same position when you meditate and make the same adjustments for an hour and see what happens. Later you can see about straightening your back and stilling your body."

As you sit down to meditate, approach the experience lightly so that your body relaxes, just as it would if you were about to slip into a bath or settle down before the television. Then choose your hand mudra, close your eyes, straighten your back, and at the same time soften your shoulders and expand your chest, so that your posture is also one of gentle openness.

Breath, posture, placement of hands, eyes open or shut: all of these techniques form the container for meditation practice. But none of them eradicates the absurd quantity and aggravating intensity of the thoughts that flood the mind when we sit down to meditate. Please expect this. Good thoughts, bad thoughts, pleasurable ones, disturbing ones—they will come and go as we sit in meditation, watching our breath, maintaining our posture. They are the weather of the mind. Our goal in meditation is not to get rid of thoughts. Rather, the goal is to abandon identifying with each thought as it comes and goes; to watch the thoughts as we would watch the weather from an observation tower.

Feelings also arise during meditation. They often rush into the empty space created when we slow down and sit still. At every retreat I have participated in, there are times when crying can be heard in the room. To an outsider it would appear strange to see a room full of people sitting in meditation on the floor or in chairs, some upright and silent, some bent over, crying softly. A strange sight, indeed. But a beautiful one also. There is something so noble about the pure expression of feelings. When drama or sentimentality is absent, tears are like a healing river moving freely through us. "The answer to anger or sadness or other negative states," says Thich Nhat Hanh, "is not to suppress or to deny them, but to embrace them with mindfulness like a mother with a baby." Suppressing feelings in meditation, as in daily life, is like blocking a stream with sticks and mud. Blocked emotions eventually gather enough pressure to break through the dams we construct. Better that they find their way out in the safe environment of meditation than in other situations, where we may be forced to act on them in thoughtless ways.

Guilt, doubt, anger, despair, and other forms of self-judgment are common visitors in meditation practice. So are our convictions, biases, and beliefs. The purpose of meditation is to step boldly into reality, just as it is in the here and now. Therefore, it is helpful to sweep the mind clean of belief systems. Strong opinions can be signs of our passion and intelligence, but sometimes they spring from that part of ourselves that wants be right, and that holds on tightly to familiar explanations. The ego wants to be a "Republican" or a "Democrat," an "American," or a "European," an "Arab" or a "Jew." It wants to judge things as right or wrong. It wants to be "for" something or "against" something. It does not want to delve more deeply into the full picture of reality. Thus, an opinion about the world can become a foe to mindfulness meditation.

When I teach meditation, I bring a box to class with quotations and poems chosen for their relevance to meditation and contemplation. I ask each person to choose one, sit with it, then share it with the group. Without fail, one of the shortest poems, by the Chinese sage Seng Ts'an, creates a big stir:

> *Don't keep searching for the truth;*
> *Just let go of your opinions.*

Inevitably some members of the class will take umbrage at the poem. One person will say, "My opinions about injustice in the world are what drive me to do good work." Another will ask, "If I don't form opinions, how will I know what is true and what it false?" Like many mystical poets, Seng Ts'an had a sense of humor and liked to overstate the case, just to get a laugh. He knew that opinions are not necessarily evil. He just wanted us to loosen the grip of our judgments, even for a few minutes, and give the whole truth a chance to reveal itself. Meditation is an opportunity to do exactly that.

As you establish a meditation practice, remind yourself every now and then why you are doing it. It is easy to fall into a rote form of practice or, even worse, to feel self-righteous or trendy just because you take a few minutes out of your day to cultivate a quiet mind and an open heart. Remind yourself that you are practicing so that you can be a peaceful person, so that the truths you discover in meditation become the way you live your life. After a while your practice will show up everywhere—from driving the car to reading a bedtime story to your child. Meditation is not separate from life; it is practice for mindful living.

One warning about meditation: Do not use it as yet another way to judge yourself. Meditation can be difficult. While it hones some of our better qualities, it also holds up a mirror to some of our worst. This is one of the reasons we do it: to see ourselves clearly; to love ourselves, warts and all; to crack through the hard crust of the personality until the gem of the self is revealed. Let your resolve to meditate spring from your longing to break open into life, not from enmity toward yourself. Let go of the burden of self-judgment by returning, over and over, to your most basic self, just as you are, with an attitude of forgiveness. Soon you will find yourself forgiving others, and forgiving the world itself.

TEN-STEP MEDITATION PRACTICE

1. **Place and Time:** Find a private and relatively quiet place where you will not be disturbed by people, children, telephones, et cetera. Choose an amount of time you are going to meditate. Set a timer or keep a clock close by. Begin with ten minutes, and work your way up over a few weeks or months to a half hour or forty-five minutes.

2. **Seat and Posture:** Assume a comfortable posture, sitting cross-legged on a pillow on the floor or on a simple chair. Keep the spine straight, and let your shoulders soften and drop. Do a brief scan of the body, relaxing parts that are tight. Relax your jaw. Choose a hand position and gently hold it.

3. **Beginning:** Close your eyes (or keep your open eyes focused gently on a spot on the floor). Take a deep breath in and let it out with a sigh. Do this three times. As you sigh, release anything you are holding on to. Remind yourself that for these few minutes you are doing nothing but meditating. You can afford to drop everything else for the time being. The pressing details of your life will be waiting for you at the end of the session.

4. **Breath:** Bring your attention to your breathing, becoming aware of the natural flow of breath in and out of the body. Observe your chest and belly as they rise and expand on the in-breath, and fall and recede on the out-breath. Witness each in-breath as it enters your body and fills it with energy. Witness each out-breath as it leaves your body and dissipates into

space. Then start again, bringing your attention back each time to the next breath. Let your breath be like a soft broom, gently sweeping its way through your body and mind.

5. **Thoughts:** When a thought takes you away from witnessing your breathing, take note of the thought without judging it, then gently bring your attention back to your chest or your belly and the feeling of the breath coming in and out. Remember that meditation is the practice of unconditional friendliness. Observe your thoughts with friendliness and then let the breath sweep them gently away.

6. **Feelings:** When feelings arise, do not resist them. Allow them to be. Observe them. Taste them. Experience them but do not identify with them. Let them run their natural course, then return to observing your breath. If you find yourself stuck in a feeling state, shift a little on your seat and straighten your posture. Get back in the saddle and gently pick up the reins of the breath.

7. **Pain:** If you feel pain in the body—your knees, for example, or your back—bring your awareness to the pain. Surround the area in pain with breath. Witness yourself in pain, as opposed to responding to the pain. If the pain is persistent, move gently to release tension, and return to your posture and breath. You may need to lean against a wall or the back of your chair, or you may want to straighten your legs for a while. Avoid excess movement, but do not allow pain to dominate your experience.

8. **Restlessness and Sleepiness:** If you are agitated by thoughts or feelings, or if you feel as if you cannot sit still, or if you are bored to distraction, come back to your breath and your posture again and again. Treat yourself gently, as if you were training a puppy. Likewise, if a wave of sleepiness overtakes you, see if you can waken yourself by breathing a little more deeply, keeping your eyes open, and sitting up tall. Sleep and meditation are not the same thing. See if you can be as relaxed as you are during sleep, yet at the same time, awake and aware.

9. **Counting Breaths:** A good way to deal with all of these impediments to concentration is to count your breaths. On the in-breath, count "one," and on the out-breath, count "two." Continue up to ten. Then begin again. If you lose count at any point, start over at "one." As thoughts and

feelings, pain and discomfort, restlessness and sleepiness arise, allow your counting to gently override their distracting chatter.

10. **Discipline:** For one week, practice meditation each day, whether you are in the mood or not. Even if it is for only five minutes, commit to a regular practice. See how you feel. If you notice a difference (or even if you don't), commit to another week. Then consider joining a meditation group or taking a retreat and receiving more in-depth instruction and support in your practice.

PSYCHOTHERAPY

I first learned to meditate when I was nineteen years old. I was terribly restless. The practice did not come naturally to me. At times I hated it. But I kept at it anyway. I did this for a variety of good and bad reasons. A good reason was that I sensed great power in the practice. I was aware that you can't get something for nothing, and I wanted the something that meditation promised: I wanted inner peace and a vaster perspective on life and death. A bad reason I continued with my meditation practice was that I felt duty-bound to please my meditation teachers—even to please God. I thought that if I meditated every day, I would be acceptable in God's eyes; if I didn't, I would be courting exile. I think many people adhere to all sorts of religious practices for the same reason and, in doing so, never really mine the deep treasures locked in the mystical heart of the great traditions.

It wasn't until I was in my thirties and had been in psychotherapy for a few years that my meditation practice became more natural and flowing. Oddly enough, therapy cleared the way for a strong and genuine meditation practice. I went into therapy because my marriage was in trouble. I discovered in therapy that the compulsion to please my meditation teachers was also at work in my marriage. Apparently, I was doing a lot of things just to please other people, and had been ever since childhood with my parents. The revelation that psychotherapy afforded me—that a life lived in order to please others ends up pleasing no one at all—changed my life dramatically. It began the process of what Norman O. Brown—one of the fathers of modern psychology—said therapy aims to do: "to return our souls to our bodies, to return ourselves to ourselves, and thus to overcome the human state of self-alienation."

Before diving into the world of therapy, I want to make a distinction between *pleasing* others and *loving* others. Pleasing another person is not always the same as loving another person, and vice versa. Pleasing another person is often about avoiding the conflict that might ensue if we tell the truth about our feelings, needs, fears, and dreams. Loving other people might involve pleasing them, but it also involves being honest with them about who we are and what we want. It does not mean getting what we want all of the time; it does mean having the self-respect to express our thoughts and feelings, and the nobility and compassion to afford that right to others.

Therapy has been faulted for its excessive focus on the needs of the self, and for putting forth an ethos by which an individual has more responsibility to himself than to his family and community. This has not been my experience. My years of therapy have helped me become a more loving mother and mate, and a more engaged member of society. Yes, the initial work I did in therapy was self-reflective, and it did push me into periods of "selfish" behavior. But in the end, self-reflection helped me become a more generous person; it led me back out into the world, and into more mature and giving relationships.

People like to make fun of psychotherapy. Cartoonists and comedians and pundits of all sorts take shots at it every day. The jokes can be funny and understandable, but because my own experiences in therapy have been close to lifesaving, I wonder why therapy, of all things, takes so many hits. People brag about going to the gym to stay healthy, eating well, and losing weight on this or that diet. They boast of their college degrees and show off their advanced thinking by talking about books they are reading and lectures they have attended. People are proud to admit they belong to a church or temple or mosque or meditation group. They readily give credit to their reliance on a trusted pastor or rabbi.

Why then is care of the psyche something that does not command as much respect and pride as care of the soul, the body, and the mind? I think it is because psychotherapy takes us into the vulnerable and volatile landscape of our emotions—an area our culture generally dismisses as inferior to the landscape of the mind. Feelings—be they of love or anger or passion or sorrow—are relegated to the domains of sentimental poets or hysterical women or hot-tempered people who live in south-of-the-border climates. Everyone else, it seems, would be wise to veer away from the labyrinthine landscape of the heart. Psychotherapy takes us into the labyrinth. It opens doors to houses that hold subjects like childhood and family, marriage and sex, power and passion. One could get stuck in houses like those—held hostage by ghosts and demons, forced to reveal shameful secrets by shamans and soothsayers. Psychotherapy awakens the Sleeping Giants bedded down in our heart's history. And the Sleeping Giants have stories to tell.

It may not seem wise at all to awaken the Giants. There is a certain logic in not picking scabs off childhood wounds. It may seem prudent to leave unexamined our current dissatisfactions, deadness, or unfelt feelings. Our lives may be hanging too close to the edge: Move one little pebble and a landslide could bring everything down. Isn't there too much at stake? The job, the family, the marriage, the complex layers of daily life? Better to keep to the known path— one false move and the pebble dislodges, the cliffside disappears.

What I learned in the safe and sacred room of my therapist's office was that the same energy I was exerting to keep things from being revealed could be used for a far more exciting and rewarding struggle: to return my soul to my body, to return myself to myself. After that, anything would be possible. And when I finally could bring my whole self—including my rich, wild, tender, and powerful emotions—into meditation and other spiritual practices, I was better able to understand and integrate what had seemed out of reach before. The combination of meditation and psychotherapy became for me a potent brew for transforming trials into revelations.

There are many forms of psychotherapy for a wide variety of psychological issues. Some people come to therapy because they feel too much, others because they feel nothing at all. Some people enter into psychotherapeutic work to bolster a weak sense of self, others because their powerful ego overshadows their ability to have loving relationships. All come to develop what is called "emotional intelligence."

Some people respond best to traditional psychoanalysis, done under the guidance of a psychiatrist. Other people love Jungian analysis because of its focus on dreams and the mythic dimensions of life. During the twentieth century, pioneering schools of psychology sprang up in America, creating a Renaissance-like revolution in the field. There are far too many kinds of therapy—including talk therapy, body-centered therapy, family therapy, and art therapy—for me to discuss them all here. For the vast majority of people interested in pursuing psychotherapy, talk therapy with a wise and responsible therapist is the most effective method. But some people—especially those with specific issues, like sexual abuse, addiction problems, and serious depression—are in need of other forms of therapy.

Many people have found that the only kind of therapy that works for them involves psychotropic medication. I am not a trained therapist and therefore not qualified to write about the use of medication for depression and anxiety. I believe that medication as prescribed by a skilled practitioner can be tremendously helpful, and I have seen it work well for several people I know. But I also believe that our fast-food culture tends to look for quick fixes and struggle-free solutions to whatever ails us. The philosopher Sam Keen warns that medications like Prozac can "deliver us prematurely from anxiety and struggle at the expense of the epiphany we need to begin again."

Psychotherapy is by nature a highly personal matter, without a one-size-fits-all formula for success. I suggest that, if you feel drawn to therapy, you do some of your own research through reading and talking to trusted friends. You may need to shop around for a while before you find a therapy and therapist that match your unique needs. My own therapy began with fits and starts before I found the best method and, more significant, the right therapist. This was not a well-conceived, strategic process. At first I had mixed feelings about being in therapy. I didn't know what I was looking for, and since one of my biggest issues was trying to please other people, I spent some fruitless months under the guidance of a therapist who was terribly wrong for me. I was so afraid of hurting his feelings that I stayed on even though I felt uncomfortable in his presence. Finally, after gathering the courage to leave and then asking around for the names of other therapists, I began work with a man whose skill and compassion helped change the course of my life.

During the difficult time of my divorce, I spent four years going to therapy once a week. My therapist helped me to slowly unravel the strands of my story—dipping back into childhood, examining my marriage, looking honestly at my behavior at work and with friends. In my own time I developed the desire to stop looking to others for salvation or for blame, and to take responsibility for my own happiness and success. This is what psychotherapy did for me. Other people will come to therapy with their own specific needs and discover parts of themselves that have gone missing for years. I found a more powerful and self-confident person through the process of therapy. Others may find a more empathetic person, or a less fearful person, or a more hopeful and lively person. Whatever it is that wants to live within you—whatever is sleeping and has perhaps been sleeping since childhood—can awaken through slow and steady work with a wise therapist.

WORKING WITH TEACHERS, THERAPISTS, AND HEALERS

Working at Omega Institute has put me in contact with some of the world's most influential psychological thinkers and spiritual teachers. I am grateful for the mystical, intellectual, and therapeutic wisdom that I have absorbed from being around these people, but you may be surprised by the most important lesson I have learned. By knowing many of Omega's teachers, I have come to understand that everyone—the saintly guru, the erudite scholar, the compassionate psychotherapist—is an imperfect human being with neuroses and problems and rough edges not unlike yours and mine. From rubbing up against the human dimension of the so-called enlightened ones, I accept now that the point of life is not to reach perfection but to befriend the fact that human beings are works in progress.

The minute an authority figure claims to be perfect, I say run fast in the other direction. That is something I have clearly learned from my close association with religious leaders, spiritual teachers, and healers of all sorts. Power corrupts, whether you are in politics, a healing profession, or a religious organization. It just does. I have seen it so many times that I have made my peace with that fact. It is a law of nature, like gravity. Drop a rock from a tower, and it falls to the ground. Give someone a lot of power, and it goes to his head. Friedrich Nietzsche warns, "Whoever fights monsters should see to it that in the process he does not become a monster." Sometimes I would like to hang that sign over the teachers' dining room at Omega. At Esalen Institute—a center in California similar to Omega—they do have a sign hanging for their faculty to see. It reads: "You always teach others what you most need to learn. You are your own worst student."

Wise leaders and healers understand this phenomenon of power. They lose their taste for having power *over* anyone and instead make it their mission to empower others. The world is moved by these kinds of leaders. We call them our heroes. But even they are not perfect. Take people like Carl Jung, or Albert Einstein, or Martin Luther King, Jr., or Mother Teresa—whomever you admire—dig a tad below the surface of their great work, and you will find real people. You will find men and women who bear typical childhood scars, who struggle with personal relationships, and who fret over the small things even as they move mountains and inspire the multitudes.

I am grateful that this insight has been ground into me through my work. It reminds me, over and over, not to be seduced into thinking that someone or some group has *the* answers to my questions. Teachers, therapists, and healers are there to help us heal ourselves. As long as we remember that, and do not expect the impossible, we will be doing ourselves a big favor.

I have seen many people come to Omega looking for empowerment and self-realization, and leave having given their power and selves away to a guide. (I will use the word *guide* here for any kind of therapist, healer, religious leader, or spiritual teacher.) But I have also seen people forgo the rewards of therapeutic work because of the mistaken notion that a guide should be a fully perfected human being. When you decide to begin working with a guide, remember that you are working with a man or a woman who has unique strengths and also normal human weaknesses. It is understandable that you would want your guide to possess all the wonderful qualities you find lacking in yourself. But this may not be the case. Sometimes the most compassionate and helpful guides are those who are only a few paces ahead of you on a healing path. Who better to lead you through the woods than someone who has struggled with similar issues?

A good guide tries to get his or her own personality out of the way. An inexperienced or self-interested guide does not. A good guide is always turning the focus away from himself and back on the student or client, always reducing the work at hand to its most simple, personal, and intimate dimensions. Good guides are not miracle workers. If they suggest they have special powers to heal you—or if the people around them prop them up as magicians—I would think twice about working with such teachers, counselors, or therapists. Oftentimes the most effective guides are what I call extra-ordinary people. They are extraordinary healers because they are profoundly ordinary people who are comfortable with their humanness. They are extra-ordinary.

The Jungian analyst Marion Woodman talks about the moment her own analysis really began. Although she had engaged in many sessions with the famous Jungian analyst E. A. Bennet, she had spent most of her time trying to prove to him that she was a good, smart, and organized person. "I had been seeing him for about six months," Woodman says, "and I was still trying to be a good girl. On Christmas Eve I learned that my childhood dog had been killed. I decided not to waste my six o'clock session that evening talking about my dog and I arrived as well organized as usual." At the end of the session, Dr. Bennet, who was in his eighties at the time, asked Woodman if anything was wrong. He had sensed that her attention was elsewhere during the session. Woodman lightly noted that her dog had died. Then the old doctor began to weep. He was weeping over her dog. This astonished her. He asked her how she could have wasted the session chattering when her "soul animal" had died. Suddenly Woodman knew what she had been doing to herself all her adult life, how she had been treating her own soul. She sat with the old doctor and wept. "That's when my analysis truly began," she says.

Dr. Bennet was a brilliant and well-trained therapist. He also was a humble and tender man. All of these are good qualities to look for in a guide.

Psychotherapy is a powerful process. If it works well, we emerge with a stronger sense of who we are in our body, mind, heart, and soul. We gather skills to help us move with less fear through the fires of life. We create a firm foundation that can support our talents, endeavors, relationships, and quests. Combined with a spiritual practice like meditation, therapy can help us develop happiness, humanity, and mastery in life. And yet, for all of our spiritual peace of mind and our psychological sanity and strength, there remains the fact that we will never quiet all our anxieties or tame all our neuroses. We are, remember, bozos on the bus.

And that is where prayer comes in.

PRAYER

Sister Alice Martin teaches gospel singing at Omega. I have taken her workshops because I love to sing, and for me singing gospel music is like diving into an ocean of bliss. Sister Alice is an electrifying singer, songwriter, and gospel choir leader. When she walks into a room, you sit up a little straighter. When she directs a group of people singing, you never take your eyes off her. During her workshops, in between leading the group in song, Sister Alice talks about prayer. "Prayer is about being hopeful," she says. "It is not a phone call to God's hotline. It's not about waiting around for an answer you like, especially since sometimes the answer you're going to get is *no*!"

My favorite advice about prayer from Sister Alice is this: "If you are going to pray, then don't worry. And if you are going to worry, then don't bother praying. You can't be doing both." When I stop and listen closely to what's going on inside my head, I often hear the buzz of worry, like the drone of bees in a wall. That's when I remember Sister Alice's words of wisdom. What would I rather being doing, I ask myself, worrying or praying? I usually choose praying. It's a lot more fun than worrying.

To pray is to let go of your belief that you are in control of your life, and to give it over to something more inclusive than your own point of view. It requires a leap of faith. Even if you have only the slightest sense that a higher power is at work in the world, you can still pray. You can name that gossamer belief "God" or not. You can pray to God, or you can pray to your own larger perspective—the part of you that trusts in the meaningfulness of life.

Sometimes I pray using other people's words. Sometimes I pray in silence. Sometimes prayer feels to me like the last resort, an act of throwing up my hands and saying, "You take over now!" Sometimes it feels like a cry of hunger or thirst. Rumi says, "Don't look for water. Be thirsty." Prayer is allowing ourselves to be thirsty; it is a longing for something we just cannot seem to find. The Sufis say that our longing for God is God's longing for us. In this way, prayer is like a conversation between friends separated across time and space.

One of the reasons I love prayer is that it is an antidote to guilt and blame. If we are unhappy with the way we have acted or been treated, instead of stewing in self-recrimination on the one hand, or harboring ill will toward someone else on the other, prayer gives us a way out of the circle of guilt and blame. We bring our painful feelings into the open and say, "I have done wrong," or "I have been wronged." And then we ask for a vaster view—one that contains within it all the forgiveness we need in order to move forward.

Sister Wendy Beckett, a marvelous Roman Catholic nun best known to the world from her books and television shows on art criticism, says this about prayer:

> I don't think being human has any place for guilt. Contrition, yes. Guilt, no. Contrition means you tell God you are sorry and you're not going to do it again and you start off afresh. All the damage you've done to yourself, put right. Guilt means you go on and on belaboring and having emotions and beating your breast and being ego-fixated. Guilt is a trap. People love guilt

because they feel if they suffer enough guilt, they'll make up for what they've done. Whereas, in fact, they're just sitting in a puddle and splashing. Contrition, you move forward. It's over. You are willing to forgo the pleasures of guilt.

You can find prayers everywhere to help you move beyond "the pleasures of guilt," and to stimulate conversations with God—poetry and song, hymns and common prayers, your own language of longing. Here are some words taken from a variety of traditions that help me enter into a state of prayer.

The Cloud of Unknowing, penned by an anonymous English Christian mystic in the Middle Ages, says this:

This is what you are to do: Lift your heart up to the Lord, with a gentle stirring of love desiring him for his own sake and for his gifts. Center all your attention and desire on him and let this be the sole concern of your mind and heart. And so, diligently persevere until you feel joy in it. For in the beginning it is usual to feel nothing but a kind of darkness about your mind, or as it were, a cloud of unknowing. Try as you might, this darkness and this cloud will remain between you and your God. You will feel frustrated, for your mind will be unable to grasp him, and your heart will not relish the delight of his love. But learn to be at home in this darkness. Return to it as often as you can, letting your spirit cry out to him whom you love. For, if, in this life, you hope to feel and see God as he is in himself it must be within this darkness and this cloud. But if you strive to fix your love on him forgetting all else, which is the work of contemplation I have urged you to begin, I am confident that God in his goodness will bring you to a deep experience of himself.

I keep this prayer by Thich Nhat Hanh on my bed stand and sometimes say it aloud when I awaken in the morning:

Waking up this morning, I smile,
Twenty-four brand new hours are before me.
I vow to live fully in each moment
and to look at all beings with the eyes of compassion.

When I am worrying a lot, I take a few minutes to slow down, breathe quietly, and silently repeat this prayer from the fourteenth-century English mystic Dame Julian of Norwich:

All will be well,
And all will be well,
And all manner of things
Will be well.

This little portion of Psalm 19, from the Bible, is a constant prayer of mine:

Clear thou me from hidden faults.

Here is a prayer from the Theosophist Annie Besant. I use it when the destructive behavior of my fellow human beings fills me with sorrow:

O Hidden Life! Vibrant in every atom;
O Hidden Light! Shining in every creature;
O Hidden Love! Embracing all in Oneness;
May each who feels himself as one with Thee,
Know he is also one with every other.

Elisabeth Kübler-Ross is best known as the medical doctor who brought death and dying out of the closet in American culture. She created a curriculum for medical students and sat with hundreds of dying people. Her faith in prayer is legendary. She says, "You will not grow if you sit in a beautiful flower garden, but you will grow if you are sick, if you are in pain, if you experience losses, and if you do not put your head in the sand, but take the pain as a gift to you with a very, very specific purpose." The only thing we can really ask for when we pray is the ability to trust in that greater purpose. We pray to have our hearts opened and our purpose revealed. We pray for gratitude when our life is good and for faith when it is not so good. We pray to trust that our pain is a gift with "a very, very specific purpose."

There is no right or wrong way to pray, and no one tradition that is favored in the heart of the Great Spirit. Václav Havel, the former Czech president and a man whose life has asked him to break open over and over again, expresses for me the true meaning of prayer. He says, "It is not the conviction that something will turn out well, but the certainty that something makes sense regardless of how it turns out." We will know if our prayers are working when we are blessed with that kind of certainty. The fruit of prayer is the realization that life is an eternal adventure, and that we are explorers, always changing, always learning, always breaking open into new vistas of clarity and peace.

Acknowledgments

Love and gratitude to:

My guides in the Phoenix Process: Pir-o-Murshid Hazrat Inayat Khan, Pir Vilayat Inayat Khan, Taj Inayat, Chögyam Trungpa Rinpoche, Joseph Campbell, Bert and Moira Shaw, Marion Woodman, Robert Bly, Babatunde Olatunji, and all the philosophers, poets, and prophets whose words have illuminated my heart.

Omega Institute and the extraordinary staff and faculty (past and present), who have added so much to my life, especially Stephan Rechtschaffen, whose creativity and energy never wane.

My steadfast readers: Grace Welkner (kudos to you), Henry Dunow, Kali Rosenblum, Sil Reynolds, Jim Kullander, Gail Straub, and Ron Frank. Thanks also to Eve Fox, Ned Leavitt, Eve Ensler, and Jane Fonda.

My agent and good friend, Henry Dunow; my editor, Bruce Tracy, whose calm discernment and support kept me steady; the team at Random House, especially Robbin Schiff; and Ann Godoff, who from the beginning trusted in me.

My beloved family: my sons, Rahm, Daniel, and Michael, and the wonderful women in their lives; my mother, Marcia Lesser; my sisters, Katy Lesser, Maggie Lake, and Joanne Finkel, and their husbands and families; and the Bullard family.

My husband, Tom Bullard, for Goethe's chain letter, for lighting the way, for making me laugh, and for loving me every day.

The friends and workshop students who shared their stories of descent and rebirth with me. Some stories are told in the book. Others inspired and informed me as I wrote. Deep gratitude to all.

My tribe of friends and my wonderful town.

And anyone now going through a difficult time. May you find the faith, the patience, and the help you need to transform pain into wisdom and joy.

Permission Credits

Also available from Rider . . .

The Road Less Travelled
A New Psychology of Love,
Traditional Values and Spiritual Growth

M. Scott Peck

Confronting and solving problems is a painful process that most of us attempt to avoid. And the very avoidance results in greater pain and an inability to grow both mentally and spiritually. Drawing heavily on his own professional experience, Dr M. Scott Peck, a psychiatrist, suggests ways in which facing our difficulties – and suffering through the changes – can enable us to reach a higher level of self-understanding. He discusses the nature of loving relationships: how to recognise true compatibility; how to distinguish dependency from love; how to become one's own person and how to be a more sensitive parent.

This is a book that can show you how to embrace reality and yet achieve serenity and a richer existence. Hugely influential, it has now sold over 7 million copies – and has changed many people's lives round the globe. It may change yours.

Buy Rider Books

Order further Rider titles from your local bookshop, or
have them delivered direct to your door by Bookpost

☐ **The Road Less Travelled**
  by M. Scott Peck   0712661158   £7.99
☐ **The Five Stages of the Soul**
  by Harry R. Moody and David Carroll   0712670912   £7.99
☐ **The Road Less Travelled and Beyond**
  by M. Scott Peck   0712670769   £7.99
☐ **The Seat of the Soul** by Gary Zukav   0712646744   £10.99
☐ **Discover Yourself** by Lillian Too   0091879485   £14.99
☐ **Loving What Is** by Byron Katie   0712629300   £10.99
☐ **Emotional Alchemy**
  by Tara Bennett-Goleman   1844130452   £8.99
☐ **Focusing** by Eugene T. Gendlin   184413220X   £7.99
☐ **Compassionate Coaching** by Arielle Essex   1844132366   £9.99
☐ **Intuition & Beyond** by Sharon A. Klingler   0712634428   £7.99

FREE POST AND PACKING
Overseas customers allow £2.00 per paperback

ORDER:

By phone: 016624 677237

By post: Random House Books
c/o Bookpost
PO Box 29
Douglas
Isle of Man, IM99 1BQ

By fax: 01624 670923

By email: bookshop@enterprise.net

Cheques (payable to Bookpost) and credit cards accepted

Prices and availability subject to change without notice.
Allow 28 days for delivery.
When placing your order, please mention if you do not wish to receive
any additional information.

www.randomhouse.co.uk